Managing People and Activities

by:

Tony Simmonds

Copyright © Open Learning Foundation Enterprises Ltd 1995

First published 1995

Blackwell Publishers Ltd
108 Cowley Road
Oxford OX4 1JF, UK

238 Main Street
Cambridge, Massachusetts 02142, USA

Every effort has been made to trace all copyright owners of material used in this book but if any have been inadvertently overlooked the publishers will be pleased to make necessary arrangements at the first opportunity.

British Library Cataloguing-in-Publication Data
A CIP catalogue record for this book is available from the British Library

Library of Congress Cataloging-in-Publication Data
A catalogue record for this book is available from the Library of Congress

ISBN 0-631-19674-9

Printed in Great Britain by Alden Press

This book is printed on acid-free paper

Contents

Introduction   1

SECTION ONE: MANAGING PEOPLE

Session One: Management and leadership   13
                  Management   14
                  Leadership   17
                  Categories of management style   26

Session Two: The culture of organisations   41
                  Culture   42
                  Power   43
                  Politics   46
                  Values and beliefs   48
                  Ideologies   49
                  Social influences   52

Session Three: Organisational development   57
                  Stages in organisational development   58
                  Future trends   66
                  Team-based organisations   69

Session Four: Individual and interpersonal behaviour   79
                  Motivation   80
                  Personality   84
                  Perception   90
                  Role theory and conflict   95
                  Organisational issues   99

Sesion Five: Teams   109
                  Teams or groups?   110
                  Group processes   111
                  Stages in the development of teams   117
                  Characteristics of teams   122
                  Team composition   124
                  Conflict resolution   130
                  Meetings as aids to decision making   142

Session Six:	Performance at work	151
	Identifying training needs	152
	Providing training	156
	Reviewing training activities	161
	Individual performance reviews	168
	Discipline and grievance	176
	Support strategies	184

SECTION TWO: MANAGING ACTIVITIES

Session One:	Work planning and organisation	193
	Strategies and plans	194
	Planning tools	198
	Effectiveness and efficiency measures	210
	Organisational analysis techniques	214
	Method study	219
Session Two:	Communications	231
	Giving orders	232
	Instruction	240
	Training and development styles	244
	Team briefing	246
	Reports	252
	Presentations	256
Session Three:	Identifying constraints and meeting objectives	261
	External influences	262
	Regulatory controls	265
	Negotiating	273
	Managerial roles	278
	Co-ordinating activities	286
Session Four:	Review and monitoring	293
	Establishing performance standards	294
	Reviewing performance standards	300
	Competences	306
	Value analysis	311
	Auditing	314
	Systems analysis	320
	The impact of new technology	322

Foreword

BTEC is committed to helping people of any age to acquire and maintain the up-to-date and relevant knowledge, understanding and skills they need for success in current or future employment.

These aims are greatly enhanced by this series of open learning books for the new BTEC HND and HNC in Business Studies.

These books will provide more students with the opportunity to successfully achieve a widely recognised national qualification in business by allowing flexible study patterns combined with an innovative approach to learning.

Our active involvement in a partnership with the Open Learning Foundation and Blackwell Publishers ensures that each book comprehensively covers the specific learning outcomes needed for a module in this Higher National programme.

Acknowledgements

Author
Tony Simmonds

Additional Material: Bob McClelland (Liverpool John Moores University)

Open Learning Editor: Peter Gaukroger

For the Open Learning Foundation:
Director of Programmes: Leslie Mapp
Design and Production: Stephen Moulds
Text Editor: Paul Stirner
Academic Co-ordinator: Glyn Roberts (Bradford & Ilkley Community College)
Academic Reviewer: Martin Gibson (University of Central Lancashire)

The Open Learning Foundation wishes to acknowledge the support of Bradford & Ilkley Community College during the preparation of this workbook.

For BTEC
Diane Billam: Director of Products and Quality Division
John Edgar: Consultant
Don Glaves: Education Adviser
Françoise Seacroft: Manager of Futures Department
Mike Taylor: Deputy Head of Department of Service Sector Management, University of Brighton

For Blackwell Publishers
Editorial Director: Philip Carpenter
Senior Commissioning Editor: Tim Goodfellow
Production Manager: Pam Park
Development Editors: Richard Jackman and Catriona King
Pre-production Manager: Paul Stringer
Sub-editorial team: First Class Publishing
Reviewers: Nadine Vikins (University of West England)
            Marilyn Farmer (West Herts College)
            Sue Gauntlett-Gilbert (Highbury College)

Parts of Section 1, Session 4 relating to personality and perception are reproduced with kind permission of the Open Learning Institute of Hong Kong.

Introduction

Welcome to this workbook for the BTEC module Managing People and Activites.

This is a book specifically designed for use by students studying on BTEC Higher National programmes in Business, Business and Finance, Business and Marketing and Business and Personnel. However, it can be also used by people who wish to learn about this aspect of business.

How to use the workbook

Please feel free to:

- write notes in the margins

- underline and highlight important words or phrases.

As you work through this module, you will find activities have been built in. These are designed to make you stop to think and answer questions.

There are four types of activities.

Memory and recall These are straightforward tests of how much text you are able to remember.

Self-assessed tasks (SATs) These are used to test your understanding of the text you are studying or to apply the principles and practices learnt to a related problem.

Exercises These are open-ended questions that can be used as a basis for classroom or group debate. If you do not belong to a study group, use the exercises to think through issues raised by the text.

Assignments These are tasks set for students studying at a BTEC centre which would normally require a written answer to be looked at by your tutor. If you are not following a course at college, the assignments are still a useful way of developing and testing your understanding of the module.

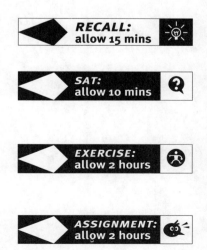

RECALL: allow 15 mins

SAT: allow 10 mins

EXERCISE: allow 2 hours

ASSIGNMENT: allow 2 hours

There are answer boxes provided below each activity in this module. Use these boxes to summarise your answers and findings. If you need more space, use the margins of the book or separate sheets of paper to make notes and write a full answer.

Managing tasks and solving problems ✔

EXAMPLE ACTIVITY

As an 'icebreaker' try this exercise.

List what you see as the main roles of managers and of leaders. How do they differ? Summarise your answer in the box below.

Commentary...

Managerial tasks include planning, communicating, analysing and organising. Managers exercise control through their positions in organisational hierarchies; this gives them authority. Leaders, in contrast, give direction to businesses and activities, providing a vision and encouraging others to follow. Not all managers have leadership qualities. Equally, some leaders are not formally recognised as managers. In Session 1, we explore more fully the key differences between management and leadership.

The emphasis of the workbook is to provide you with tasks that relate to the general operating environment of business. The work that you do on these tasks enables you to develop your BTEC common skills and a skills chart is provided at the end of this introduction for you to note your practice of each skill. One sheet is probably not enough, so cut this sheet out and photocopy it when you require new sheets.

Aims of the workbook

This workbook is concerned with increasing your ability to understand and evaluate techniques for managing people and activities. The two are interrelated in that effective individuals and teams are essential to the planning, organising, co-ordinating and monitoring of workplace activities.

The book has two sections which are designed to cover the learning outcomes (as shown in bold in the boxes below) for this core module. These are as given in the BTEC publication (code 02–104–4) on the Higher National programmes in Business Studies. Where appropriate, BTEC's suggested content may be reordered within the sections of this book.

SECTION ONE: MANAGING PEOPLE

On completion of this section, you should be able to:

> ▶ **evaluate the effectiveness of alternative styles and approaches to managing people**

> ▶ **analyse the factors influencing the effectiveness of individuals and teams**

> ▶ **evaluate alternative approaches to motivating people at work, improving performance and dealing with staff work problems**

> ▶ **work with a team and identify techniques for team building**

> ▶ analyse and evaluate the effect of team members' and others' behaviour on interpersonal relationships at work.

Content

Management styles: major categories of styles, effectiveness and appropriateness of each within different situations, contingency theories, changes in working patterns: flexibility, multi-skilling, team-working, empowerment

Individual and interpersonal behaviour: motivation theories, personality, perception, attitudes to work, internal and external factors

Teams: stages in group development, group dynamics, decision making in teams, team building, team roles and selection, internal and external influences

Performance at work: coaching skills, training and development, counselling, discipline, monitoring and reporting individual and group performance.

SECTION TWO: MANAGING ACTIVITIES

On completion of this section, you should be able to:

> ▶ use techniques and methods of work planning and organisation

> ▶ identify the importance of management information and communications in the effective management of activities

> ▶ co-ordinate human, physical and financial resources in carrying out activities

> ▶ identify major constraints on effective management of activites

> ▶ review effectiveness of self and others and improve the way activities and tasks are organised.

Content

Work planning and organisation: PERT, CPA, method study, flow of work, measures of efficiency and effectiveness, changing and amending plans

Communications: giving orders and instruction, briefing individuals and teams, giving and receiving feedback

Co-ordinating: interrelationship of dependent activities, achieving balance between activities

Constraints: deadlines, regulatory control, scarcity of and internal competition for resources, external changes

Reviewing and monitoring: value analysis, systems analysis, performance standards and indicators, impact of technology.

In working through the BTEC Higher National programme in Business Studies, you will practise the following BTEC common skills:

Managing and developing self	✔
Working with and relating to others	✔
Communicating	✔
Managing tasks and solving problems	✔
Applying numeracy	✔
Applying technology	✔
Applying design and creativity	✔

You will practise most of these skills in working through this module.

Recommended reading

SECTION ONE

Session One
Bennis, W. and Nanus, B., 1985, *Leaders: The strategies for taking charge*, Harper. and Row.

Thompson, R., 1993, *Managing People*, Butterworth Heinemann.

Session Two
Pheysey, Dianna, 1992, *Organisational Cultures, Types and Transformations*, Routledge.

Session Three
Cross, K., Feather, J. and Lynch, R., 1994, *Corporate Renaissance*, Blackwell Publishers.

Stewart, A. M., 1994, *Empowering People*, Pitman.

Session Four
Cooper, C. L. and Makin, R., 1984, *Psychology for Managers*, British Psychological Society and Macmillan.

Robertson, I. T., Smith, M. and Cooper, D., 1992, *Motivation Strategies*, Institute of Personnel Management.

Session Five
Belbin, M., 1993, *Team Roles at Work*, Butterworth Heinemann.

Stott, Kenneth and Walker, Alan, *Teams, Teamwork and Team Building: A manager's complete guide to teams in organisations*, Prentice-Hall.

Session Six
Anderson, G. C., 1993, *Managing Performance Appraisal Systems: Design, implementation and monitoring for effective appraisal*, Blackwell Publishers.

Reddy, M., 1987, *The Manager's Guide to Counselling at Work*, British Psychological Society and Methuen.

SECTION TWO

Session One
Currie, R. M., 1972, *Work Study*, Pitman.

Lockyer, K., Muhlemann, A. and Oakland, J., 1988, *Production and Operations Management*, Pitman.

Session Two

Adair, J., 1988, *Effective Communicator*, Industrial Society.

Parry, Howell, 1991, *Successful Business Presentations*, Croner Publications.

Session Three

Martin, D. M., 1993, *Tough Talking: How to handle awkward situations*, Pitman.

Session Four

Oakland, J. S., 1993, *Total Quality Management: The route to improving performance*, Butterworth Heinemann.

National Council for Vocational Qualifications, 1989, *National Vocational Qualifications – Criteria and Procedures*, NCVQ.

GENERAL READING

These two readers cover many aspects of this module.

Armstrong, M., *Management Processes and Functions*, Institute of Personnel Management.

Koontz, H. and Weihrich, H., 1990, *Essentials of Management*, McGraw Hill.

Name

Module

BTEC Skill	Activity No./Date	Activity No./Date	Activity No./Date	Activity No./Date	Activity No./Date
Managing and developing self					
Working with and relating to others					
Communicating					
Managing tasks and solving problems					
Applying numeracy					
Applying technology					
Applying design and creativity					

Managing People

Management and leadership

Objectives

After participating in this session, you should be able to:

▶ describe the key differences between management and leadership

▶ describe the main components of the role of manager

▶ identify the main components of the role of leader

▶ discuss a range of management styles.

In working through this session, you will practise the following BTEC common skills:

Managing and developing self	✔
Working with and relating to others	
Communicating	
Managing tasks and solving problems	✔
Applying numeracy	
Applying technology	
Applying design and creativity	

Management

Peter Drucker (*The Practice of Management*, Heinemann Ltd, 1955) commented: 'Management is a practice rather than a science.' This is somewhat self-evident, but to try to make rules for successful management, in the same way as a chemical process, ignores the main element of variability – namely the people involved. The activities and the role of a manager will vary depending on the organisation and its culture. Sales organisations tend to give the title of 'manager' very freely, while manufacturing industry has been reluctant to do away with the traditional 'tall' hierarchy where there are far less management positions to be had, and where titles like foreman/woman, and supervisor are more common.

Management is a broad concept. Trying to encapsulate it in a single definition is bound to be a tricky process. Some commentators have attempted to explain the concept by first defining what 'management' is not. They have identified the following roles that, on their own, do not make up a 'manager':

- business person

- administrator

- accountant

- specialist

- shop steward

- politician.

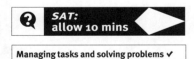

SAT:
allow 10 mins

Managing tasks and solving problems ✔

ACTIVITY 1

Consider the six roles given above and under each one, list one or two activities related to that role, which you imagine a typical manager might have to perform. For example, the 'business person' will also be looking for opportunities to expand, develop and improve the business or his or her part of the business.

Commentary...

The 'business person' and 'administrator' elements within a managerial role may be fairly obvious. As an administrator, a manager always has a significant amount of checking, controlling, monitoring, and reporting to do, and as a 'business person' may be looking for opportunities to expand, develop and improve the business or his/her part of the business.

'Specialist' roles (usually considered to refer to technical specialists) are still prevalent in many organisations, where the technical specialist may be seen to manage by having a monopoly on knowledge. Most managers also have a requirement to control budgets and general finances and, therefore, need to adopt an accountant role from time to time.

The 'shop-steward' role for a manager may be considered to be the 'people' activity, but it is highly unlikely that this alone will lead to the effective decision making. The political games-playing that takes place in most organisations will need to be recognised within the 'politician' role although it is arguable that an effective manager should be advised to recognise the politics within the organisation but avoid joining in. To the list of six on page 14, the role of 'amateur psychologist and counsellor' could also be added.

Having defined what it is not, the list, nevertheless, provides a guide to the range of activities for which the manager needs to have skills. These skills need to be present if the person is to carry out one of the fundamental purposes of management: to exercise control. This is not purely defined as having power over the people under their authority; the manager must also ensure that overall goals are met by the allocation of appropriate resources. This will often lead to yet another of the key management roles: resolving conflict. A more comprehensive definition of the role of the manager could be described as follows:

- Seeing the 'wood for the trees'.

- Providing a structure or framework by which objective decisions can be made.

- Recognising that most business problems are unlikely to be unique.

- Providing a pragmatic, intelligent approach to problem solving.

- Using the basic tools of decision making where appropriate.

- Answering the six keys questions: What? Where? How? Who? Why? When?

- Providing a reference point for solutions.

If you examine this list, you should recognise that, within each of these seven sub-roles, there are some key skills of:

- planning

- disseminating

- analysing

- organising.

These are essentially the skills of doing things correctly and properly. Some current jargon words which we have not used in these descriptions are **vision** and **empowerment**. This is because they are concerned with 'leadership' rather than 'management'. These attributes are equally essential for the effective achievement of success but are more concerned with the skills of doing the right things (i.e. leadership) rather than doing things right (i.e. management).

RECALL:
allow 10 mins

Before we move on to look at the alternative ingredients of leadership and the differences from management, it would be useful to test how much of the definitions of management you are able to recall. Make notes which summarise the skills and activities that define management.

Leadership

Leadership, as distinct from management, is, as we have already suggested, primarily concerned with 'doing the right thing' and these 'right things' are the key concerns of vision and empowerment. These are complex issues which require many skills and attributes, and we shall examine each of them separately later.

Over the last 20 years, a wide range of thinking on the subject of leadership has taken place as a result of research and practical observation. Here are a few of these researchers' thoughts.

Warren Bennis (*Leaders – The Strategies for Taking Charge*, Harper and Row, 1985): One of the most influential thinkers who identified four main abilities of effective leaders: vision, communications, trust and self-knowledge. These four elements are referred to in different ways by many of the other 'experts', and we shall be examining each of them in more detail.

David McClelland (Power is the Great Motivator, *Harvard Business Review*, March–April 1976): Demonstrated that most effective leaders had exceptionally high needs for power and influence, not just to benefit themselves, but to achieve positive results for their organisation and their members. He called this 'social power' since it is aimed at benefiting everyone in the organisation. This is a slightly different perspective, but it highlights the importance of power in the whole process of leadership while emphasising that this power need is not necessarily a self-indulgent one.

Warner Burke (*Executive Power*, Jossey-Bass, 1986): Refers to the key process of leadership as empowering oneself. In recent developments, the word empowerment is a commonly used expression to describe the process of 'taking charge'. Burke suggested that leaders tend to be those who have sufficient presence and self-belief to be able to recognise the many ways of controlling and directing situations, from the position of a clear understanding of themselves.

Robert House (*Charismatic Leadership in Management*, Jossey-Bass, 1988): Identified charisma in effective leaders. The word has become widely used in many different ways, but House considered it to be mainly concerned with an individual's capacity to create a vision that appeals to others and to communicate that vision in a striking and unforgettable manner.

Elliott Jacques (*The Form of Time*, Crane, Russak and Co, 1982): Provided the basis for the concept of the 'visionary leader' when he identified that authentic visionary leaders can develop realistic visions covering decades for large organisations. Jacques referred to the leader's 'span of vision' and talked of the ability of some gifted leaders to be able to hold out a vision that not only dealt with the current issues facing the organisation, but also had, within it, the ingredients essential for its long-term survival. This implies the existence of some strong moral or ethical rationalities within the vision, with which most people are able to agree.

Edgar Schein (*Organisational Culture and Leadership*, Jossey-Bass, 1985): Suggested that one of the most important functions of a leader is to shape an organisation's culture by inculcating specific values and beliefs. Once again, this implies some form of rational thinking by the leader, or at least some attractive thinking which will appeal to the vast majority of people affected. It is only by exhibiting this characteristic that a culture may successfully be changed.

In recent years, people like **Charles Handy** (*The Age of Unreason*, Hutchinson, 1989) have carried out more detailed research and have published their findings on a range of different situations, the vast majority of which supports the conclusions of these earlier researchers.

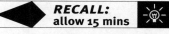
RECALL:
allow 15 mins

One of the common threads within each of the above versions of leadership is vision. Before you move on to look at vision, it would be useful to test how much of the definitions of leadership from the management gurus mentioned earlier you are able to recall. In about six words for each guru, list the key principles as outlined by:

Warren Bennis

David McClelland

Warner Burke

Robert House

Elliott Jacques

Edgar Schein.

VISION

What is it that enables good leaders to do the right things? What are these somewhat intangible qualities that constitute the charisma of a leader? Warren Bennis in his seminal book *Leaders – the Strategies for Taking Charge* (Harper and Row, 1985) concludes, after interviewing 90 recognised leaders from all walks of life, that attempts to ascribe common traits to leaders is more difficult than it would appear.

Bennis found that the 90 leaders comprise some who dress for success and some who do not; well-spoken, articulate leaders and laconic inarticulate ones; some John Wayne types and some 'who are definitely the opposite'. Nevertheless, despite what he termed a profound diversity, he did conclude that there were four main traits which were shared to a greater or lesser extent by all of them: attention, meaning, trust and self-awareness.

Attention (or providing a vision)

Leaders are able to communicate an extraordinary focus of commitment which attracts people to them. They provide a clear picture or vision of what is possible, usually of something which others, the followers, did not previously regard as feasible. The vision is not a mystical or religious one; it is usually in the form of an outcome, a goal or a direction. Leaders' intentions are always evident and their own passionate commitment to those intentions is infectious.

Meaning (understanding the vision)

The leader's skill is not in the mere explanation or clarification of the goal or direction, it is the creation of meaning. It is in the interpretation of the vision in terms which everyone not only understands but associates themselves with. Communication, of course, does not only take place through words or pictures but through actions; good leaders are able to portray their aims through the way they behave.

Trust (believing the vision)

Consistency is the basis of trust. Skilled leaders are absolutely consistent. People know where they stand with them. They do not shift ground or change their underlying focus. A recent study showed that people would much rather follow people they can count on, even when they disagree with that viewpoint, than people with whom they agree but who shift position frequently.

Self-awareness (achieving the vision)

Self-awareness is mainly concerned with having a good awareness of one's own skills and patterns of behaviour. It is to do with using these skills (and occasionally the patterns) and avoiding the more compulsive and conditioned behaviours. Good leaders know their strengths and nurture them and they do not try to hide their weaknesses in pretence. Like incompetent doctors, incompetent leaders can make things worse for people. They can act as carriers of stress and other problems.

The ability to hold out an exciting vision based on values and beliefs that appeal to people at every level – not only in a particular department, but also in the organisation as a whole, in the market place and in the world at large – is what leadership is about.

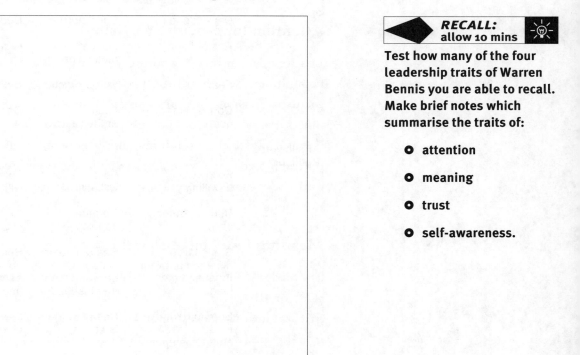

RECALL:
allow 10 mins

Test how many of the four leadership traits of Warren Bennis you are able to recall. Make brief notes which summarise the traits of:

- attention
- meaning
- trust
- self-awareness.

EMPOWERMENT

Leadership can move organisations from current to future states, create visions of potential opportunities for organisations, instil within workers commitment to change and instil new cultures and strategies in organisations that mobilise and focus energy and resources.

Most people generally perceive leadership in three basic ways:

- **coercive leadership** – the power-wielding, dominating autocrat
- **manipulative leadership** – the devious politician
- **real leadership** – the visionary, participative enthusiast.

The true nature of these three leadership types can also be identified through the behaviour and attitude of their followers.

	Coercive Leaders	Manipulative Leaders	Real Leaders
Followers show:			
	Submission	Caution	Involvement
	Dependence	Suspicion	Dedication
	Resignation	Lack of motivation	High involvement
	Fear	Self-protection	Enthusiasm
	Concern for own goals	Lack of enthusiasm	Commitment
Followers' attitudes:			
	Follow unwillingly	Follow less willingly	Follow willingly
	Require autocratic style	Require supervision	Respond to charisma
	See a large distance between them and the leader	See a medium distance between them and the leader	See little or no distance between them and the leader
	See authority in the use of reward and punishment	See authority in status	See authority as rational

FIGURE 1.1: *Behaviour and attitude of followers to different types of leaders.*

It has to be recognised that real leaders are, unfortunately, in a minority. Sadly, the types that still make up the vast bulk of leaders in current society are either manipulative, or coercive.

The real leader is concerned with the enabling process by which people may develop their full potential. This process is called empowerment. Real leaders encourage followers to see no distance between themselves and the leader; they encourage followers to become leaders. Real leaders are leaders of leaders. Once one is empowered, one is a leader, so the process of empowerment is the process of releasing people's leadership potential.

Tom Peters in *Thriving on Chaos* (Macmillan, 1988) lists ten points for the achievement of flexibility by empowering people:

- Involve everyone in everything.

- Use self-managing teams, i.e. relinquish authoritarian leadership.

- Listen, celebrate and recognise.

- Spend time lavishly on recruitment.

- Train and retrain.

- Provide incentive pay for everyone.

- Provide an employment guarantee.

- Simplify and/or reduce structure.

- Reconceive the middle-manager's role as a facilitator.

- Eliminate bureaucratic rules and humiliating conditions.

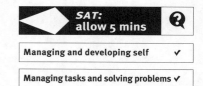

SAT:
allow 5 mins

Managing and developing self ✓

Managing tasks and solving problems ✓

ACTIVITY 2

The Institute for New Leadership Initiative lists twelve attributes of leaders:

- Develop a vision of the future.

- Decide to see to it that everything goes well.

- Develop practical action plans.

- Ensure plans are implemented and review their effectiveness.

- Stay open to learning.

- Develop high self-esteem.

- Build close desirable relationships with everyone.

- Become a leader of leaders.

- Take positive initiative instead of complaining or blaming.

- Put your attention on other people and the task in hand.

- Appreciate yourself and others well and often.

- Recognise attacks and deal with criticism, elegantly and well.

It suggests that every individual can aim to develop these attributes. It also stresses that this definition of leadership applies to all aspects of life and not solely to those within an industrial, commercial or political environment. This means that, as a student or as a manager, you can consider yourself against these characteristics. Using the list above, rate yourself out of 10 against each of the points. Score 10 if you rate yourself exceptionally high, down to 0 if you rate yourself with no ability in that attribute. You may consider that some of your points are influenced by the resources available to you and the organisational culture in which you may work. Nevertheless attempt an assessment against each item. Remember that being a leader does not depend on your being employed as a manager.

Commentary...

The higher your total score the more you are a real leader. The checklist you have just completed was developed by the Institute for New Leadership Initiative (INLI, 71 High Street, Saltford, Bristol BS18 3EW) and is based on the assumption that it is possible for each and every person to achieve a position of leadership in life.

Good leadership may be recognised in all walks of life: it is revered and its essential qualities much sought after. There is a basic principle which separates the titles of manager and leader: the issue of status. In order to be a manager in most organisations you must normally be located fairly highly in the organisational tree or hierarchy. To be a leader, you can be located anywhere. In fact, you can be a leader in any aspect of life in general, rather than specifically within a working context. There are some important implications of this principle:

Leadership is not the prerogative of a manager – management is

There are plenty of excellent managers operating within the world of work, who are keeping businesses alive and maintaining the systems and procedures. Very often, however, they are not leaders.

Leadership is not the prerogative of one single person

Each individual within an organisation may be a leader in one or more aspects of the operation. Any individual, irrespective of organisational status – director, manager or office cleaner – can assume leadership and take charge of their situation.

Leadership is not a title given to anyone within an organisation

Leadership is something which is assumed and comes about as a result of personal confidence and self-assuredness. As such, it is often not recognised overtly in any way, but is accepted by people, particularly the followers, through quiet respect and support.

SAT:
allow 15 mins

Managing tasks and solving problems✔

ACTIVITY 3

Try to remember three clear instances where you have identified, in other people, managerial behaviour, i.e. someone who was 'doing things right', and three instances of someone behaving as a real leader, i.e. someone who was 'doing the right things'. You may be able to recognise such behaviour in people in your learning institution, or even in your friends and relatives.

Commentary...

In practice, it was probably very difficult for you to identify many instances in which the distinction between manager and leader is significantly highlighted and distinguishable since effective people are often also efficient. In other words, when someone is a manager they are also probably leading reasonably well. However, the emphasis may have been somewhat different in each set of instances.

Let us summarise the differences between management and leadership.

Management is:

- concerned with 'doing things right'
- largely work-oriented
- comprised of skills which are capable of being learnt and of being taught.

Leadership is:

- concerned with 'doing the right things'
- includes activities to do with family, social life, sports or politics, as well as work
- concerned with 'personality', attitudes and values which are more capable of being 'released'.

This message was published in the *Wall Street Journal* recently:

People don't want to be managed.

They want to be led.

Whoever heard of a world manager?

World Leader, Yes

Educational Leader, Political Leader, Religious Leader, Scout Leader, Community Leader, Union Leader, Business Leader.

They lead. They don't manage.

The carrot always wins over the stick.

Ask the horse.

You can lead your horse to water, but you can't **manage** it to drink.

If you want to manage somebody, manage yourself.

Do that well, and you'll be ready to stop managing and start leading.

Categories of management style

In the remainder of this session, we look at a range of different management styles and develop an understanding of the different ways in which managers can operate.

MᴄGʀᴇɢᴏʀ's ᴛʜᴇᴏʀʏ X ᴀɴᴅ Y

McGregor, a management researcher and psychologist, believed that the way we manage others is decided by the views we have about people in general: in other words, the assumptions we make about each other. McGregor carried out some research and came to the conclusion that there were basically two different views of the world which could be summed up by the statements:

- People are basically lazy and prefer to do nothing.

- People are basically enthusiastic and like achieving things.

He called these views theory X and theory Y assumptions respectively.

It should be stressed that McGregor talked about beliefs and not what we observe. In this way, he suggested that a manager's style was dependent upon his or her assumptions about others, and not necessarily what people actually did or how they actually performed. For example, if you hold the view that people are basically lazy, then in managing you will probably constantly watch over them and even do the job for them at the first sign of difficulty.

Some examples of the beliefs are listed in table 1.1.

Theory X Beliefs	Theory Y Beliefs
People are basically lazy and prefer to do nothing.	People are basically active and like setting targets for themslves.
People work mainly for money and status.	People look for many things in work including pride in achievement, enjoyment, friendship or new challenges.
The main force keeping people at work is their fear of being fired.	The main force keeping people at work is the desire to achieve their own goals.
People are dependent on leaders.	People like to be independent.
People do not want to think for themslves.	People know what is needed and can think for themsleves
People need to be supervised closley.	People will do a good job if they are trusted.
People resist change and like to stay in ruts.	People get tired of routines and enjoy new experiences.
People need to be pushed or driven.	People need to be encouraged and helped.

TABLE 1.1: *Examples of theory X and theory Y beliefs*

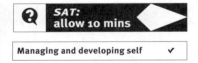

SAT:
allow 10 mins

Managing and developing self ✓

ACTIVITY 4

Take an honest look at yourself and tick the boxes in Table 1.1 that you believe represent your beliefs about people. Consider for a moment whether these beliefs have, or would have, a significant effect on the behaviour you adopt while managing people.

Commentary...

You may find that you have a predominant set of beliefs, either X or Y; alternatively you may find yourself with a mixture of the two.

One of the main criticisms of McGregor's theory is that it is too simplistic; it attempts to categorise beliefs under only two headings rather than face the fact that people tend to have a mixture of views about people. Indeed, when managers are asked to carry out similar self-awareness tests, the most common view that emerges is that either 'Some people are Theory X and others are Theory Y' or 'Some of the time people are lazy (theory X) but under other circumstances they are enthusiastic and hard working (theory Y)'.

In fairness, we should state that McGregor was simply making the point that we all tend to have a preference for one view or the other, and that most of our management actions are influenced by those assumptions.

AUTOCRATIC/DEMOCRATIC CONTINUUM

Another way of looking at management style is the autocratic/democratic continuum. This continuum has two extremes of management styles: **total authority** with no discussion and no employee involvement in decision making at one end and **total participation** in decisions at the other. In between is a range of alternative styles as shown in figure 1.2. It shows that there is no one way of acting when making decisions.

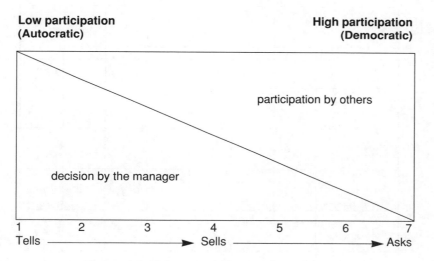

FIGURE 1.2: *The autocratic/democratic continuum.*

The way a manager behaves can depend on the expectations of the individuals and the group with whom he or she is working, and his or her own ideas about being a manager. Choosing the appropriate style along the continuum can be a problem, particularly if you are naturally inclined towards one style and not very familiar with the other.

The style that operates within a group may vary according to the needs of the situation, so that a highly authoritarian style (with low participation in decision making) may be appropriate during an

CATEGORIES OF MANAGEMENT STYLE

emergency (if, for example, a building catches fire) or when it is otherwise essential that all members of the group do the same thing (for example, during a surgical operation). In such cases the members of the group can achieve the objective most readily by acting in unity, even though the action taken may not be theoretically the 'best' action.

Blake's grid

Another look at management style comes from an idea by Blake who, like McGregor, was interested in the attitudes of managers. He saw that the basic problem for the manager is in balancing the need to finish the job with the needs of the people doing the job.

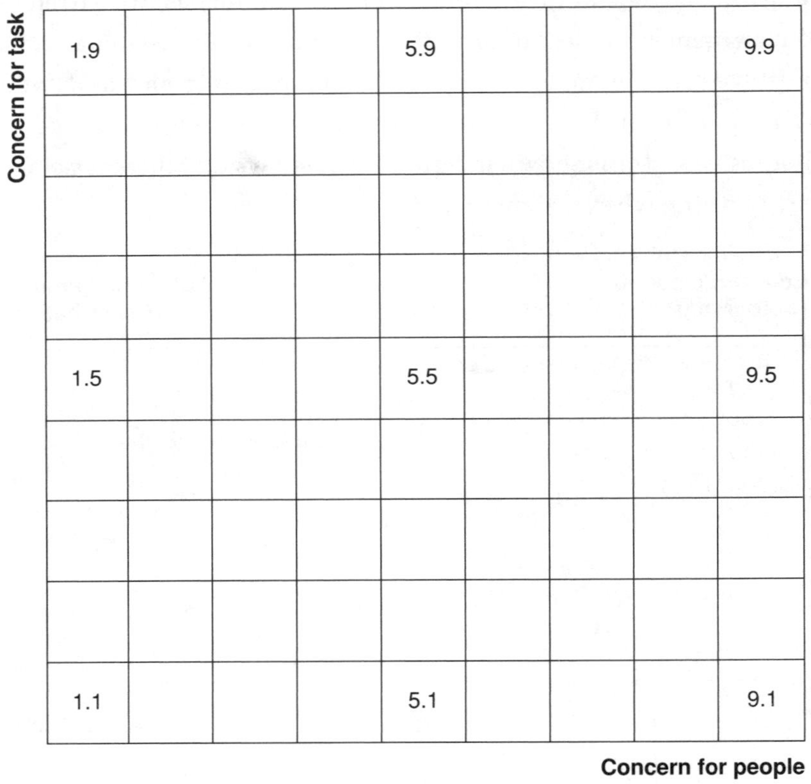

FIGURE 1.3: *Blake's grid.*

In Blake's grid, we can see several combinations of numbers which refer to slightly different styles of management, with the first figure relating to people and the second to task.

1.1 – total abdication: no concern for task or people

1.5 – some concern for task but none for people

1.9 – high concern for task but none for people: the harsh autocrat

5.1 – some concern for people but none for task

5.5 – a medium concern for both task and people

5.9 – some concern for people but a higher concern for task

9.1 – high concern for people but none for task: 'the social-club manager'

9.5 – some concern for task but a higher concern for people

9.9 – a high concern for both task and people: 'the ideal manager'

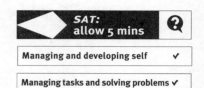

SAT: allow 5 mins	❓
Managing and developing self	✔
Managing tasks and solving problems	✔

ACTIVITY 5

The three ways of examining management style looked at so far, could be said to be observations of individuals' attitudes rather than specific managerial traits. On this basis, each of us possesses attitudes in one form or another even if we are not currently managing anybody or anything.

With this in mind, and as an exercise in self-awareness, identify your style in each of the three theories described in this section.

- **Are you predominantly theory X or theory Y?**

- **Are you an autocrat or democrat?**

- **Are you task-oriented or people-oriented?**

Attempt your self-analysis in the context of a current or recent activity you have undertaken with others, either as a manager or as a student.

Commentary...

There are some broad correlations between the three theories which should show in your self-analysis.

If you identified yourself as predominantly Theory X then one would expect a judgement on participation to lead towards the autocratic end of the spectrum. Equally, your style assessment on Blake's grid would lean towards 1.9 rather than 9.1 or 9.9.

If on the other hand you identify as a Theory Y person, then your Blake's grid position would be 9.1 or 5.1 and you would probably see yourself as democratic.

A more complex mixture of these theoretical types might suggest that you have a more flexible, situational style.

REDDIN'S 3D GRID

The 3D management style is a Canadian theory of management behaviour and is based on similar principles to Blake's grid in that two key characteristics are task orientation and people orientation. Reddin, however added a third dimension of effectiveness, so that each predominant task/relationship mix also has an alternative in less or more effective behaviour. This is an interesting nuance since all the other style theories mentioned so far do not make any reference to effectiveness, only to broad behaviour.

People		
Missionary	Compromiser
Deserter	Autocrat

Task

FIGURE 1.4: *Reddin's grid – the less effective matrix.*

In the less effective matrix shown in figure 1.4, the four styles are: deserter, missionary, autocrat and compromiser.

Deserter

These managers often display lack of interest in both task and relationships with people, and are ineffective not only because of their lack of interest but also because of their effect on morale. They may not only desert, but may also hinder the performance of others by withholding information.

Missionary

The missionary managers put harmony and relationships as an overriding priority to such an extent that in order to ensure that they feel good about themselves, and in an attempt to make others feel good about them, they are prepared to risk ignoring the task.

Autocrat

This type of manager sees the task as the overriding priority; they are almost totally unconcerned about people and relationships. They have no confidence in others; people dislike them, and so are only motivated by the autocrats when direct pressure is applied to them.

Compromiser

While having a concern for both task and people, these managers find it difficult to make decisions. They are usually influenced by the most recent or heaviest pressure, and tend to compromise rather than find the optimum answer.

These four management styles have some similarities to those which may be derived from the Blake's grid theory:

- Deserter: 1.1

- Missionary: 5.1

- Autocrat: 1.9

- Compromiser : 5.5

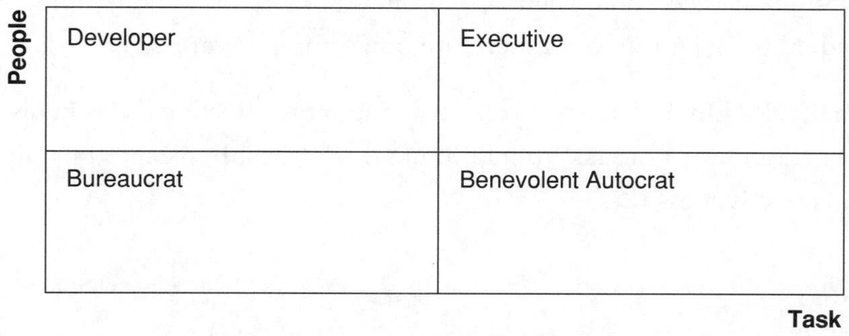

People		
Developer	Executive
Bureaucrat	Benevolent Autocrat

Task

FIGURE 1.5: *Reddin's grid – the more effective matrix.*

In Reddin's more effective manager styles (figure 1.5) we have four more descriptions: bureaucrat, developer, benevolent autocrat and executive.

Bureaucrat

These managers are more effective than deserters in that they at least follow rules and procedures (though often to minimum effect), while at the same time giving little attention to people or task. They follow regulations, appear to be involved and try not to let it affect morale.

Developer

These managers can be seen as the facilitators and empowerers since they see their role primarily to develop the skills of others and to provide a workplace environment which ensures motivation and job satisfaction. While these managers are usually very effective through other people, occasionally their focus on relationship issues may temporarily lead them to avoid dealing with important tasks.

Benevolent autocrat

These managers are fairly common in that they strive to achieve the tasks before them while appearing to be concerned about people. Their people concern however, is often a more manipulative one rather than reflecting a genuine participative approach. They have a basic implicit trust in their own ability to resolve matters.

Executive

This style is the one which embodies the maximum attention to both task and people as they see their role as maximising the effort of others in relationship to the short- and long-term tasks. They set high standards but equally recognise that people are different and have different expectations. Their commitment to both task and people is evident to all and they are therefore powerful motivators.

Finally, Reddin links the less effective and more effective styles in his 3D grid in terms of task orientation (X), relationship orientation (Y) and effectiveness (Z).

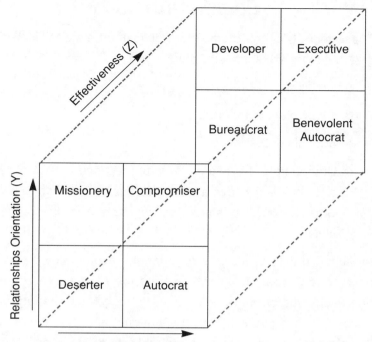

FIGURE 1.6: *Reddin's 3D grid.*

ACTIVITY 6

Consider the four more effective styles and try to make a direct comparison with those derived from Blake's grid.

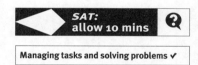

	People	Task
Developer		
Benevolent autocrat		
Executive		
Bureaucrat		

Commentary...

These four styles are a little more difficult to relate to Blake's grid, but there are some similarities:

- ◉ Developer: 9.1

- ◉ Benevolent autocrat: 5.9

- ◉ Executive: 9.9

- ◉ Bureaucrat: This is an awkward one since the 1.1 style does not easily have a more effective comparison within Blake's grid. If pushed, you could say that it is a 3.3 style.

In Reddin's theory, there is no strongly recommended style preference, apart from the excellence of the executive approach. Rather, there is the implicit suggestion that styles have their own use in different situations, and that having a flexible repertoire of styles is probably more important than being fixed in one.

SITUATIONAL STYLE THEORY

Leaning heavily on some of the previous theories for its emphasis on task and relationship orientations, the situational style theory suggests that no one style is best. Successful managers are those who can choose to adapt their behaviour to meet the demands of their own unique situations.

The model developed from this theory is based on two factors:

- ◉ the amount of task behaviour and personal relationship behaviour the manager must provide

- ◉ the level of development apparent in the subordinates' behaviour.

Task behaviour is the extent to which the manager engages in one-way communication, explaining what each subordinate is to do as well as when, where, and how tasks are to be performed. Relationship behaviour is the extent to which managers engage in two-way communication by providing support and encouragement.

The subordinates' level of development is defined by:

- ◉ the extent to which they are motivated to achieve the task

- their ability and desire to accomplish the task

- their knowledge and skills available in order to complete the task.

In the model shown in figure 1.7, there are four quadrants defining the different situational styles, where the relevant style of management would be dependent upon the level of development of the subordinate.

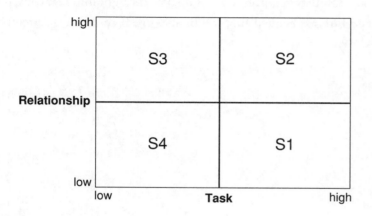

FIGURE 1.7: *Situational style matrix.*

S1: High task/low relationship

S1 is referred to as the 'telling' style because it is characterised by one-way communication in which the manager defines the roles of the subordinates and tells them what, where, when and how to do the various tasks.

S2: High task/high relationship

S2 is referred to as the 'selling' style because in this situation, although the manager is primarily still directing the subordinates, there is also a strong attempt at two-way communication and support in order to encourage the subordinates to become committed to the decisions.

S3: Low task/high relationship

S3 is the 'participation' style because the subordinates, who have all the necessary skills and knowledge to complete the task, share in decision making through two-way communication and more facilitating behaviour from the manager.

S4: Low task/low relationship

S4 is described as 'delegation' because it implies the subordinates taking complete charge of the situation, mainly as a result of their demonstrable maturity, and willingness to take responsibility.

Some subordinates may be at different levels of development for different tasks and, as a result, the manager will have to change style. However, changes must be gradual, because sudden changes may undermine or confuse the subordinate. Choosing the appropriate style is a skill that requires a great deal of thought and effort by the manager, but it is argued that it will also produce the most effective results.

This session has covered five different theories related to management style. Before moving on to the next session, see if you can briefly summarise each of the five theories.

summary

This session has covered the concepts of management and leadership.

- ▶ We have seen that managers can occupy a variety of roles. Key managerial tasks are to exercise control and to resolve conflict. Key skills include planning, disseminating information, analysing problems and organising activities.

- ▶ Leaders provide vision and empower organisations and individuals. They instil commitment to organisational objectives and focus energy and resources.

- ▶ Leaders must command attention, provide meaning in communicating their vision, instil trust in others and need to be aware of their strengths and weaknesses.

- ▶ Management skills are capable of being learnt, but leadership is assumed and comes about as a result of confidence and self-assuredness. Managers' authority comes from their position in the organisational hierarchy, but anyone in the organisation may display leadership.

- ▶ Managers can adopt a range of styles. In this session, we looked at five ways of analysing different approaches: McGregor's theory X and theory Y; the autocratic/democratic continuum; Blake's grid, Reddin's 3D grid; and situational style theory.

The culture of organisations

CULTURE

POWER

POLITICS

VALUES AND BELIEFS

IDEOLOGIES

SOCIAL INFLUENCES

Objectives

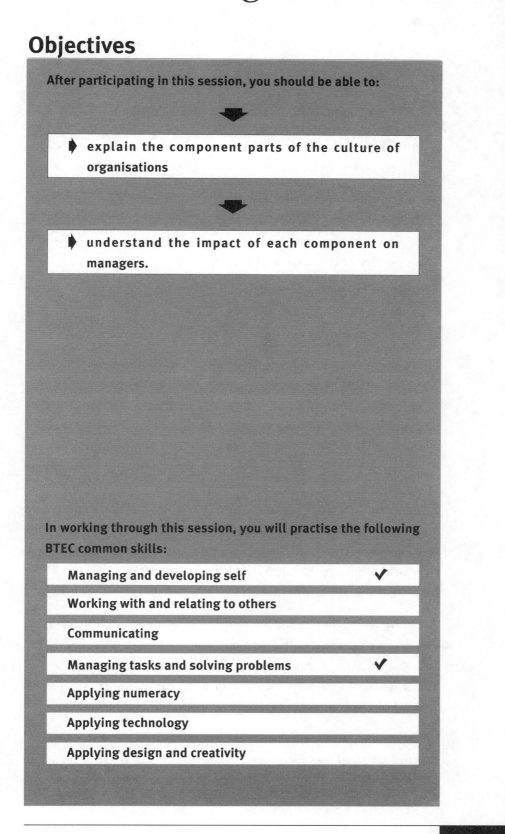

After participating in this session, you should be able to:

▶ explain the component parts of the culture of organisations

▶ understand the impact of each component on managers.

In working through this session, you will practise the following BTEC common skills:

Managing and developing self	✔
Working with and relating to others	
Communicating	
Managing tasks and solving problems	✔
Applying numeracy	
Applying technology	
Applying design and creativity	

Culture

Organisational culture is an extremely difficult issue to define since there are so many inter-relating components:

- **Power** – Who holds the legitimate authority and who makes the decisions in the organisation? These authority figures and decision makers may not be the same people.

- **Politics** – What types of different relationships exist in the organisation and whose views have unofficial influence?

- **Values and beliefs** – What do the decision makers believe in, and how well are these values accepted by the rest of the people in the organisation?

- **Ideologies** – What underlying philosophies influence management style and procedures? Is there a recognisable policy of how to deal with people?

- **Social influences** – What are the different social pressures on behaviour? These could include issues of style, fashion and taste, as well as more deeply ingrained social elements.

Large organisations tend to have a dominant 'culture' which all employees share to one degree or another. They also have subcultures in individual departments or divisions where the members of that department share the same values. We could call this subculture or a 'rogue' culture. Of course, in some situations, the values of one department may clash with those of the predominant organisational culture. Where this happens, there usually has to be either accommodation of the 'rogue' culture by the organisation's culture, or conflict between the rogue culture and the organisation's culture. In the latter case, the staff within the rogue culture can attempt a take-over of the dominant culture or, alternatively, the strength of the rogue culture will be diminished.

An example of this would be where a research and development department operates with a strong team identity, and a relaxed and casual approach to rules, procedures, and standards of dress, as contrasted with the organisation in which it operates as a whole which has a strong hierarchy, adherence to rules, and formal dress.

In *In Search of Excellence* (Harper & Row, 1984) Tom Peters talks about 'organisational skunk-works' where groups of like-minded organisational 'skunks', or rebels, band together to influence change. Peters argues that, although it is often healthy for organisations to encourage 'skunk-works', they are usually discouraged and extinguished by predominant cultures.

Organisational cultures can be weak or strong. Their strength can be measured on the basis of:

- the extent to which the culture is shared and accepted by everyone in the organisation

- the depth and intensity in the sense of acceptance and commitment to that culture by everyone.

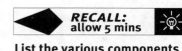

RECALL:
allow 5 mins

List the various components of organisational culture.

Power

An organisation may be viewed as a set of human systems in which there are three contributory factors: power, interests and conflict.

Power

Looked at in human terms, power is the medium by which individuals can pursue their interests and deal with any conflicts. This recognises that individuals are likely to have different aims from those of the organisation as a whole, and they will use their membership of the organisation for their own ends.

Interests

We can look at these in terms of the work to be performed, the career interests of individual employees, and their activities outside the immediate work situation. These vary widely from person to person. Such interests are likely to be influenced by individual personalities, commitments, values and beliefs. For example, if you have a job, sometimes you may be asked by your manager to stay late (he or she is using power) to complete an important task and you are quite happy to do so. On other occasions, the request conflicts with a social or family matter. Your father or mother might be ill and need you to help. This is the kind of difficult decision, we all have to make from time to time.

Conflict

This view of organisations proposes that conflict is likely to be perpetual. Therefore, some means of control and regulation need to be set up.

There are two ways in which power operates:

- **Authority** legitimises power so that a person in authority has the right to give orders and expect people to obey.

- **Influence** is much broader in scope than authority, and is normally associated with the definitions of leadership.

It is possible for people to advance in organisations by using the avenue of politics, and, in turn, organisational politics can be used to acquire power. This usually happens through powerful people giving power and opportunities to others in return for their support.

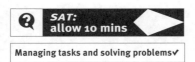

SAT:
allow 10 mins

Managing tasks and solving problems✔

ACTIVITY 1

Read the case study below. Identify ways in which power and opportunity have been given to people within Cuddly Toys.

CUDDLY TOYS

Jim Bannion is sales director of Cuddly Toys and has worked for the company for 15 years. He was initially recruited by the chairman, who is a friend of Jim's father. Jim started in the store room as a labourer but was soon shifted to a supervisory role and after three years, found himself in charge of administration. With a little help from the chairman, Jim was encouraged to apply for the job of quality manager to which he was appointed and in which he stayed for another four years, until moving to take up the vacant position of sales director.

Jim likes people around him who think the same way as him and so he has appointed some of his colleagues from his previous department into some of the more important posts in sales. When it comes to the annual appraisals, Jim always makes sure that his supporters are rewarded with above-the-norm pay rises.

Jim also has an assistant who is responsible for the company car fleet. Although the policy of the company is for every salesperson to have a Ford saloon, Jim's assistant has found a way around this and some of the high-flyers in the sales force have been given BMWs.

Commentary...

You may have identified some of the following methods: patronage, favouritism and nepotism.

- **Patronage** is helping to appoint someone to office and supporting their careers.

- **Favouritism** is singling out people for rewards.

- **Nepotism** is when family members are supplied with jobs, opportunities and rewards in preference to others.

Many people join organisations for the sole purpose of acquiring power, as they believe it can lead to monetary rewards and influence. This raises the question of ethics. Business ethics are the codes of behaviour adopted by an organisation (as well as by individuals and the professions). These codes may set out how a company negotiates for contracts, for example, or whether it will deal with certain countries or regimes. They can also apply internally to how employees ought to behave towards each other.

It is crucial that ethical standards are maintained when a quest for power is taken to extremes. These situations can often have a negative affect on the organisation. Managers often spend time on acquiring 'power' and are successful at obtaining promotion, but their subordinates are less satisfied, and this can result in low morale and decreased productivity.

Politics

When considering the effects of politics on managers, we must first take a close look at the manager's personal position in the situation. There are some strong arguments for managers to avoid becoming involved on a personal level in any organisational politics, mainly because of the potential damage to trust and image. Sometimes, however, it may be extremely difficult to stay completely aloof.

Politics, as described by Tannenbaum (*Social Psychology of the Work Situation*, Tavistock, 1966), is concerned with any process whereby the aims of individuals are achieved through influencing others. Here, we are describing the ability of one individual to both understand thoughts and feelings of people who are different from him or her and also behave in a different manner according to the needs of the situation. The basic principle of this school of thought is that people develop certain strategies which determine their work behaviour and until these strategies are understood, it is impossible to be successful in organisations; instead, you will be politically inept.

Three distinct strategies have been identified which characterise the way people in organisations operate: alpha, beta and zeta.

Alpha strategy

These people have a short-term view of the future and prefer to try to maintain the *status quo*. In doing so, they tend to accept the organisational constraints and power dependencies. They concentrate on very specific task and people skills within their jobs so that they are seen, and want to be seen, as being very good at their jobs, and as one of the 'boys/girls'.

Beta strategy

This strategy involves people adopting an approach which accepts the overall values and beliefs of the organisation, while at the same time questioning the constraints and power dependencies that others create for them. These people interact with others who are basically different from them, and they understand the ways in which various parts of the organisation operate. They need the skills involved in appreciating organisational systems and dealing with different people. They tend to take a medium-term view of the future.

Zeta strategy

These people have a long-term view of both their organisations and the future generally. They have an appreciation of marketing and the marketplace, and are able to negotiate changes in the organisation required to meet future needs. They have a fundamental questioning approach to the task, values and philosophy of the organisation and do not accept the existing constraints and power dependencies.

SAT:
allow 5 mins

Managing tasks and solving problems✓

ACTIVITY 2

Identify three 'power bases' or sources of power, which a person may be able to use in order to influence others. For example, expertise or track record could be two bases upon which to build power and influence. Now list three more.

Commentary...

Apart from expertise or track record, you may have identified such things as:

- credibility, e.g. from qualifications or from prominence in professional bodies
- informal contacts
- control over information
- control over the work flow
- group support
- being available
- being known as a winner.

Values and beliefs

Another key component of culture is the value system which underpins an organisation, and this system is a complex mixture of many individual value systems. If the values and beliefs of the decision makers coincide with those of their subordinates, then harmonious relationships should exist. If not, there may be the seeds of conflict present.

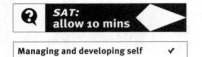

SAT:
allow 10 mins

Managing and developing self   ✔

ACTIVITY 3

Here is a checklist of cultural values which cover a wide range of issues. Each pair of statements represent values at either end of a continuum.

Underneath each pair of statements, ring the number on the 1–9 scale which signifies what your personal values are in relation to those statements. Then, for the top five items only, cross the number which you believe equates to, either the values of the organisation in which you work or, if you are a student, the values which you suspect are held by decision makers in companies.

Problem solving
Rational/Logical   Instinctive/ Impulsive
1   2   3   4   5   6   7   8   9

The environment
Can be controlled by humans   Beyond human control
1   2   3   4   5   6   7   8   9

Authority
Resentment/Rebellion   Valued/Respected
1   2   3   4   5   6   7   8   9

Time
Only the present important   Future planning valued
1   2   3   4   5   6   7   8   9

Science and technology
The servant of humanity   The enemy of humanity
1   2   3   4   5   6   7   8   9

Work
A necessary evil   Humanity's highest expression
1   2   3   4   5   6   7   8   9

Material objects
Of utmost value   Of little value
1   2   3   4   5   6   7   8   9

Life
All life highly valued   Individual life less important than group survival
1   2   3   4   5   6   7   8   9

Child-rearing
Strict control   Permissiveness
1   2   3   4   5   6   7   8   9

Death
A meaningless waste   Enriches life
1   2   3   4   5   6   7   8   9

Commentary...

Clearly, these ten issues raise a number of important points that are specific to the cultures you find in western societies. They touch on factors like nationalism, social class, religious beliefs, and upbringing. The number you circle for each item does not reflect a right or wrong answer. It is more a reflection of differences between cultures. In a multicultural society, you would expect to find a huge variety of responses.

When you compare your own answers to the values which you consider are held by decision makers in companies, is there much of a discrepancy? If there is, it may indicate the possibility of current or potential stress for you at work, or at least potential conflict.

Ideologies

The culture of any organisation has something to do with its history: the path it has taken, its successes and failures, and the original 'mission' of the organisation. Also it has something to do with goals and values, and the direction the organisation is currently taking. These sorts of influences determine what are regarded as appropriate relationships between an individual and all the other people in the organisation. As a result, a sort of 'social contract' is established in which the values are established, and in which the rules and controls over them are agreed.

Roger Harrison (How to describe your organisation, *Harvard Business Review*, September 1972) has identified four distinct organisation value systems or ideologies which are often competing:

- power orientation

- role orientation

- task orientation

- people orientation.

He states that the politics played, and the strategies and tactics adopted within each of these ideologies, will be very different.

Power orientation

The organisation is set up to compete. It dominates its environment and vanquishes all opposition. It is competitive and jealous of its territories, markets, land area, products and access to resources. It seeks to expand at the expense of weaker organisations; it is concerned with hierarchical distinctions and strives to have more of everything than its neighbour. Organisations such as IBM in USA and Rupert Murdoch's media empire could be termed power-oriented.

Role orientation

These organisations aspire to orderliness and rationality. They are preoccupied with legality, legitimacy, responsibility, dependability and correctness. Competition and conflict are regulated or replaced by agreements, rules, regulations and procedures, and the rights and privileges of all people are carefully defined, limited and adhered to. There is often a strong emphasis on hierarchy and status, but this is moderated by the system of promotion and the legality of career development. The Civil Service and large educational organisations are examples of this type of ideology.

Task orientation

These organisations regard achievement and accomplishment of goals and targets as the most important values. The goal could be economic, reforming the government or helping the poor, and it is important that the structure, function and activities are all evaluated in terms of their contribution to the achievement of the goal. Nothing stands in the way of accomplishing the task, even if there are outdated roles, rules and regulators; these will be changed. If individuals do not have the skills, abilities or knowledge to perform a task, they will be trained or replaced. Authority is considered legitimate only if based on power or a position in the hierarchy. Examples of this type of organisation include major charities, political parties and some of the specialist automobile companies.

People orientation

These organisations exist to serve the needs of their members. The growth and success of the organisation are not valued as ends in themselves but are valued because the organisation is useful to its members. The organisation provides the system and support for members (employees) to realise their potential. Authority and power (in the role) is eliminated as far as possible. People are expected to influence each other through helpfulness and care. In general, people should not have to do things that are incongruent with their own values and goals; consensus in decision making predominates. An artists' co-operative is an example of this type of organisation.

ACTIVITY 4

Take a look at your own organisation (or one you are reasonably familiar with, e.g. your college or university) and consider if any of Harrison's four ideologies describe the situation within the place. Can you recognise one predominant ideology or are there several in operation?

Commentary...

In examining these ideologies, you may have considered some of the following factors within each type of ideology.

Power:	Role:	Task:	People:
● competition ● jealousy ● ruthlessness ● desire to expand ● hierarchical ● acquisitive	● procedures ● rules ● agreements ● responsibilities ● regulations ● status	● goals ● achievements ● focus ● reward and sanctions ● train or replace ● targets	● personal influence ● care ● mutual support ● consensus ● helpfulness ● realising potential

These four types of orientation are used to describe the dominant theme of an organisation. It is possible for one organisation to contain elements of more than one of these orientations in different departments or divisions or even at different levels in the hierarchy. It is also possible for all four orientations to exist in one organisation.

SAT:
allow 5 mins

Managing tasks and solving problems✔

ACTIVITY 5

Tick the features in the list above to see how many of each type occur within the organisation you chose for Activity 4.

Social influences

The society in which we live can have an important influence on the culture of our organisations. Organisations must change and adapt to fit the demands and behaviours of host countries.

Geert Hofstede is a well-known researcher of cultural differences. His research (*Culture's Consequences,* Sage, 1980) shows significant differences between countries on a number of dimensions:

- power distance
- individualism/collectivism
- masculinity/femininity
- uncertainty avoidance.

Power distance

Power distance refers to the hierarchical nature of power in some organisations with seniority giving legitimacy to power, and where the higher a person is in the organisation, the greater the relative difference in power from someone in the lower reaches of the company. Britain tends to have high power distance where, traditionally, senior managers generally have power and authority, and this is accepted by their staff. Over the last 30 years, however, this situation has gradually changed, mainly due to imported ideas from Japan about participation and involvement. These have been linked with theories emanating from management gurus about flatter, non-hierarchical structures. Even though the economic recession of the 1990s has slightly diminished the importance of these ideas, the power distance is still receding, and British companies are becoming less hierarchical. There is, however, a suggestion that in some companies the distance between the very top layers of management and the rest is becoming greater, while in the rest of the organisation, power is more shared.

Individualism/collectivism

By individualism/collectivism, Hofstede means the principle of individual power and empowerment on the one hand, and the principle of the common needs, collected power and empowerment of groups on the other. Some would argue that individual freedom is not incompatible with a group or collective ethic. In business, for example, the 'quality revolution' of the last ten years has been fostering the notion of individual responsibility while at the same time extolling the virtues of teamworking. It has been shown, in some progressive organisations, that the apparent paradox between individualism and collectivism can be reconciled satisfactorily.

Masculinity/femininity

Some people would see Britain as a masculine society with some feminine aspects, such as concern for the family and work group. The masculine side is often demonstrated within organisations, in the often harsh and cold decision making, and the feminine side outside of work, in the activities involving mutual support and enjoyment. Of course, in many societies, there remains a strict division of labour along gender lines. This has led to the predominance of males in positions of power and authority – and, more generally in paid work – with women left in supportive, nurturing roles outside of work.

Uncertainty avoidance

A further dimension is uncertainty avoidance where avoidance of risk and adherence to the tried and trusted ways can often take precedence over innovation and change. Much has been documented on the principles and theories of change and resistance to change. Despite many attempts to encourage risk-taking and innovation, most of the established bastions of Western industry and commerce have remained in a position of uncertainty avoidance.

RECALL:
allow 15 mins

Describe briefly Hofstede's four dimensions of social culture attributes:

- power distance

- individualism/ collectivism

- masculinity/femininity

- uncertainty avoidance.

In this session, we have explored the complex issue of culture and ideologies in the context of organisations. Cultures evolve and change, and they can also be planned and influenced by many factors. An organisation's culture, if appropriate, assists an organisation to realise two purposes: its objectives and its stakeholders' goals.

- To meet its objectives, an organisation has to cope with the external environment.

- To meet its stakeholders' goals, an organisation has to differentiate between and meet the different needs of shareholders, suppliers, customers, workers and the community.

To achieve its objectives, an organisation has to focus on its outputs, methods and costs. No matter whether it is a profit-making organisation, a government department, or a voluntary body, in order to meet the needs of its stakeholders, it has to focus on everything in its external and internal environments.

As we have seen, most of the cultural/ideological/social influences not only have a subtle but none-the-less profound effect on the nature of the organisation, but also may significantly affect the nature and style of management itself.

We have seen that various ideologies and cultures can develop in order to reconcile the aims of an organisation. An additional dimension is the problem of adjusting the structures and processes of the organisation to meet the volatile demands of the internal and external environments, and the next session addresses this key dimension.

summary

This session has looked at how the organisational culture can impact on managers and influence the ways in which they can operate. Organisational culture can be analysed by studying five different components or attributes:

▶ Power is the medium by which individuals can pursue their interests and deal with conflict. In organisational terms, it may be exercised directly through authority or indirectly through influence.

▶ Organisational politics can be defined as the process whereby the aims of individuals are achieved through influencing others. We studied three strategies – alpha, beta and zeta – which characterise the different ways in which people operate.

▶ A key component of organisational culture is the value system that underpins an organisation. Organisational values may not be shared by all employees. In a multicultural society, you would expect to find a wide range of core values.

▶ Organisational ideologies refer to the mission of the organisation, its goals and values. Harrison identified four distinct values systems: power orientation, role orientation, task orientation and people orientation.

▶ Social influences have an important bearing on organisational culture. Hofstede showed how cultural differences can effect organisational behaviour. Important social dimensions are attitudes to power structures, to collectivism as against individualism, to gender – and the roles of men and women, and to risk and innovation.

Organisational development

Objectives

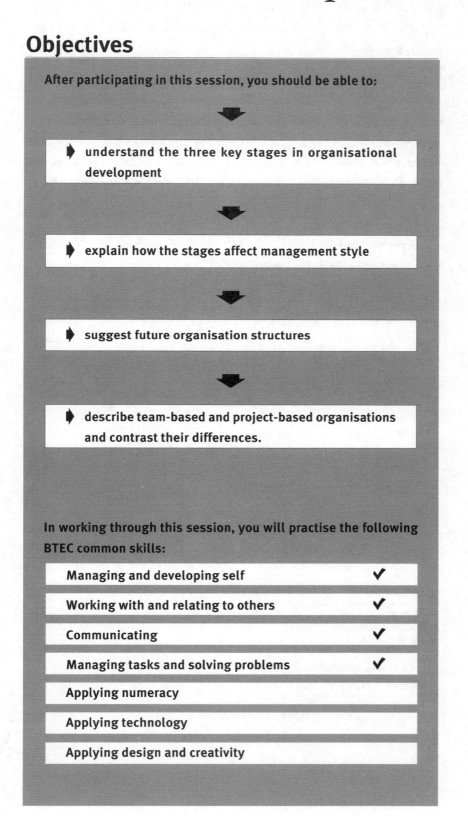

After participating in this session, you should be able to:

▶ understand the three key stages in organisational development

▶ explain how the stages affect management style

▶ suggest future organisation structures

▶ describe team-based and project-based organisations and contrast their differences.

In working through this session, you will practise the following BTEC common skills:

Managing and developing self	✔
Working with and relating to others	✔
Communicating	✔
Managing tasks and solving problems	✔
Applying numeracy	
Applying technology	
Applying design and creativity	

Stages in organisational development

Any organisation – in industry, commerce, education, politics, charity, or even the military – develops and changes over time. Such changes are often related to an organisation's growth. It is possible to build up a picture of the principles of development which a typical organisation will follow.

From its inception, any organisation develops by way of several 'phases'. At a particular stage of development, its management style, structure and processes follow a pattern which changes as the organisation develops. The move from one phase to another is a natural but often difficult process. As the company develops, its current approach no longer copes with the changing demands made upon it. The resulting problems force the company to change its approach, and thus move into the next phase of development. Three main phases can be identified: the pioneering phase, the scientific phase and the integrated phase.

These principles and ideas cannot be rigidly applied since every organisation is different, and also departments and divisions of organisations can be at different stages of development at one point in time. They are of value, however, in interpreting company problems and assisting in the change process.

Integrated Phase

Flexible, risk-taking, and empowering

Scientific Phase

Organised systematic and departmentalised

Pioneer Phase

Entrepreneurial and controlled by the owner

FIGURE 3.1: *Stages in organisational development.*

THE PIONEERING PHASE

New organisations, or relatively small ones, are usually led by an entrepreneur. The entrepreneur, by autocratic leadership and decision making, produces very clear organisational goals and an informal organisation with rigidly defined lines of communication. Few procedures or methods are standardised and forward planning is minimal. Little or no formal management development takes place, and managers are selected on the basis of their willingness to accept dependency and autocratic leadership.

The following are characteristics of the pioneer organisation:

- The structure is not rigidly defined.

- The pioneer runs the organisation like a family – a potential autocrat.

- Most employees are in direct touch with the top people, whether it be the pioneer him or herself or a small group of powerful leaders. Even in this stage, there will be an attempt to enforce a hierarchy with managers or supervisors appointed to certain functions.

- In practice, the pioneer is still likely to make day-to-day contact with every employee and may make instantaneous decisions without reference to the manager, thus rendering the hierarchy meaningless.

- Managers' and supervisors' jobs normally cover a range of tasks and functions (such as purchasing, production, technical, personnel) and they tend to develop their own personal systems, styles and techniques. This lays the foundation for the inconsistency and the poor communications which are at the root of the pioneer crises.

- Jobs are not formally defined, and duties vary and overlap. Within limits, each new entrant shapes the job to his or her personal inclinations.

- The direct control of all activities by the pioneer means that the organisational chart at that stage may well be a wheel (circle) with the pioneer at the hub.

SUPERGEAR ENGINEERING

Supergear Engineering is a 100-employee company having been started by the owner, Judith Frampton, seven years ago with five staff. The company has been extremely successful because of its engineering skills and its quick response to customers, many of whom have an excellent relationship with Judith. In fact Judith maintains regular contact, in a sales role, with all her major customers even though she has an enthusiastic (but increasingly frustrated) sales team. Judith also has a personal interest in the technical side of the business, being a chartered engineer herself.

She works at least 12 hours a day and expects everyone else to be equally committed. Judith is an autocrat but is fair to her employees, although she can be ruthless with people who she believes let her down. The business is expanding and there is a need for new premises as well as more modern equipment and machinery. The only computer in the company is a PC in the sales office, and there have been a few complaints from suppliers about late payment of invoices and incorrect quantities of goods delivered.

Judith is very energetic and is currently taking on the role of technical director since this person recently left the company. She has also been regularly visiting the bank manager to seek extra funds for financing expansion – so far with little success.

Organisations at this stage are often very successful for a period until external pressures tend to force changes. These pressures include growth in size, a need for specialist technology and better planning, lack of technology, and the introduction of professional managers who are not prepared to function within the paternalistic style. These factors contribute to what can be described as a **pioneer crisis**. The retirement or death of the original pioneer often causes further pressure for change

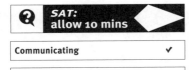

SAT:
allow 10 mins

Communicating   ✔

Managing tasks and solving problems ✔

ACTIVITY 1

List at least three of the symptoms of pioneer crisis in Supergear Engineering. Describe the style of management you would expect to find in this type of company.

Commentary...

The key symptoms of the pioneer crisis, as experienced by this company are:

- the dominating and all-pervasive role of the owner

- the lack of a more participative culture in which other managers are empowered to take charge

- the need for some basic systems and procedures in the company, e.g. in recruitment and selection, market research, purchasing, and management controls

- the lack of immediate cover for key people off sick

- the lack of clear job delineation especially with Judith's relationship with customers

- the need for quick expansion

- the need for money to finance this expansion

- the need for computerisation.

There may be a few more symptoms of crisis in this particular company that you may be able to spot, but even the above list is sufficient to warrant strong cause for concern. The scenario suggests a major requirement for change especially by the boss herself. If this can be achieved, then some progress may be made through acquisition of new plant and machinery, some new systems and through training interventions.

Judith Frampton herself is a major obstacle to change. She should consider moving herself from the scene, allowing staff to exercise more managerial responsibilities. She should consider possibly bringing in a partner or two (with an equally important injection of capital). This is often unlikely in these companies even though it is possibly the largest single potential obstacle to business growth.

Management style in this sort of organisation will be characterised by people who are exasperated and frustrated. The culture that Judith has cultivated will probably produce some defensive attitudes from managers, who are either forced to keep quiet in order to preserve their jobs, or choose to leave. The paradoxical situation is, however, that the managers will probably be ejected from the company anyway by Judith if they are not perceived as delivering the right performance; it is a typical 'no win' situation for the managers.

Because the pioneer insists on keeping very close to all proceedings in the company, it would be very difficult for a manager to establish a clear identity, and even more difficult to take unilateral decisions and deal creatively with problems.

THE SCIENTIFIC PHASE

In this stage, the pioneer has recognised the frailties of the unstructured, loose arrangement and has installed a clear hierarchy with each employee responsible for a specific area. Authority is still retained by the senior people, including the original pioneer, but all levels of staff can make decisions within defined limits. Jobs are clearly defined with tasks apportioned, so that there is no duplication. Scope of authority and levels of responsibility are outlined. There are specific areas of control with each individual having defined spheres of responsibility.

Companies in this phase may be characterised by the following attributes:

- New systems and procedures are introduced, and processes are mechanised.

- Standardisation, specialisation and co-ordination become major attributes of the company.

- Management operates through a clear hierarchy and an obvious span of control with everyone responsible to one manager in the hierarchy.

- Responsibility and authority are vested in managers.

- Specialists are seen as having an advisory role.

- Formal communication systems operate in a number of different forms.

Despite its lack of flexibility and loss of the personal touch, this type of organisation may continue to operate effectively for a long period. Most medium and large companies in the UK have scientific management characteristics, and many companies would argue that this style suits them. However, at some point, if the company continues to develop, a crisis can result from a breakdown in co-ordination and communication through inflexible staff/line relationships, a lack of motivation and inertia. This crisis may take the shape of a drop in customer goodwill, scheduling problems, industrial relations problems, or even something as serious as financial difficulties.

DESKTOPS PLC

Desktops is a major market leader in the office furniture business. It operates from a large head office in Bradford and has 20 large superstore outlets, each of which has an annual turnover of at least £36 million.

There are central purchasing, marketing, personnel and finance functions, and each store makes detailed daily, weekly and monthly reports to head office.

New product development is also based in Bradford and this causes some problems; the stores feel there is insufficient sensitivity to their local market demands and needs.

The personnel procedures are seen as inflexible and unresponsive to individual difficulties. This causes staff relations problems resulting in high labour turnover in most stores.

One or two of the earlier established stores are currently being sold with the intention of developing more superstores on the outskirts of towns and cities. Younger managers are being sent out to run these new stores, and the older managers are being made redundant.

Sales are beginning to fall in a worrying way, and despite many frustrated suggestions from the store managers, the hierarchy in head office believes it can weather the storm with only the minimum of store closures. One or two of the more progressive senior managers are toying with the idea of devolving power to the stores and setting up a regional structure to the organisation. This, however is meeting stiff resistance from the older well-established directors. In the meantime, sales are still falling.

Desktops plc is typical of an organisation in the scientific phase. Its managers are effective, task-oriented, well-qualified, and assertive: in other words, they are 'professional'.

If it is not careful, Desktops plc will soon be in a significant crisis. It needs to adopt a more customer-responsive approach and develop a more flexible organisational structure if it is to meet and overcome market problems, and halt falling sales.

Some key managers often leave organisations at this stage because of a lack of flexibility and loss of the personal touch. Some managers may persist with 'tried and trusted' methods but these will have increasingly less effect until the need for a new approach with a radically different culture is reluctantly acknowledged.

In general, an organisation in the scientific phase typically displays a role orientation (in Harrison's theory). Managers will specialise in a particular type of role (policy making, organising, executive) and function (production, sales, engineering, personnel). Technical specialists advise rather than command, so the staff/line relationship is clear. Rules and procedures are emphasised so the organisational chart at the scientific stage is normally the classic hierarchy.

Multi-functional teams may be used to implement organisational initiatives. In companies experiencing the symptoms of crisis, project teams are often used in attempts to resolve the current problems; but the very fact that there is a crisis sometimes leads to the poor direction, motivation and resourcing of the projects themselves.

THE INTEGRATED PHASE

During the integrated phase, flexibility, informality and teamwork are established while retaining a systematic approach to planning and control. Very few organisations reach this stage because most large organisations prefer to pour resources into maintaining and supporting an increasingly creaking structure.

The 'quality' revolution in recent years has brought a new attempt by many organisations to move into the integrated phase.

The integrated phase is characterised by:

- a management philosophy based on understanding human motivation and applying the concepts to enable the staff to achieve the company goals

- management development programmes which focus on team-building activities and personal development workshops

- self-managing teams and forms of leadership based on 'empowerment' becoming the norm.

MICROMESH

Micromesh is a rapidly expanding computer company. The business was started by two young colleagues, five years ago in Cardiff, and it now has a major portion of the 'office systems packages' market.

The original two founders are now based in London and still focus their attention on new design and exploring new markets. Meanwhile, there are three small product development, customer service, packaging and distribution centres in different parts of the country, each of which is run by a team of young managers with a small staff of approximately 20.

The founders spend a day a week at each centre in order to consult with employees, and any strategic initiatives are planned with the teams from each centre.

The scientific crisis of lack of flexibility leads to the integrated organisation which requires a more adaptable format. In the case of Micromesh, the integrated phase was reached very rapidly as a conscious decision by the pioneers.

SAT:
allow 10 mins

Managing tasks and solving problems ✓

ACTIVITY 2

What type of decision making would you expect to take place in a company such as Micromesh? What implications does this carry for its management style?

Commentary...

All operational decisions in the centres in Micromesh are likely to be made by the workers who would only refer to the managers for extra information when required.

Policy decisions are made by a representative group of workers and managers, and if the organisation grows any further, then the centres will probably not be expanded, but rather new centres will be opened along the same lines.

In these types of organisation, the management style is, by necessity, extremely participative and facilitative. In fact, it would almost be true to say that this is the type of organisation in which leadership attributes will be more prevalent than management characteristics.

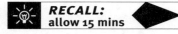

RECALL:
allow 15 mins

Let us test how much of the three stages of organisational development you are able to recall. Make notes which summarise the nature of management within:

- the pioneer phase
- the scientific phase
- the integrated phase.

Future trends

The structures of the more modern organisations are closely related to concepts of leadership and empowerment. Encouraging individuals to 'take charge' and exercise responsibility for 'seeing that everything goes well' obviously requires change, and it can be assumed that it will not happen easily or effectively if there is excessive organisational structure.

Tom Peters says that there are three key things that must happen to an organisational structure if an organisation is going to respond quickly to changed circumstances:

- Layers of management must be radically reduced. No more than five layers are necessary regardless of organisation size, with layers in any facility limited to three at most.

- Most 'support' staff (accounts, personnel, purchasing, etc.) must be assigned to the operations of the business, reporting to line managers. They should be encouraged to be 'business team members' rather than narrow functional specialists.

- A radically increased ratio of non-supervisors to supervisors must be established so that there is a wide span of control particularly at the organisation's front line. The minimum span should be one supervisor to every 25–75 non-supervisors.

The apparent paradox, of comprehensive teamworking on the one hand and individual responsibility and empowerment on the other, can be shown to be reconcilable, but there is certainly no way that rigid hierarchies can be reconciled with current organisational thinking. Indeed, it is probably one of the main reasons why some of the early attempts at implementing concepts such as total quality foundered or are experiencing major difficulties.

Empowerment of individuals is not something which can be achieved overnight, so some of the more traditional organisational structures will need to be kept in place, at least in the early stages of organisational design and implementation. Eventually, these structures will begin to break down and change as individuals and teams start to assume more power and leadership.

There is probably no ideal organisation structure since the internal and external pressures for change will always demand flexibility in organisational design. It is, however, possible to describe some key structural principles which, at least to our current way of experience and learning, seem to be appropriate to the way society is moving:

- Decision making needs to be as quick and as near to the point of action as possible. This inevitably means a move towards flatter organisational structures and, at the early stages of organisational development, extremely quick and effective communication between layers.

- A focus on meeting customer requirements and co-operation in achieving that aim necessitates teamworking. Not only does the organisation have to operate as a total team but it begins to become team-based.

- A requirement for quick access to specialist functions within the organisation means that these functions or people need to be within teams.

A number of management thinkers have produced their own views on the future shape of organisations:

- **Charles Handy** (*The Age of Unreason*, Hutchinson, 1989) refers to 'shamrock' organisations which possess several separate parts which are nevertheless attached to a whole.

- **Michael Porter** (*The Competitive Edge of Nations*, Macmillan, 1990) describes groups of smaller organisations clustered together in a 'honeycomb' appearance such as in Silicon Valley, California, or the M4 corridor in England.

- **Meredith Belbin** (*Team Roles at Work*, Butterworth/Heinemann, 1993) comes to the conclusion that the pre-eminence of teamworking in current and future scenarios will inevitably lead to 'trapezium' organisations, where autonomous work groups or teams are supported by a small number of operational managers, and where decisions of a strategic nature are taken by a small group of separate managers in a balanced team.

There are many other projections and predictions of organisational structures, shapes and cultures, but they all seem to have common ingredients in that they are predominantly based around flatter, non-hierarchical structures with heavy emphasis on teamworking and empowerment of individuals in decision making. The other key dimension is that of continuous change and adaptability where not only basic structures may change frequently, but also job-descriptions, methods, systems, procedures, relationships, technology, leadership and style.

The classic structure recommended for empowered, and empowering, organisations is an inverted triangle drawn in such a way to illustrate the role of the board of directors and the facilitators (note, not middle managers) all in supporting positions rather than authoritative managing positions.

FIGURE 3:2: *The empowering organisation.*

An organisation which is team-based, especially one with self-managing teams does not require managing; instead, it requires its managers and maybe even front-line supervisors, to become people who are skilled at:

- facilitating

- diffusing good news

- breaking down barriers

- providing expert information.

For some organisations, the concept of a flatter, non-hierarchical organisational structure is difficult to absorb, and an inverted hierarchy even more difficult. Even if the senior management has a commitment to the need for this structure, there are likely to be many objectors at middle-management level who view this approach as threatening their roles, their authority and, ultimately, their jobs.

Team-based organisations

Organisational culture has been highly influenced in recent years by a number of issues:

- the emergence of the 'team' as a key feature within organisations

- the speed of development of information technology enabling rapid access to information

- the removal of layers of management to produce flatter organisations

- the shift from physical work to mental work in many organisations.

In any organisation, everyone has something to offer, and the person doing the job usually has the clearest picture of what is happening. It is, therefore generally accepted that organisations must begin to find a way by which their employees may be listened to and their knowledge and experience effectively used. Organising them in teams or groups is an accepted method of achieving greater employee involvement and increased productivity.

Self-managing teams are not an easy concept for many traditional organisations to accept, since they fly in the face of the established 'boss–subordinate' culture as illustrated in the case study. Normally, they render the more conservative middle manager virtually redundant, and therefore need a great deal of effort, training, and careful planning. The concept of self-managing teams is still a relatively new one, and as such there are not too many examples in the UK. However as empowerment develops as a concept, there will inevitably be a demand from staff to be allowed to operate in more democratic and participative environments.

The range of teams and groups that may operate in team or project-based organisations include:

- **self-awareness and learning groups** – to deal with newly introduced concepts, philosophies or practices in an organisation

- **learning sets** – regular meetings for people on similar study or learning paths

- **communications groups** – to enable speedy and efficient means of transmitting essential information

- **negotiation groups** – to introduce democratically new ways of working, and new terms and conditions

- **decision-making or problem-solving groups** – to deal with complex problems or difficult situations democratically

- **co-determination groups** – set up in progressive and democratic organisations in order to agree a mutually beneficial plan of action.

We shall now explore briefly the nature of some team or project-based groups, and then examine how they may affect the role and style of the manager.

QUALITY CIRCLES

A quality circle is usually a group of four to ten employees who work in the same department and who meet typically for an hour once a week, led by their supervisor, to identify and solve their own departmental problems. The features of quality circles are as follows:

- The system is entirely voluntary.

- Management gives support and listens to presentations from circles, but the circles themselves decide how they will operate, what problems they will examine, and what solutions they feel are appropriate. There is no interference from management.

- Circles may work on any problems which directly affect the quality of working life in the department; this might, for example, include energy conservation, productivity, safety and communication issues.

- Quality circles do not present suggestions; they present clear answers to problems, backed up with evidence and costings.

- Members are trained to identify key problems, to use simple techniques to analyse and solve them, and to present their conclusions to management.

- Quality circles tend to be set up in organisations where there is a genuine willingness to empower people to take decisions. Circles will be asked to tackle any problem that they wish to (within certain limitations, like wages or individual personalities).

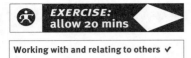

EXERCISE:
allow 20 mins

Working with and relating to others ✔

Managing tasks and solving problems ✔

ACTIVITY 3

For the team members, quality circles offer an opportunity to become involved and to increase job satisfaction, with less frustration. Can you think of some of the ways in which the nature of the job of management might be changed by the existence of these types of teams?

Form into groups of four to discuss this issue. Summarise your conclusions in the box below.

Commentary...

For managers, quality circles can make their job easier. Quality circles are seen as superb vehicles for releasing individual potential and for encouraging leadership. The sustaining of a circle regime in an organisation requires a great deal of sensitivity and skill and, in particular, the role of middle managers needs to be very clearly agreed prior to embarking upon such a programme.

Managers in organisations where there are quality circles need to adopt a strong facilitating role in which they should support and encourage others in a largely non-directive way.

PROJECT TEAMS

Project teams have been in operation in many organisations for some years now but they are currently becoming a major feature of organisations. Where project teams are established, they are multidisciplinary and are concerned with overcoming major organisational problems or concerns.

A project may be described as:

- a defined activity involving the conversion of material or data resources over a constrained time frame

- a non-repetitive activity.

Projects may be internally generated, e.g. concerned with developing a new computer network. Alternatively, they may be externally generated, e.g. concerned with the development of a particular product for a customer. They may involve departmental project teams or multi-functional project teams.

A project usually involves:

- change

- a recognisable life cycle

- ripple effects – a project will have consequences for many parts of the organisation, not just those directly concerned with its execution

- a degree of novelty

- personnel temporarily in assigned project roles.

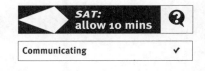

ACTIVITY 4

Think about a project that you have been involved with at work, in your social life or your learning institution. How does it differ from your day-to-day activities? Did it involve any of the above features? Write down a few words about the features you have identified.

Commentary...

There are a number of ways in which a project differs from a normal management task.

- **Time** – a project has a defined start and finish time as opposed to an ongoing operational activity. This requires a more involved and tighter controlling function from the manager.

- **Resources** – a project needs a much higher degree of financial accountability. However, because of the complexity of most projects, and the time-scale involved, they will often be far more difficult to cost and control than ongoing operational activities.

- **Project team members** – often the personnel can be from different functions and have different skills and experience. They may also be from various levels of organisational hierarchy.

It is increasingly clear that projects will be a feature of the business and commercial landscape in the next ten years. The effects of project working on management style are significant in that it influences managers to become more participative while at the same time, focusing on task achievement. In other words, there could be a distinct move towards the Blake's 9.9 manager (see page 30) with high concern for both task and people. The nature of most project teams is multi-functional and multi-status so that it will be difficult for a teamleader to exercise too much of an autocratic approach based on either his or her position in the hierarchy, or on job knowledge.

Tom Peters suggests the following elements will be observed in the future business environment.

- Most of tomorrow's work will be done in project teams.

- Traditional functional staff units will almost disappear and will be encompassed by project teams.

- A project team is not a committee, and the difference is team member dependence.

- Trust is essential.

- The life span of a project team can be long or just a few hours, but dynamic, short-lived configurations will be commonplace.

- The average project team will often include 'outsiders'.

- There will be constant reorganisation of project team structures.

FACILITATORS

The aim of a facilitator is to encourage and enable people to learn for themselves and to decide what they will do with the learning or, to put it another way, 'to help people find their own wisdom'.

The facilitator is not the same as a traditional manager in that the facilitator aims to enable a team to reach its own conclusions through being concerned with the quality and the process of the discussion. The intervention of a facilitator might be appropriate if a project team is formed, or if an established team is thought to be working ineffectively.

In this type of situation, the role of the facilitating manager is to help a team to develop its skills and behaviours. This can be in the context of problem solving, creativity, team building, effective meetings or other aims. So, the activities of a facilitator that you may have listed would include: process observations, feedback to the team, short inputs and interventions.

Process observation

This is the key skill; it can be practised in several ways using a range of techniques. These can include observations on:

- the individual levels of contribution within the team

- the style of contribution of various team members

- the type of decision-making techniques used

- the levels of creativity within the team

- the extent to which the team focuses on the past, present or future

- the degree of satisfaction the team has with outcomes

- the clarity of purpose and achievement.

Feedback to the team

Feedback can be practised personally and subjectively or in a formal, factual and statistical manner. In either case, if the feedback is to be of any use, it should be focused on helping the team to review its performance and improve its planning and operation.

Short inputs

These might cover problem-solving methods such as brainstorming, cause and effect analysis, etc.

Intervention

In some situations, the facilitating manager might be asked to chair a meeting or lead a group in an activity, and this requires additional skills. The facilitator role requires someone who can remain neutral and objective, who can withstand and interpret the processes of group interaction, who has the confidence to intervene when appropriate and the self-control not to intervene when the team is working well.

By contrast, a traditional manager's role might normally include:

- managing the agenda

- controlling levels and types of contribution from group members

- managing potential or actual conflict

- summarising progress

- managing the use of problem-solving tools.

SAILBOARDS LTD

Alan Groves, the managing director and owner of Sailboards Ltd, is keen to keep his business at the frontiers of any new developments. He has introduced all the latest computer-control systems into his factory, his design department are using computer-aided design, and the sales department have been liaising with the Department of Trade and Industry about possibilities of exploring European markets.

All is going well and Alan has decided that his internal management processes should be improved by introducing a team-based approach. Alan has been on a one-day seminar on the subject and, on his return, has instructed his senior managers to set up self-managing teams.

To begin with, Alan decides to select the members of his first team himself, including the appointment of a team leader (though this is not appreciated by the team members). Alan also decides to join the team himself as an observer.

There is great pressure on all managers at work so Alan decides that the teams will have to work outside of normal hours, and that he will give them the topics on which they are to work. The one-day seminar he attended, suggested that teams would need training, so Alan hires a trainer to carry out training in problem-solving techniques. The training is set up for the next two weekends. After the training the teams are asked to start their work, and Alan expects them to provide answers to the problems they are given very quickly. He hints strongly that if money-saving solutions are not identified, the managers will be downgraded at their next appraisals.

The teams do not last very long, and although Alan wishes they would work, he reluctantly agrees to abandon the idea – but not before two managers have resigned and one has been dismissed.

ACTIVITY 5

ASSIGNMENT:
allow 1 hour

Managing and developing self	✔
Communicating	✔
Managing tasks and solving problems	✔

Read the case study above on Sailboards Ltd.

You are a consultant that has been appointed by Alan Groves to examine the company's management problems. The introduction of the team-based approach did not work. Alan Groves wishes to repeat the experiment but this time he wants to the new approach to be a success.

Produce a 1,000 word report which sets out how Sailboards might develop a team-based management style. Your report should have three sections covering:

   (a) the reasons from the outline given why the previous attempt to introduce a team-based approach was unsuccessful;

   (b) a strategy for re-introducing team-based methods, outlining for example any training and development programmes that might be needed both for managers and staff;

   (c) an explanation of how Alan Groves will need to change his own role and management style.

Conclude your report by summarising the potential benefits to Sailboards of adopting this new approach.

Use separate sheets of paper to record your answer. Summarise your findings in the box below.

summary

▶ The three stages of organisational development are the pioneer phase, the scientific phase and the integrated phase.

▶ Organisations in the pioneer phase are usually new or relatively small. They tend to be informal organisations, with few standard procedures and methods and little forward planning.

▶ In the scientific phase, organisations adopt clear hierarchies, jobs are clearly defined, and areas of responsibility are clearly outlined. Managers are increasingly 'professional': effective, task-oriented and well-qualified.

▶ In the integrated phase, flexibility, informality and teamwork are established while retaining a systematic approach to planning and control.

▶ It is expected that organisations in the future will have smaller and flatter management hierarchies and make much greater use of team structures.

Individual and interpersonal behaviour

Objectives

After participating in this session, you should be able to:

⬇

▶ describe the motivational theories of Herzberg and Maslow

⬇

▶ briefly review the main theories of personality

⬇

▶ describe the major theories of perception

⬇

▶ relate personal factors, role theory and conflict to individual attitudes and behaviour

⬇

▶ describe the organisational issues relating to individual attitudes and behaviour.

In working through this session, you will practise the following BTEC common skills:

Managing and developing self	
Working with and relating to others	
Communicating	✔
Managing tasks and solving problems	✔
Applying numeracy	
Applying technology	
Applying design and creativity	

Motivation

Most of the research into human motivation has been carried out in respect of work. Some of these ideas and research results are complex. Researchers have attempted to identify the factors that motivate, or prevent motivation in people. They identified a number of factors that increase or decrease motivation:

- early environment – the encouragement and love, or lack of them, that you receive as a child

- education – your first experiences of learning

- understanding – the need to know and understand how things happen or work

- aesthetics – your feelings about beautiful objects, designs, scenes, music

- self-esteem – belief in your ability

- heredity – the genetic make-up you inherit from your parents

- experience – the range of activities you have taken part in or situations you have been in.

Researchers have also identified that all people have unfulfilled needs which have to be satisfied, and these needs lead to strong motivation. The two most famous researchers in the field of motivation are Herzberg (*Motivation to Work*, John Wiley, 1959) and Maslow (*Motivation and Personality*, Harper and Row, 1954) and we shall explore their theories in some detail.

HERZBERG'S THEORIES

Herzberg concluded, from his research in the United States, that there are two types of factors influencing workers' motivation: hygiene factors and motivators.

Hygiene factors

The hygiene factors are the conditions needed before successful motivation can take place. Although they do not contribute to the level of motivation, these factors must be present within an organisation and they include issues such as:

- company policy

- administration

- supervision

- salary

- working conditions

- job security.

Motivators

The motivators only affect the level of motivation if the hygiene factors are present. These motivators include:

- advancement

- recognition

- responsibility

- the work itself.

Hygiene factors, like good working conditions and salary, do not automatically raise motivation, but if they are absent workers are unlikely to make much effort.

You should be aware, however, that Herzberg's work took place in the United States in the 1960s and comprised a small research base of accountants and engineers, and that his ideas have since been strongly challenged.

MASLOW'S THEORIES

There have also been a number of attempts to categorise and list individual needs, and Abraham Maslow's work is probably the most respected. Maslow saw people's needs in a hierarchy comprising five levels, with the most basic physiological needs at the bottom: physiological needs, safety, love, esteem and self-actualisation.

It is important to remember that Maslow's five needs are hierarchical. So, starting from the bottom with physiological needs, you have to satisfy each level of need, before you can start to meet the needs at the next level up.

The needs apply in the following ways:

- **Physiological needs** (i.e. food, water, air, sleep) are essential for survival.

- **Safety needs** lead to a threat-free, just, ordered and stable environment.

- **Love needs** include affection and belonging to a group.

- **Esteem needs** refer to both public and self-esteem.

- **Self-actualisation** is the need for self-fulfilment and achievement of one's potential.

The implication of this theory is that if you want to motivate someone, you help them to fulfil one or all of their needs. If you can identify their most important need at a given time, this one, which you are helping them to meet, is their best motivator. As with Herzberg, it is important that you should appreciate that Maslow's proposals have also been subject to criticism.

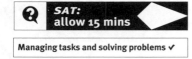

SAT:
allow 15 mins

Managing tasks and solving problems ✓

ACTIVITY 1

Read the following cameo of Les Taylor. In the light of the principles of motivation which you have just read, what motivational influences are affecting him at present, and what might be the most motivating thing that could happen right now?

LES TAYLOR

Les Taylor is the manager of a data processing department. He works in the Hampstead head office of an international trading company. He has been with the company for 25 years and runs an efficient DP service. However, the company has been going through a difficult patch, and Les is aware that several parts of the organisation have been recently closed down in a cost-cutting exercise, resulting in several management redundancies. He has been told by his boss that his job looks safe, but 'nothing is certain these days'. In his department, there are several younger people who are ambitious and skilled, and Les knows that they are looking for promotion. At 48, Les has some ambition left and hopes that he might still make the senior management ranks. He is now feeling less convinced that this is possible.

Les has always led a fairly frugal life style even though his salary has steadily increased over the years. His one financial extravagance has been his house which is large and expensive; he has a very large mortgage. Outside of work, Les is a fine tuba player in a local brass band, which has won many competitions. Les is also the arranger of the music and the band's publicity officer. He has often thought of becoming a full-time musician with the band and living his life as he would really wish, albeit on a lot less income.

Currently, Les is feeling depressed at the company circumstances, and at his own fragile position.

Commentary...

You may have taken account of Les's personal circumstances as well as the company circumstances.

Les does have some needs that could be called self-actualisation needs: making a living as a full-time musician with the brass band. He also has some self-esteem needs: to make it to the senior ranks in the company. Perhaps his needs for belonging are met through his contact with colleagues in the band, as well as relationships at work. All of these needs are Les's motivators (in Herzberg's terms), and one could argue that the lowest level of motivator – the belonging need – is probably being satisfied, leaving the two higher needs of self-esteem and self-actualisation unfulfilled.

However, the most pressing problem for Les at present is his job security. Though he currently earns a good salary and copes with living expenses very well, the future looks bleak. He worries about his ability to continue paying the mortgage if he is made redundant. It could, therefore, be concluded that the key area of personal difficulty for Les at the moment is security. It is not as basic a need as a physiological need since he still has a job and is receiving a salary, but this is under threat so the hygiene factor of security is the most important. If you were trying to motivate Les, there would be no point in offering him more companionship, more seniority, or even more personal fulfilment. It would probably be equally useless offering him more money. The main motivational issue for Les is to be assured of some job security – and that is not even motivating – rather it is a hygiene factor which has to be satisfied before any motivators may be brought into action.

Personality

When you first meet other people you very quickly form an impression of what they are like. Young, old, tall, short, fat, thin, friendly, surly, helpful, aggressive, defensive, open – these are some of the adjectives you might use when describing them. Much of the impression that you form is concerned with what we term personality, and the way in which you form the impression is, in itself, influenced by your own personality.

Your first impressions of other people are very powerful, but you come to these situations prepared. You bring with you a battery of experiences, presumptions, expectations and attitudes arising from your experiences and previous influences: your parents, grandparents, brothers and sisters, aunts and uncles, friends, teachers, classmates and work mates. By the time we are adult and settled into work, most of us have adopted a clear set of attitudes called a **value system**. Because we find it very difficult to abandon these attitudes, we presume they are based on logic and we tend to reject data that does not fit with our value system.

When you meet new people, you rapidly gather some first impressions, and by noting their dress, manner, speech, etc., you put together a mental profile that makes you quite certain that you know how they will behave in the future. You might be quite wrong, but these first impressions are very hard to shift.

PERSONALITY THEORIES

Psychologists disagree about the nature of personality and its origins. Here, we briefly review the main theories.

Freud

In Freud's model, the personality arises from the dynamic interplay of three elements: the id, the ego and the superego.

- The **id** is the purely physical part of ourselves, motivated by the immediate pleasure principle and likely to go berserk if frustrated as shown by the unrestrained behaviour of tiny children.

- The **ego** is a more realistic sense of self which tries to satisfy the id but which is aware of reality and future possible outcomes.

- The **superego** is a kind of conscience imposing standards and duties, making high demands which the ego has to keep in balance.

The **libido**, a sexual or life-force, was seen by Freud as the driving force behind the development of the personality in which mechanisms (e.g. defence mechanisms) were developed to protect the ego.

It is difficult either to prove or disprove many elements of the theory because it can apparently explain many aspects of behaviour. However, it cannot predict them. Later psychoanalysts proposed a number of modifications to Freud's theory.

Carl Jung

Jung was one of Freud's students, and he started analytical psychology. Jung's views can be summarised as follows:

- Jung objected to Freud's emphasis on sexual impulses and believed that a number of other instincts were equally important.

- Jung stressed the importance of humanity's ideas and aspirations.

- Jung's theory of personality borders on the mystical as he proposed a 'collective unconscious' which consists of all the memories and patterns of behaviour inherited from humanity's ancestral past. So, all human beings have the same collective unconscious which predisposes them to act in certain ways.

- Jung was the first to distinguish between extroverts and introverts and because of his overall optimistic and mystical flavour, he gained more popularity.

- Jung had a more positive view of humanity than Freud, and was to some extent a predecessor of the humanistic psychologists.

Adler, Horney and Fromm

Other influential psychoanalysts such as Adler, Horney and Fromm placed more emphasis on the ego and reality testing than they did on the id. Some of them feel that the ego develops independently of the id and has its own source of energy. By and large, the neo-Freudians were more optimistic than Freud about the nature of humankind and the ability to change.

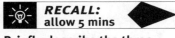

RECALL:
allow 5 mins

Briefly describe the three constituents of Freud's personality theory:

- id

- ego

- super-ego.

Eysenck

Eysenck's work is different; it is based on the use of questionnaires, from which Eysenck attempts to measure the respondents' traits and to group them to produce some overall categories of personality type. This analysis enables comparisons to be made between people. (Self-assessment questionnaires can be found in Eysenck's books.)

The main criticism of Eysenck's approach is that the outcomes might be too rigid and too simplistic. They also do not allow for the changing nature of personality in different situations.

Isobel Myers and Katherine Briggs

This mother and daughter partnership worked in the 1950s on producing a more easily recognisable range of personality types. Their work resulted in a **psychometric test** which arguably allows a little more freedom to the concept of changing nature. It is called the **Myers–Briggs type indicator**.

Although the indicator refers to personality type, it does offer an analysis of traits in people in terms of how they prefer to operate. The theory is largely based on the work of Carl Jung, and through a large number of questions presents a profile of an individual in terms of four continuums.

FIGURE 4.1: *The Myers–Briggs continuum.*

The Myers–Briggs questionnaire is used extensively in personal and interpersonal development activities. It offers insights into many facets of an individual's preferred approach to life, work, learning environments and, in particular, learning groups.

HUMANISTIC THEORIES

These theories are useful because they try to take account of human potential and the dynamic nature of personality.

Carl Rogers

Rogers was interested in the fact that people strive to grow throughout their lives. This views can be summarised as follows:

- Rogers argued that personality problems arise when people are consistently prevented from developing their potential.

- In his experience, personality is not so much a series of unrelated factors but a coherent 'whole' which requires 'positive regard' from other people in order to be healthy.

- 'Unconditional positive regard' and the sense of being loved, especially by parents during the formative years, are particularly important for the growth of the healthy personality.

- Help with personality disorders is based on assisting people in a non-directive manner to bridge the gap between the person they think they are and the one they would like to be.

- This work led to the formation of encounter groups which enabled many people to experience great personality changes later in life when their circumstances changed.

Abraham Maslow

Abraham Maslow was one of the most influential humanistic psychologists; his theory of needs was discussed earlier.

Maslow studied mature, competent, self-fulfilled individuals and came up with a definition of a 'self-actualiser' as someone who had no neurotic or psychotic symptoms and was in the healthiest one per cent of the population. These people experience transient moments of self-actualisation or 'peak experiences', comprising values of wholeness, perfection, uniqueness, effortlessness and self-sufficiency.

Maslow's views are much more positive and optimistic than Freud's since he maintains that none of our innate needs are antisocial. Aggression, for example, arises only when attempts to satisfy basic needs are frustrated.

Personality factors can affect how we learn and how effective we are at learning. An individual will not be an effective learner if he or she has a personality disorder, or has been bullied or threatened in early life so that all curiosity and enthusiasm have been stifled.

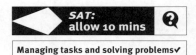

ACTIVITY 2

Take a few minutes to think about two or three people with whom you come into contact: a lecturer, an acquaintance, or someone at work or college. Try to sum up their personalities in the light of the research we have just covered and jot down your thoughts.

Commentary...

We cannot give an answer to your personal assessment. However, when you meet new people, you try to fit them into the pattern of behaviour you would expect in the light of your own experience and value systems. If the new people do fit your value system, you tend to like them and assume that in work situations you will be able to co-operate with them. You need to be very careful with your initial assessments, however, especially if you are meeting people from other countries and other cultures.

Perception

There is no single theory of perception. Instead, there is a range of competing theories, each claiming to explain phenomena observed by psychologists.

There are three main groups of theories:

- those developed in the last century, based on views of the person and mental discipline

- those arising from behaviourist analyses, based on observations of how people react to stimuli

- those arising from Gestalt analyses, based on ideas on how the mind works and the nature of understanding.

These three main groups are now considered in some detail.

NINETEENTH-CENTURY THEORIES

Early beliefs about the nature of human beings varied widely. In many ways they persist today and still affect the way we 'see' people. They include some very simple beliefs, e.g. that human beings are:

- essentially evil and have to be brought under control

- essentially good and the goodness determines their behaviour

- blank sheets of paper upon which the teacher draws.

Overall, these are philosophical views and are not supported by modern scientific method. However, a good deal of teaching and learning still appears to be based on these views.

A teacher might think all students are 'evil' and have to be forced to learn or they are 'good' and need no external pressure. The 'blank sheet' approach exists where the teacher is regarded as a great 'expert'.

BEHAVIOUR ANALYSIS THEORIES

Towards the end of the nineteenth century, some psychologists in the USA and Europe focused on observations of behaviour which could be scientifically verified. They wanted to support their conclusions with real evidence, similar to that produced in the repeatable experiments of physics or chemistry.

This psychological approach to learning is called **behaviourism**. It arose from studies of animals which indicated that their behaviour could be modified with an appropriate system of rewards. The arguments have two aspects:

- the processes are transferable to humans

- conditioning is a biological process in the brain and nervous system, not a mental process in the mind.

Pavlov

The work of Pavlov became very influential among psychologists seeking a model of mankind which could contribute to the arguments about ability and learning. He noticed that a hungry dog salivated when presented with food. If a bell were sounded repeatedly alongside the presentation of the food, before long the sound of the bell alone would cause the dog to salivate. From this starting point, he and other researchers developed laws of learning based on their observation that a stimulus caused a response. Pavlov's work is known as **classical conditioning**.

The stimulus–response links were used to show that if you wanted to train a dog to sit up at the command 'up,' you could make the dog sit up by offering a piece of meat on a string, accompanied by the call 'up'. When this was satisfactorily achieved, you could simply withdraw the meat and use the call alone. In this way, the dog could be taught to perform any other action of which it was capable by substitution of the stimulus. It was asserted that this principle of stimulus substitution was equally applicable to mankind.

Edward Thorndike

Edward Thorndike's work set the scene for **instrumental conditioning**. His cat experiments were also influential with educators because they established a basis for trial and error learning.

It was found that if a hungry cat was shut in a cage which could be opened by a lever and some food was placed outside, the cat would strive at random to escape until it opened the gate by chance. Repeating the experiment would result in the cat gradually reducing the time of random activity until it went immediately for the gate-opening mechanism.

Thorndike asserted that this reinforcement of the response to the stimulus created a physical bonding in the nerve or brain system. It was not thought to be related to insight. Further repetition strengthened the link. Being rewarded for success, 'positive reinforcement', was found to be longer-lasting in the strengthening than being punished for failure, 'negative reinforcement'.

Other behavioural psychologists developed the notion of **operant conditioning**. They showed that the response could be modified by reinforcement. This might be the satisfaction of a need like hunger, sex, security or recognition. Reinforcement in the training situation takes the form of praise to strengthen the behaviour, and punishment to discourage it.

These are the three contrasting functions:

- **classical conditioning** – the substitution of the stimulus like the bell for the food

- **instrumental conditioning** – the modification of the response by positive or negative feedback

- **operant conditioning** – the reinforcement of a series of responses or behaviours.

Research shows that success reinforces achievement. Whenever that happens, there is a greater chance of the learner repeating the behaviour.

In this sense, you can regard the social system as a set of reinforcers because we respond to the very powerful influences of our family and peer groups. Many small businesses are successfully run in the traditional manner of the family with power clearly in the hands of the owner.

In the light of the work of Pavlov and his followers, you will now be able to appreciate how conditioning has influenced the thinking of behavioural psychologists. If you find the above ideas of particular interest, you may like to spend some time referring to organisation behaviour modification which develops the techniques of conditioning within an organisational context.

RECALL:
allow 10 mins
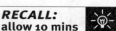

Describe the three forms of conditioning:

- classical conditioning

- instrumental conditioning

- operant conditioning.

B.F. Skinner

Professor B.F. Skinner, a leading proponent of the behaviourist approach, has asserted in his writings that in order to shape the behaviour of their students, teachers and trainers should focus on the relationship between the stimulus and the response.

Skinner argues that you should ignore any psychology that makes mental links. For Skinner, psychology is purely the science of observable behaviour. For the behaviourists, man is simply an accumulation of tiny learnt behaviours or responses. People are just machines reacting in a predictable manner to stimuli.

The key messages arising from a behaviourist approach, as described by Skinner, are:

- if you want people to learn, you must encourage positive stimulation

- you must also ensure that positive reinforcement of approved behaviour is given within a short time of the initial act

- you must then develop a strategy of reinforcing desired behaviours which accumulate into the overall pattern of behaviour you are seeking

- generally you must reinforce desired behaviour whenever possible.

GESTALT ANALYSIS THEORIES

The word 'Gestalt' means 'pattern'. Look at a triangle and you will see that it consists of three straight lines. When these lines come together in the shape of the triangle, you can say the whole is greater than the sum of its parts. The pattern, the layout of the lines or the configuration, adds to the meaning.

If you took all the components of a inter-city train and laid them out on the ground, you would only have a set of the parts. But, if you put them together in the correct manner, you would have a vehicle, a whole, which could transport passengers. The whole is greater than the sum of the parts.

In contrast to the behaviourists, Gestalt psychologists noticed that people always try to give 'meaning' to phenomena. If you show people three dots on a piece of paper they will mentally organise the dots and see the points of a triangle.

It is now known from later research that we try to organise information according to its meaning for us. We find it easier to learn and remember meaningful information than random data. If something we see or hear does not make sense, we try to make it make sense, even if it is wrong.

Checking against mental models is an aspect of learning. If new information fits your mental model, you will accept it. If it does not fit, you will probably reject it. A teacher, aware of this phenomenon, can help a learner to change perceptions and develop new mental models in order to accept the changes underlying the new information.

Building on the concepts of Gestalt, cognitive field theorists have developed a view of learning as a combination of:

- cognition, i.e. understanding oneself and one's environment, and

- field, i.e. the interrelationships of oneself and one's psychological perception of the environment.

Cognitive field theory defines learning as an interactive process within which a person attains new insights or cognitive structures. You learn from your experiences. You learn as your understanding of yourself and your perception of your environment changes and develops.

In this sense, learning takes place as a result of the insight gained from the doing of an act. New concepts come through experience and the developing of an appropriate cognitive field. Examples of this kind of learning and understanding might include:

- in a bank – the concepts of debit and credit

- in mechanical engineering – a left- or right-hand thread

- in computer aided design – the spatial concept of vectors

- in catering – the difference between clean and hygienically safe.

Role theory and conflict

In an earlier part of this session on individual and inter-personal behaviour, we examined the issues of personality and motivation. However, perhaps we ought to ask the question: What is it that brings people to work in the first place, and to what extent are their goals and aspirations met by the organisations for which they work?

The ability and willingness of individuals to become involved at work are influenced not only by organisational factors, but is often affected by a range of different personal factors:

- **physical make-up**, i.e. health, physique, appearance, bearing and speech

- **attainments,** i.e. education, qualifications

- **general intelligence**, i.e. fundamental intellectual capacity

- **special attributes**, i.e. mechanical, manual dexterity, use of words, or figures

- **interests**, i.e. intellectual, practical, constructional, social, artistic

- **disposition**, i.e. acceptability, influence, steadiness, dependability, self-reliance

- **personal circumstances**, i.e. marital status, children, leisure interests.

These seven points form **Rogers' 7-point plan**, named after Alan Rogers who first described it. His plan is used by organisations involved in recruitment, to produce a person specification.

Another such framework used for personnel specifications is the **Munro–Fraser five-fold grading system** which covers:

- **impact** on others, i.e. physical make-up, speech, manner

- acquired **qualifications**, i.e. education, vocational training, work experience

- **innate abilities**, i.e. natural quickness of comprehension and aptitude for learning

- **motivation**, i.e. kind of goals set by the individual, his or her consistency and determination in following them up, his or her success in achieving them

- **adjustment,** i.e. emotional stability, ability to manage stress, ability to mix well with people.

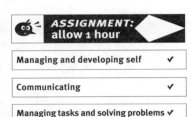

ASSIGNMENT:
allow 1 hour

Managing and developing self	✔
Communicating	✔
Managing tasks and solving problems	✔

ACTIVITY 3

You work for a brewery. The tenancy for one of your public houses becomes vacant. Use the Rogers' plan to write a person specification for a pub manager. You might find it useful to use the following grid in planning your answer.

	Essential qualities	Desirable qualities
Physical make up		
Attainments		
General intelligence		
Special attributes		
Interests		
Disposition		
Personal circumstances		

The company is keen to attract good quality candidates. Review the ideas on motivation discussed earlier in this section. What factors would you stress in recruitment literature? How would you sell the benefits of working for the brewery to potential applicants?

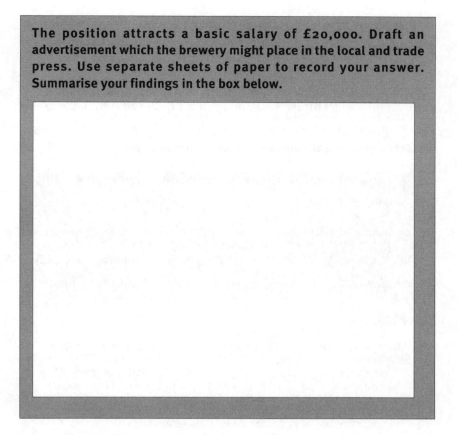

The position attracts a basic salary of £20,000. Draft an advertisement which the brewery might place in the local and trade press. Use separate sheets of paper to record your answer. Summarise your findings in the box below.

ROLE THEORY

Role theory is a term used by social psychologists to describe the way in which people manage the many roles in their lives.

> Every member of an organisation occupies a position, e.g. computer analyst, shop-steward, personnel manager. For every position, there is a role, i.e. a pattern of behaviour typical of people in that position. The role may include the work done, ways of behaving towards people in other positions, styles of non-verbal performance, attitudes and beliefs, clothes or uniforms worn, and styles of life outside work.

> **Michael Argyle**, *The Social Psychology of Work*, Penguin, 1967.

Role theorists believe that the nature of the job largely defines people's behaviour at work; jobs can only be performed in certain ways. For example, if one office manager was replaced by another, the person would probably carry out the job in more or less the same way.

Role conflict

Role conflict occurs when different people have different expectations about how a role should be performed (and, of course, this can happen within a work role or within other roles outside work). Research by **Parker and Childs** in the 1960s and more recently by

Willis serves to confirm that a worker's apparent loss of interest, effectiveness or morale, may have its origins in changes, pressures and stresses outside the workplace. People have roles at work, but they also have many other roles outside of work, each of which has its own strains and expectations. The ability of an individual to balance the effects of these roles, and to manage the stress involved will largely affect his or her contribution in a working situation.

SAT:
allow 15 mins

Managing tasks and solving problems ✓

ACTIVITY 4

Read the case study below and state at least three areas where you think there may be potential for role conflict in respect of working and non-working roles.

MARIO

Mario is 45, married and has two children (a boy and a girl) in their late teens, both living at home in the village of Dunkersley.

He has a job as sales manager with the Spangle Company. He has worked for Spangle for 20 years, and has been in his present demanding role for five years. The company is expanding its business into Europe and this will mean a great deal of travelling on the continent as well as occasional trips to America.

Mario's wife does part-time work at the local school, and the two of them are very involved in the Parish council. Mario is also keen on rugby. An ex-rugby player himself, he now coaches the school sixth form team, for which his son is scrum-half, in the evenings and at weekends.

Mario's daughter is disabled and needs assistance in travelling to school as well as extra attention at home.

Commentary...

There are a number of potential role conflicts:

- The increasing demands of the job of sales manager and the demands of being a father and husband.

- The demands of the work and non-work situations. At work, Mario is in charge, whereas at home he is a partner and shares responsibilities.

- Travelling or stability? Mario will shortly be expected to travel over Europe which means staying away from home, but he is also required at home to be a stabiliser (coach, councillor, carer).

- Short-term versus long-term? Mario has a daughter who will need help and care into the future. He also is established in the village and at the school. Against that, the job is developing fast, but for how long, and does Mario want this type of stress for much longer?

Organisational issues

We have just looked at the potential of role conflicts within any individual. Ideally, an organisation will take note of such conflicts and attempt to assist in their reconciliation. On the other hand, there are many organisations currently suffering in the wake of recession and from the resultant financial pressures, in which very little attention has been paid to the personal needs of the employees.

Thankfully, however, many managers have realised that people are the central resource in a successful business. You can change the systems, introduce technology, change structures, manipulate finances and segment markets but at the centre of everything are the employees. As a result of this realisation, most progressive organisations have adopted human resource development (HRD) strategies.

The following organisational factors affect individuals:

- **The move towards non-hierarchical organisations**
  Those organisations with self-managing teams and empowerment of individuals at all levels have made the concept of leadership more important than management. Currently, one of the main HRD concerns is the idea of encouraging leadership within every employee so that they have the commitment, willingness and ability to 'take charge' of their workplace.

- **The recent impact of standards of performance**

  The introduction of performance targets and customer standards (or charters) is having a big impact on employees. The pressure to perform and meet set targets is reflected in a greater emphasis on management development, leadership development, team building and communication.

- **The concept of quality assurance**

  This is leading progressive organisations to increase the participation of employees in the businesses in which they work.

- **Global competition**

  More intensive competition both from other Western countries and the emerging economies in East Asia is placing pressure on all businesses. This is a prime mover for change.

Manager development and management development activities designed to alleviate and deal with some of these influencing factors.

> **\?/ Manager development** considers the position of the individual manager and the issues which affect his or her personal development.
>
> **\?/ Management development** refers to learning activities which are primarily concerned with meeting organisational objectives whether they be in the business plan or are simply cultural or style objectives. Management development activities usually involve groups of managers or the entire management staff of an organisation.

Manager development should take into account a manager's:

- career needs

- need for greater adaptability

- values and aspirations

- job

- potential.

We now look at these factors in turn:

CAREER DEVELOPMENT

There are two kinds of career development:

- **Organisational career development** is focused on training individuals to meet the anticipated skill needs of the company or organisation.

- **Individual career development** is mainly concerned with the individual's personal career, irrespective of the needs of an employing organisation

Both these approaches have value, and it is important to take a balanced view. Training should be primarily to meet the needs of the organisation, but at the same time recognising the interests and ambitions of the individual employee.

The trend towards empowering employees and operating flexible systems of work allows individuals to become an integral part of a highly adaptable team with a wide repertoire of skills and knowledge. This might be a satisfactory career opportunity for many employees.

ADAPTABILITY

The current demand for a manager to demonstrate great adaptability and resourcefulness is an important characteristic of organisational survival. Businesses are confronting rapid and traumatic change, brought about by vacillating markets, innovative technology, powerful competition, recession and political and environmental demands. Most managers' early education and training does not prepare them for this challenge. Junior and middle managers, particularly, bear the brunt of sudden change. Flexibility is a rare skill or attitude. In organisations which are ill-equipped to deal with change, managers have to deal with the upheaval alone and survive or perish. In progressive companies, coping with change is seen as a major task.

THE MANAGER'S VALUES

The values of the chief executive and senior management permeate an organisation. The way in which individual managers accept or reject this value system may have an influence on manager development activities. In some cases, a new managing director means a new set of values applied from the top and the installation of a whole new programme of training and development for newly recruited and existing managers regardless of whether they want it or not. Their commitment to such development activities is likely to vary, as will the learning that results.

The issue of values is an extremely difficult one to define, but it will always play a large part in the way in which a manager organises and enacts the job. It will be the source of possible conflicts and disagreements with other people in the organisation – subordinates, peers, and bosses – and it sometimes leads to a manager deciding that his or her own values are incompatible with those of the organisation. This can lead to dissatisfaction resulting in the manager leaving or being dismissed.

THE MANAGER'S JOB

Managers control resources to achieve specified objectives. This controlling element distinguishes manager's tasks from non-manager's tasks. The higher the job is placed in the organisation, the greater the creative elements of the job. All managers deserve to know what their responsibilities and quantitative performance criteria are, and should be allowed latitude in defining their jobs. This means allowing them to contribute to the organisation using the full range of their abilities and experience. This is best illustrated at the top of the organisation where a newly appointed chief executive would be expected to be creative and bring new ideas and approaches to the organisation and not merely to fulfil the expectations of the previous job holder. The same should apply to any manager in the system.

THE MANAGER'S POTENTIAL

It is arguable that assessment of potential is impossible for the following two reasons:

- Human potential is immeasurable and we realise only small aspects of it within an organisation. This is a reflection of the inability of industrial society to deal with the complexities of human beings.

- In addition, even if it were possible to identify potential in an individual, it would remain a snapshot taken at one moment of time. In subsequent days, months and years, the personal, organisational and environmental circumstances surrounding each individual will change so much that the original snapshot is rendered useless.

But organisations still need to work on the basis that every manager entering employment has enormous potential. Manager development activities should operate on this principle rather than match any newcomer with the person who previously held the job. Matching with the past is a recipe for stagnation.

Every job has the potential for the development of the job holder. The key is to suit the potential of the job to the potential of the applicant. This is difficult since it is impossible to assess potential accurately, even though massive resources have been devoted in recent years to this aim, using a range of techniques including:

- assessment centres

- psychometric tests

- trial periods

- in-depth interviews

- test projects.

Nevertheless, an organisation which realises that its long-term future success depends on the quality of its managers, must commit itself to a process that centres on the individual so as to enhance effectiveness and reduce conflict.

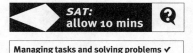

SAT:
allow 10 mins

Managing tasks and solving problems ✔

ACTIVITY 5

Read the case-study. Try to identify a few things that could be done to improve the organisation's approach to dealing with individuals and the organisational pressures on them.

FEMALE FOUNDATIONS

Female Foundations, a women's underwear manufacturer, has a fairly flexible organisation where everyone helps each other out with problems, and there is little paperwork. Most of the planning and development activities are informal and not documented, but there is a strong commitment to training. The company has what it considers is a solid approach to manager development:

- It has a clear policy on the manager's role in mentoring and in coaching subordinates.

- There is a statement in the policy that each employee (including managers) has at least five days of training per year.

- There is a standard induction programme for all new managers.

- Secondment is often used as a method of manager development.

- All managers have a reasonably clear idea of their responsibilities from their selection interview.

- Informal discussion on careers is encouraged between managers.

Commentary...

In the case study of Female Foundations, there are many good aspects of systematic manager development, but there are a few areas which could possibly be improved:

- clearer job descriptions for all managers

- a performance review system (appraisal scheme)

- formal meetings on career development issues

- a policy on internal promotions

- the use of assessment centres or psychometric tests to aid counselling interviews on development issues

- the use of projects as a tool of development.

RECALL:
allow 5 mins

List the five factors which
should be taken into account
in planning a manager
development programme.

The degree to which the HRD approach in an organisation is
'systematic' will inevitably depend on the culture and the awareness
of the concepts of manager and management development at senior
levels. Regrettably, there are many companies which fail to address
adequately manager development issues.

- Successful **career development** in today's economic
  environment is extremely rare, since the traditional notion of a
  'job for life' is no longer operable. Many organisations are,
  however, attempting to compensate for this by offering a
  breadth of experiences and development opportunities in order
  to equip people for future life.

- The need for **adaptability** can also be squeezed by economic
  factors. Some organisations are attempting to equip managers
  to be able to deal with rapidly changing circumstances, by
  extending their repertoire of skills. But because of the pressure
  of the economic situation and the relative shortage of time,
  resources and people, this is a relatively rare occurrence.

- **A manager's values** have, in recent years come to the forefront
  of many organisations' development activities as a result of
  issues such as quality customer care, empowerment and
  environmental pressure. However, although much effort has
  been applied, the results have been disappointing and it has
  revealed that values are difficult things to change.

- **The manager's job** is probably the easiest issue to deal with
  because it lends itself to traditional analysis and identification
  of needs. This, of course, does not necessarily mean that the

analysis is done well or that the results of the analysis are always acted upon. In fact, the economic situation has turned many organisations attention to other apparently more urgent issues, with the result that many managers are expected to 'sink or swim'.

- The issue of **a manager's potential** is a difficult one and, although many larger organisations do use significant resources in attempting to identify this potential, much of this effort is used at the recruitment stage where, despite the increasing range of techniques, tools and tests, the longer-term results are still poor. Even where ongoing attempts are made to identify potential, the activity is more often used for promotion/demotion purposes or for reward systems, than it is for individual development planning.

summary

▶ Managers need to understand human behaviour. Theories about motivation, personality and perception contribute to an understanding of how employees might react under different management regimes.

▶ Work by Herzberg and Maslow describes factors which influence employees' motivation. Maslow identified five basic needs: physiological, safety, love, esteem, and self-actualisation.

▶ Role conflict occurs when people have different expectations about how jobs should be performed.

▶ Pressures and stresses outside the workplace can influence employees' effectiveness and morale.

▶ Organisational factors can impact on individual performance and generate role conflict. Current issues which may generate conflict include the move towards non-hierarchical organisations, the introduction of job standards and performance targets, new quality assurance systems and increasing intense national and international business competition.

Teams

TEAMS OR GROUPS?

GROUP PROCESSES

STAGES IN THE DEVELOPMENT OF TEAMS

CHARACTERISTICS OF TEAMS

TEAM COMPOSITION

CONFLICT RESOLUTION

MEETINGS AS AIDS TO DECISION MAKING

Objectives

After participating in this session, you should be able to:

▶ describe group processes

▶ identify the stages of team development

▶ recognise the characteristics and key abilities of effective teams

▶ distinguish between effective teams and co-operative groups

▶ describe the roles people play in teams

▶ recognise the ways of resolving conflict

▶ discuss factors which influence meetings positively

▶ identify behaviour which helps decision making.

In working through this session, you will practise the following BTEC common skills:

Managing and developing self	✔
Working with and relating to others	✔
Communicating	✔
Managing tasks and solving problems	✔
Applying numeracy	
Applying technology	
Applying design and creativity	

Teams or groups?

What is the difference between a team and a group? You may be wondering why such an apparently pedantic question is asked. However, the distinction between a team and a group has many implications for organisations and, in particular, the role of the manager, and is therefore worth exploring in some detail.

In this session, we shall explore the development of a collection of individuals who are gathered together from different parts of an organisation in order to fulfil the aspirations of senior management in pursuit of business excellence. Everyone at work, whether they be a typist or a managing director, has, at some stage, to work with others in a group. This may be a permanent group (such as a small department) or it may be a group which meets infrequently and which changes from time to time.

But before we look at the distinctions between team and group, we need to examine briefly why an organisation needs to bring together a collection of people in the first place.

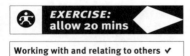

EXERCISE:
allow 20 mins

Working with and relating to others ✔

ACTIVITY 1

Form into groups of four. Discuss what you think are the advantages of working in a group. What activities are best undertaken by individuals? Would this exercise be easier to do on your own? Summarise the group's findings in the box below.

Commentary

You may have considered some of the following:

- **Task achievement**

  Groups are not very good for dealing with simple, repetitive tasks; individuals are generally far quicker. However, groups come into their own when faced with complex problems; there are several reasons for this, outlined below.

- **Quality of decisions**

  A group can generate more ideas than any single individual. It is, therefore, better able to consider a choice of possibilities, and the ultimate quality of the chosen way of doing things is likely to be better than an individual's decision.

- **Better judgements**

  Group judgements are better than individual judgements on tasks that involve random error because the group average takes into account each individual's error of judgement; in other words, an average of guesses would be closer than most individual guesses.

- **Motivation**

  It is suggested that the mere presence of others in a group, motivates individuals to perform at a higher level.

- **Speed of learning**

  Groups learn faster than individuals; there is the capability to explore and evaluate many more possible solutions than an individual can experience in working alone.

Group processes

Working with others in groups is often not as simple as it sounds. Many groups have problems which are not usually anything to do with the ability of the members to understand and to cope with the task they are carrying out. The problems that occur are rather more to do with members often not knowing very much about the group process.

The task or job of the group is what the group is trying to achieve. The process however, consists of all the things which determine how the group goes about achieving the task, and what influences it while doing so. There are many aspects to group process: the group structure, the nature of the individuals within the group, the environment and the way decisions are made.

The structure of the group

- If there are a large number of group members, it is often difficult to have a reasonably fair discussion, which leads to a failure to achieve objectives. In this situation, examples of poor group process would include domination of the discussion by one or two people, or frequent restating of the same points by different members.

- If there are too few people in the group, there may be a series of silences.

- If some of the group members are of a higher status in the company than others, then this could inhibit discussion.

- If there is insufficient expert knowledge in the group, then opinions rather than facts will be offered, which can lead to poor decisions.

The nature of the individuals

- Differences in personality and mood often show up in a group; angry types, talkative types, domineering types, and shy types respond differently in group situations.

- Some people cannot seem to stop talking, while others keep quiet, and others try to act as umpires or referees.

The environment of the meeting

- The size of the meeting areas is important to establish an appropriate atmosphere for the meeting.

- The shape of the room, heating, ventilation, lighting, seating, acoustics and decorations can all affect the efficiency of the meeting.

The way decisions are made

- There are different sets of behaviours that can take place in a meeting which is trying to reach a decision.

- Some behaviours are more effective than others; certainly, the most effective in terms of fairness and commitment is **consensus**.

TYPES OF TEAM OR GROUP

So, having explored the reasons for bringing together a collection of individuals in a group and the phenomenon of group process, it is appropriate now to focus on how a group of individuals actually becomes a team. A group begins to become a team when the individuals each recognise and become committed to:

- the purpose for their being together

- the subsequent improvement in effectiveness of the group process.

When both of these things happen there is an inevitable movement towards, and ultimately the achievement of, a team.

As we shall see later, there are many stages in the development of a team, but it might be useful, at this point, to consider the subtle differences between a group of people who are not in conflict or being deliberately fragmented – we could call this a **co-operative group** – and a group of people who are totally committed to the task and to each other – let us call this an **effective team**.

SAT:
allow 20 mins

Managing tasks and solving problems✔

ACTIVITY 2

Form into groups of four to perform the following task.

Read the case study and distinguish between the effective team and the co-operative group. Make a list of the different characteristics of each.

ASHAR AND GRAHAM

Ashar and Graham are sales managers of computer equipment in the Thames Valley area and each of them is in charge of a group of six salespeople.

Ashar's meetings are always lively and the group has been together for a couple of years. They tend to be argumentative but friendly, and they always spend time resolving any disagreements between themselves. Graham's group, on the other hand, are newer to the job and are more cautious of each other, even though several of them are close friends outside of work. Their meetings tend to be fairly formal and unexciting, although they always finish their work in the time allowed.

Graham's group are extremely highly motivated and totally committed to the job in hand. On a day-to-day basis, they keep to themselves and only contact Graham when they have a serious problem. In contrast, Ashar's group often set up informal gatherings after normal working hours and combine a little socialising with some work matters. They try to reach total agreement on work issues and will spend as much time as is available to thrash through any disagreements.

In Graham's group, each person has his or her own way of working and they are happy to check with Graham on his views of their procedures. Graham has noticed that one or two of his group – the ones who are longest serving members – tend to look upon some of the others as outsiders. Ashar's group has a reputation for 'navel-gazing' but no one doubts their sincerity and their commitment, even though their meetings are often longer than anyone else's, and they insist on reviewing their 'meeting effectiveness' at the end of each session.

Commentary...

You may have recognised a range of different behaviours and attitudes taking place in these two collections of people. Ashar seems to have an effective team and Graham a co-operative group. These, then, are the somewhat different characteristics between Ashar's team and Graham's co-operative group.

In **effective teams:**

- people trust each other
- feelings are expressed freely
- process issues are part of the work
- commitment is high
- conflict is worked through
- decisions are by consensus
- listening is high
- objectives are common to all.

In **co-operative groups:**

- trust and openness are measured
- feelings are not part of the work
- process issues are worked on covertly
- commitment is conditional
- conflict is accommodated
- people negotiate
- information is passed on a 'need-to-know' basis
- people co-operate to complete the work.

Let us now explore the benefits of having a fully committed and enthusiastic team, one in which people pursue mutually agreed goals. The overriding consideration for having a team rather than an assorted collection of individuals is **synergy**. In simple terms, synergy happens when a collection of people have joint 'ownership' of a task, are committed to the achievement of it in the most effective way, and are committed to each other's development and satisfaction in achieving the goals. The activity is likely to be more rewarding not only to the business as a whole but to each individual member, than it would be if a grudgingly accepting collection of reluctant hard-pressed managers and specialists were ordered to meet together to tackle a task which none of them recognise as being particularly important either to themselves or to the company as a whole.

SAT:
allow 15 mins

Managing tasks and solving problems ✔

ACTIVITY 3

Take an initial look at a group in which you currently operate; it could be a formal one at work or in college, or it could be a more informal one outside of work or study, in a social environment. Examine the characteristics and decide whether it is a team or a group. Use the list of characteristics given in the commentary to Activity 2 to come to your decision.

Commentary...

You may have found that there are times when your chosen group appears to operate as an effective team, and other times, in different circumstances, that it reverts to being a simple, but nonetheless, co-operative group. You may already be asking whether you really need a team in some areas of work or your social life.

Some organisations have people operating in short-term, short-lived groups whose aims are to achieve limited goals, rapidly in a task-oriented culture. It may be that, in some organisations, the work objectives make the development of effective teams important.

Stages in the development of teams

It is virtually impossible to set an effective team up from scratch. You may be lucky and be able to collect together a group of harmonious and effective people who all share the same objectives but there is a special ingredient which builds a true team – **trust** – and trust can be difficult to establish.

Teams develop over a period of time, which may be short or long dependent on the resources put into team-building, the commitment of the original members, the nature of the project and the skills of the team leader.

We now explore the various stages in the development of a team.

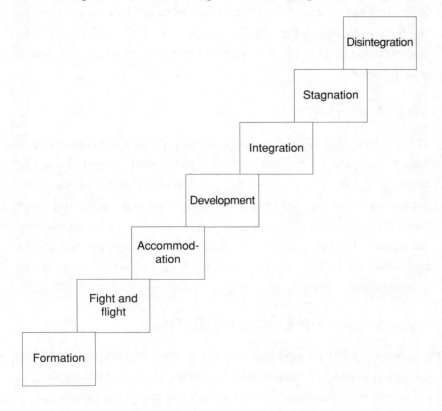

FIGURE 5.1: *Stages in the development of teams.*

Stage 1: formation

When a group of individuals are brought together to form a 'team' they are likely to come from a range of different backgrounds and functions, each with different skills. With these potentially conflicting aspects, it would be difficult to imagine an early meeting taking place without some degree of competition occurring – not necessarily violent but nevertheless obvious examples of people vying for position, or alternatively, trying to escape.

Stage 2: fight and flight

Shortly after the initial phase, comes a stage when some of the members are beginning to see the potential of the project in either positive or negative terms. These individuals can react in different ways: they can stand and fight, argue and reposition themselves in relation to the tasks; or they might feel that they want little or nothing to do with the project and will attempt to move out or, at best, simply switch off their attention.

Stage 3: accommodation

At some point in the process, members become accustomed to the task they have been given and adjust their functional situations to 'accommodate' the project requirements. They accept, with reservations, the aims of the project and the efforts of the leader/manager. The predominant behaviour in these circumstances is compromise.

Stage 4: development

This is a critical stage in the process. It occurs when each member has openly accepted the project terms (or has contributed to amending them) and has agreed to work systematically on improving the process of the group. Up to and including this stage, the collection of individuals has simply been a group. This stage usually signifies the emergence of a co-operative group but not a team even though the predominant behaviour of members is co-operation verging on collaboration.

Stage 5: integration

This is the zenith of development of the group in that it follows an intense development phase in which every aspect of effective team process is examined and worked upon with the aim of producing an effective team operating on full throttle.

Teams are now in their most productive phase. Project activities run very effectively and extremely efficiently. Everyone is collaborating with each other and task and people orientations are optimised.

It is obviously in every organisation's interest to reach this stage with every project team as soon as is possible and to maintain it as long as it is possible. One of the major influences on the sustaining of an integrated team is the continuity of members.

Stage 6: stagnation

At some point, a team becomes disillusioned, no matter how committed and integrated they were at one stage. The disillusionment may come about through boredom as a result of the time the team has been together. It may come about through frustration as a result of circumstances such as reduction in resources. It may arise through demotivation as a result of lack of feedback or clearly observed results. Unfortunately, once a team starts to stagnate, attempts to restore it are often thwarted by apathy or lack of resources.

Stage 7: disintegration

Inevitably, there must always be a point where any team finishes. In some cases, this happens at a point earlier in the process – during integration, for example. This is excellent if it is possible, because each member leaves the team with fond memories and enthusiasm still bubbling through their veins. However, if this does not happen, disintegration occurs naturally. Disintegration can take place 'spiritually' rather than physically in that the team may actually be meeting regularly but the enthusiasm has completely disappeared and been replaced by antagonism, resentment and, sometimes, sabotage.

These, then, are the seven stages in the development and demise of a project team. It is a natural process which usually occurs over a long period of time. However, it can be made more acceptable and can be influenced by awareness and commitment on the part of team members and through team development activities.

It is possible to speed the process through the first four stages to the integration stage. It is also possible to sustain the team in this stage for a long period. It is, however, also possible to misread the signals and to invest time and other resources into propping up a team which has reached a point of terminal decline.

STAGES IN THE DEVELOPMENT
OF TEAMS

  *RECALL:*
allow 15 mins

Briefly describe each of the seven stages of team development:

- **formation**

- **fight and flight**

- **accommodation**

- **development**

- **integration**

- **stagnation**

- **disintegration.**

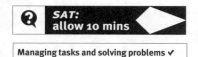 *SAT:*
allow 10 mins

Managing tasks and solving problems ✓

ACTIVITY 4

Consider the group of students in which you may currently find yourself or, if you are working, the group of people with whom you currently work. Try to identify where your current team (or an important team from your past) fits in the seven stages of development.

Commentary...

It is easy for some people to pretend that the group in which they operate, or which they lead, is an effective team when in fact it is simply a group of people who are compromising with each other.

One of the simple tests of this type of pretence is to ask the basic questions: How much time does the team spend during each meeting reviewing and evaluating the process of the team meeting rather than the content? It is the focus on development activities that often differentiates a group from a team, so that we could say that a group does not start on the road to being a team until the fourth of the development stages described above.

To summarise, we can say that formation, fight and flight, and accommodation are all group stages of development, whereas development, integration, stagnation, and disintegration are all team stages of development.

There are significant benefits to be gained from working in effective teams, but it should not be forgotten that some extremely useful and materially rewarding projects can also be carried out by co-operative groups.

Characteristics of teams

We have already distinguished between effective teams and co-operative groups. If we briefly describe the common characteristics of all teams, we can then move on to explore what makes them effective.

All teams are characterised by:

- a reason for formation in the first instance – a purpose

- a group of individuals selected to meet that purpose

- individuals in the team selected for particular roles

- time allocated for meetings

- some expectation of output or outcomes from team meetings

- an informal or formal method of working.

EFFECTIVE TEAMS

If each of these common characteristics are examined, it can be seen that there are many ways in which effectiveness can be influenced. Effective teams have some peculiar characteristics. Let us take a closer examination of the typical characteristics of an effective team:

- Its members share explicit, common team objectives.

- It tackles problems which concern individuals as well as those which concern the team as a whole.

- It does not just swap information, but tackles problems, makes decisions, and produces specific plans of action.

- It has a strong, but democratic, and sensitive leader.

- It is not, however, leader dependent; all members share responsibility for success or failure.

- Members are clear on roles and relationships within the team.

- A flexible and explicit working procedure exists which is understood and adhered to by all members.

- It thinks 'results' first, then 'methods' but acknowledges both are equally important.

- Time is allocated to review process issues, e.g. concerns about leadership, relationships, structure, procedures, objectives.

- Honesty and 'openness' is such that relationship issues can be discussed in a mature way, at any time.

- Each member values and respects the contribution of other team members.

- Members enjoy team meetings.

ACTIVITY 5

Before we move on any further, make an assessment of the team you dealt with in the last activity. For your selected team, rate its characteristics out of ten and identify key areas in which there may have been, or still may be, a need to focus in future.

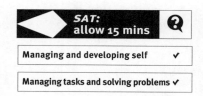

SAT:
allow 15 mins

| Managing and developing self | ✔ |
| Managing tasks and solving problems | ✔ |

Commentary...

If you found yourself marking your selected team consistently low on each characteristic, you may need to reconsider whether your team actually is a 'team'.

Team composition

For a team to operate effectively, it needs a balanced mix of personalities. The team is an entity that ought to be more than the sum of its parts: it needs synergy as discussed earlier. The different parts of a team's 'personality' can be within different individuals and each can be called upon at the appropriate time. These different qualities, such as drive, prudence, enthusiasm, understanding, opportunism and reliability, all have their parts to play.

Nobody can claim to be perfect, but a team has the opportunity to emphasise the strengths of each individual and eliminate the weaknesses. Properly orchestrated, a team acquires a mental and emotional strength that provides a significant 'edge' to tackle problems and devise innovative solutions.

Different team roles start to emerge when the team begins to form and work together, but **Meredith Belbin** (*Team Roles at Work*, Butterworth Heinemann, 1993) found, to his surprise, that there were only eight key roles in successful teams. When individuals accept the existence of a team, then one or more of Belbin's roles are open to them:

- The **chair** ensures that the best use is made of each member's potential. The chair should be self-disciplined, dominant but not domineering.

- **Shapers** look for patterns and try to shape the team's efforts in this direction. They are outgoing, impulsive and impatient. They make the team feel uncomfortable but they make things happen.

- **Innovators** are the source of original ideas. They are imaginative and uninhibited. They are bad at accepting criticism and may need careful handling to provide that vital 'spark'.

- **Evaluators** are more measured and dispassionate. They like time to analyse problems and mull things over.

- **Organisers** turn strategies into manageable tasks. They are disciplined and methodical but can sometimes be inflexible.

- **Entrepreneurs** go outside the group and bring back information and ideas. They make friends easily and have a mass of contacts. They prevent the team from stagnating.

- **Team workers** promote unity and harmony within a group. They are more aware of people's needs than other members. They are the most active internal communicators and form the 'cement' of the team.

- **Finishers** are compulsive 'meeters of deadlines'. They worry about what can go wrong and maintain a permanent sense of urgency which they communicate to others.

The successful team is a well-balanced group containing the appropriate mix of these roles. It is important to emphasise that all these characteristics are equally valuable, although in a given situation certain roles may be seen as more valuable than others.

ACTIVITY 6

Examine again the team you chose in the last two activities and try to recognise some of the roles in operation. In doing this, you may realise that some people within a team carry out more than one role. Take two of the roles and examine the people filling the roles in terms of their strengths and weaknesses in that role.

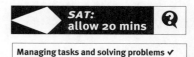

SAT:
allow 20 mins

Managing tasks and solving problems ✔

Commentary...

Not all teams need the same mix of roles. For new groups, the main requirement is for the drive and energy of the shaper. A good combination for a new team might be: shaper, finisher, organiser and team worker.

As the group grows and expands its activities, the innovator is needed to generate new ideas, and the evaluator to ensure the group avoids costly mistakes.

That there are eight roles does not mean that the ideal group comprises eight people, each taking one of the main team roles. In fact most people may adopt more than one role as you have seen and can vary their performance to suit the situation.

SIZE OF GROUP

How many members should there be in a team? The answer depends both on the team objectives and on how many people are available. As a general rule, however, effective teams are composed of four to ten members.

- If it is smaller, it becomes difficult to cover all the necessary team roles and functional areas. There is no slack, the team is dependent on the individual personalities involved and vulnerable to one member leaving.

- If it is larger than ten, it becomes unwieldy because people have very little opportunity to contribute; a few members dominate the proceedings and the rest of the group are cast in a fairly passive role.

Groups of five or more members usually need a chair. This change in direction, from the project leadership of the shaper to the social leadership of the chair, may cause difficulty for the group and can be painful for some of its members.

MARGERISON AND MCCANN'S TEAM ROLES

We have spent time looking at Meredith Belbin's team roles but we can take a slightly different view. **Margerison** and **McCann** (*Team Management Index*, NCB University Press, 1985) have also carried out extensive research into operational roles within effective teams. Drawing much from the Myers–Briggs analysis and profiles, they have described eight key roles within their 'team wheel'.

- **Reporter/advisers** tend to enjoy gathering and reporting information to meetings.

- **Creator/innovators** enjoy generating and experimenting with creative ideas.

- **Explorer/promoters** typically spend a lot of time making contacts exploring alternatives, persuading others and generating resources.

- **Assessor/developers** want to assess alternatives to see how they can work in practice.

- **Thruster/organisers** are impatient, always wanting to move forward, knocking down any barriers in order to complete tasks as quickly and effectively as possible.

- **Concluder/producers** want to ensure that tasks are concluded so that plans and ideas are brought to fruition. They want things to run in an orderly way.

- **Controller/inspectors** exert a controlling influence to ensure that tasks are inspected, checked and done according to rules, regulations and standards.

- **Upholder/maintainers** are strongly supportive of friends and colleagues who believe in their ideals. They uphold the standards values and traditions of the organisation.

In addition to the above eight key roles, there is a control role. People who adopt the control role like organising, but know the value of advising. They like exploring opportunities, but they know when to consolidate and how to control and monitor events.

SELECTION OF TEAM MEMBERS

In selecting the best people for a team, there are a number of important issues that the manager must bear in mind:

- technical skills and knowledge required for the team task

- personal skills and style required for a balanced 'team'

- degree of commitment of individuals to the task

- the 'spread' of involvement of members for organisation-wide projects

- willingness of individuals to work with others including the manager

- the mix of perceived and actual status and accountabilities within the team

- authority of individuals to be able to commit their functions

- track record.

To a large extent, most of these criteria can only be judged subjectively, and through discussion with other people in the organisation such as the prospective team-members, manager, colleagues and subordinates. Some judgements will be made on perceived behaviour and past relationships, as well as current enthusiasm and energy.

There are also, however, a number of more objective assessments which may be made in at least a couple of the criteria.

- The technical competence of the individual can be measured in a number of different ways, through, for example, qualifications, achievements in current and past employment, performance appraisal records, documented performance evidence and observations.

- The personal skill and style of an individual within a team may be assessed.

Different people bring different talents to group work. Some people are good at generating ideas, others have the push and drive to make things happen, while others possess the social skills to lead the group and make sure it slides together. Characteristics which would be incompatible in one individual can combine well in a group. To be successful, a group or team needs a balanced mix of people whose skills and personalities match and mesh. These different styles and personalities in operation within a team or group can be examined and assessed in more detail using questionnaires of various types. The two main techniques for assessing styles are Meredith Belbin's questionnaire and Margerison and McCann's team roles questionnaire.

GRAHAM HURLEY'S TEAM

Graham Hurley's sales team are in one of their regular meetings, which are held once a fortnight. The members are becoming increasingly frustrated with the boring bureaucracy of the meeting which Graham does little to eliminate. He works steadily through the agenda, without allowing too much time for debate and then finishes with a flourish on time. Unfortunately, there are several members who would prefer to finish later if only they could have more opportunity to contribute.

James, for example, loves to involve himself in deep discussions, and indulges himself in pursuing a few red herrings occasionally. Mary is also that way inclined, and if the discussion seemed to be moving towards a conclusion, then she would often add another contribution to the argument thus pushing it into even further discussion. She enjoys debate and the company of her colleagues.

On the other hand, Jeremy is a quiet, meticulous person who is always supportive of Graham in his attempts to finish the meeting early. He derives great satisfaction from summing things up, which he does at regular intervals. Unfortunately, Jeremy and Graham are in a minority in their group, since most of the team are often looking forward to the gathering in the offices after a hectic two weeks on the road. They like to explore problems and operational plans, instead of working through quick decisions.

Frequently, there are emotional outbursts from some of the group, especially when judgements appear to be made about their performance without the opportunity for them to comment. Graham is a strong chairperson, although he is not particularly influential in the way in which decisions are made. In this respect it is nearly always Sarah who makes the running. Sarah is a strong-willed extrovert who interrupts most people, speaks loudly, and holds views which are difficult to shift. Most members of the group feel that the meetings are becoming a charade.

ACTIVITY 7

Is Hurley's team effective? Are there some obvious weaknesses or gaps in the repertoire of skills and styles available?

If you were given the task of strengthening the group and improving its effectiveness, what additional personality or personal skills would you be seeking in new members?

How would you advise Graham's manager on how the group could be made more effective? Write a 200-word report setting out your recommendations. Use a separate piece of paper to record your answer. Summarise your findings in the box below.

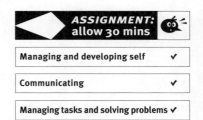

ASSIGNMENT:
allow 30 mins

Managing and developing self	✔
Communicating	✔
Managing tasks and solving problems	✔

Conflict resolution

How conflict is dealt with in teams is, of course, heavily influenced by the style and approach of the manager. It is also influenced by a number of other elements, including the pressure of the group as a whole or power exerted by one or more individuals within the group or even from outside the group.

Before we examine ways of dealing with conflict in groups or teams, let us first describe the nine stages of escalation of conflict: discussion, debate, deeds not words, fixed images, loss of face, strategies of threat, inhuman, no retreat and no way back. These are illustrated in figure 5.2.

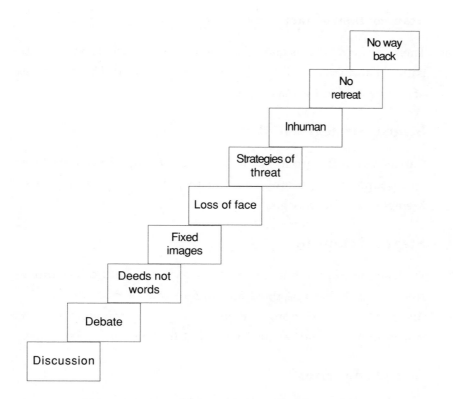

FIGURE 5.2: *Stages in the escalation of group conflict.*

Stage 1: discussion

This occurs where a group is convened to tackle a task. Signs of tension may be apparent. There is caution and verbal confrontation. Although there is a basis of co-operation, there is often an element of incidental competition.

Stage 2: debate

Psychological pressure begins to mount. There is a keenness on picking up on the weak points in others; group members indulge in some 'point-scoring'. Co-operation is still in existence but it is now matched by competition.

Stage 3: deeds not words

Non-verbal behaviour has become more important; also people are saying one thing and doing another. Boundaries start to be drawn and competition begins to dominate.

Stage 4: fixed images

Perceptions of others and their motives have begun to change and solidify so that stereotyping becomes prevalent. Everyone is put into 'boxes' and dealt with as though they are inflexible.

Stage 5: loss of face

There are huge doubts and contradictions; dissenters from the 'right path' are thrown out. Rituals begin to be established. There is a sense of 'seeing behind the mask' of people.

Stage 6: strategies of threat

Threat within the group has now arrived. Bridges have been burnt and people react to others' actions by doing something worse. Members in conflict begin to 'up the stakes'.

Stage 7: inhuman

Destruction of others is now seen as legitimate. Rules are broken freely. People become fixed and immovable in their views. They distance themselves from each other so that they can view the other side as inhuman and can justify fairly radical measures as defence.

Stage 8: no retreat

Attacks on the sources of power become important. People anticipate retaliation and tend to cut off any means of retreat. There are attempts to burn the bridges of others as well as your own.

Stage 9: no way back

Totally irrational behaviour begins; it is considered that withdrawal is a fate worse than destruction. The result is that the other side must be dragged towards disaster with you.

Of the nine stages, it is clear that the last three or four are so bad that, under normal circumstances, any typical organisational team would have ground to a halt before reaching that point. However, the first five or six stages of conflict can be observed very readily in many groups and organisations.

There are a number of options for dealing with such conflict:

- With the **structural approach**, a group is re-organised with different rules and procedures. If necessary, people can be removed and new personnel added.

- With the **perception approach**, attempts are made to clarify misconceptions, and people are allowed to let off steam in controlled circumstances.

○ The **moralising or missionary approach** is aimed at attitudes; an appeal is made to people's 'inner-self' or core values. It is only successful if the appeal is made to basic values which have not been abandoned.

○ The **law and order approach** is aimed at unacceptable behaviour. Physical controls are brought in, or status and power is used to force people into controlled behaviour. The more controls there are, however, the more energy tends to be put into finding loopholes.

○ With **attitude training**, attempts can be made to introduce sensitivity training to conflicting parties, but this can often have disastrous results.

Some of these approaches are more successful than others. It depends greatly on the surrounding circumstances to the conflict for their efficiency. In the early stages, conflict may be resolved if the manager is able to operate in a clear facilitator role. In most of the later stages of conflict as described above, the team leader would find it difficult to solve conflict without external help. Once the conflict has moved past Stage 3, it would be difficult for anyone internally to deal with it. Normally, an external facilitator or process consultant would be required. At later stages, a therapist and even an arbitrator or mediator may be needed.

ACTIVITY 8

Think of the recent conflict situations in which you have been involved either at work, in the learning institution, in social life or in another part of your life. Can you recognise these conflicts moving through the stages? How were each of them eventually resolved and by whom?

Perhaps you can spot a current disturbance in one of your work, learning or social activities with the potential for escalation. How can you prevent this?

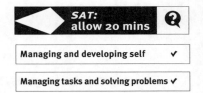

SAT:
allow 20 mins

Managing and developing self ✔

Managing tasks and solving problems ✔

Commentary...

Conflict will often occur within organisations, especially when there are difficult business circumstances, e.g. where targets are not being met, when finances are tight, or where people are being made redundant. Conflict can also occur where there are significant disagreements between managers about the way forward.

Prevention of conflict, or at least the restriction on the likelihood of conflict escalating once it has started, is always the best action to take. It is to be preferred to attempting to resolve a highly complex and emotional 'war'.

There are a number of ways conflict can be actively prevented from arising and they are either concerned with good planning or in the use of appropriate behaviour. On the business and operational planning side, the manager needs to make sure that all the basic rules are followed, including adequate consultation and briefing. Extra care also needs to be taken over recruitment and selection of individual employees based on personality compatibility and, where appropriate, a balance of natural team roles. Care also needs to be taken over the allocation of adequate resources, including time and finance.

Finally, extra care needs to be taken over clarification of roles at work, particularly as far as authority, responsibility, and accountability are concerned. By setting out clear roles and lines of responsibility, such clarification works to the benefit not only of the individual employee but also his or her functional boss and colleagues.

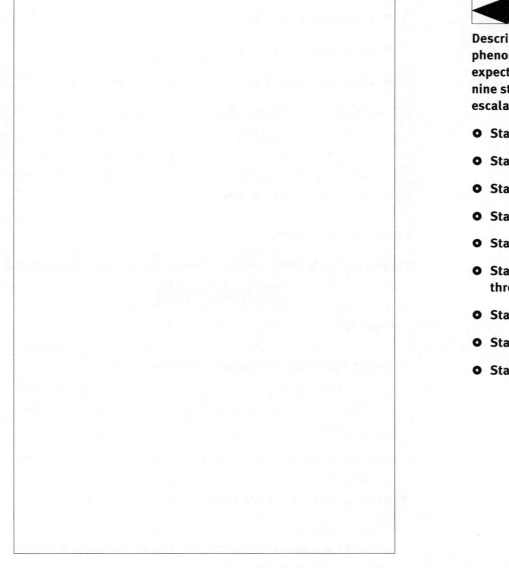

RECALL:
allow 15 mins

Describe briefly the phenomena that you might expect to occur at each of the nine stages of conflict escalation.

- Stage 1: discussion
- Stage 2: debate
- Stage 3: deeds not words
- Stage 4: fixed images
- Stage 5: loss of face
- Stage 6: strategies of threat
- Stage 7: inhuman
- Stage 8: no retreat
- Stage 9: no way back

Conflict situations are those in which the concerns of two or more people appear to be incompatible. In such situations, we can view a person's behaviour against two basic dimensions:

- **assertion** – the extent to which the individual attempts to satisfy his or her own concerns

- **co-operation** – the extent to which the individual attempts to satisfy the other person's concerns.

These two basic dimensions of behaviour can be used to define five specific methods of dealing with conflict, or 'conflict handling modes', as defined by **Thomas Killman**:

- **Competing**: 'I win – you lose'

- **Accommodating**: 'I lose some – you win'

- **Avoiding**: 'I lose – you win'

- **Collaborating**: 'I win – you win'

- **Compromising**: 'I win some – you win some'

A quick look might suggest that the best two modes to pursue are competing or collaborating since in both cases there is a predominance of 'I win'. However, some situations may require a more diplomatic or long-term strategy which could involve the use of the other modes. Let us look at each of the modes.

Competing: 'I win – you lose'

Competing is assertive and uncooperative. An individual pursues his or her own concerns at the other person's expense. This is a power-oriented mode; a person uses whatever power seems appropriate to win his or her own position.

Accommodating: 'I lose some – you win'

Accommodating is unassertive and co-operative – the opposite of competing. When accommodating, an individual neglects his or her own concerns to satisfy the concerns of the other person: there is an element of self-sacrifice in this mode.

Avoiding: 'I lose – you win'

Avoiding is unassertive and uncooperative. The individual does not immediately pursue his or her own concerns or those of the other person and so does not address the conflict.

Collaborating: 'I win – you win'

Collaborating is both assertive and co-operative – the opposite of avoiding. Collaborating involves an attempt to work with the other person to find some solution which fully satisfies the concerns of both persons. It means exploring an issue to identify the underlying concerns of the two individuals and to find an outcome which meets both sets of concerns.

Compromising: 'I win some – you win some'

Compromising is intermediate in both assertiveness and co-operativeness. The objective is to find some expedient, mutually acceptable solution which partially satisfies both parties. It falls on a middle ground between competing and accommodating.

SAT:
allow 10 mins

Managing tasks and solving problems ✔

ACTIVITY 9

For each of the five key styles of conflict resolution, write down at least two examples of the types of comment you would use in conversation (or negotiation) in attempting to resolve a problem.

For example, in an accommodation style, you may use a statement like: 'I agree with you there.' In a collaboration style, you might say: 'Let's find some common ground.'

Commentary...

Suggestions for each style are given below.

Competing

- I'm not prepared to change my position.
- I must make my position quite clear.
- My view is the most rational.
- If you don't do this, I'll ...
- I know best, you'd better ...
- Do as you're told.
- I'm sure mine is the best way.

Accommodation

- I concede that point.
- I agree with you there.
- I'm prepared to accept that.
- I will do as you say.
- I don't want to offend you.
- What is your preferred outcome?

Avoidance

- I can't take responsibility for this.
- I'd prefer not to discuss that.
- Let's talk about that later.
- That is outside my brief.
- I won't be drawn on that.
- I'm not in a position to discuss ...
- I don't want to talk about ...
- I don't see your point.

Collaboration

- Let's work together on this.
- What is mutually acceptable.
- What do we disagree about?
- Let's find some common ground.

- Let's investigate the problem.

- My position is ... What's yours?

Compromising

- Let's find a quick solution.

- I'll give you ... if you give me ...

- Let's split the difference.

- I suggest we meet halfway.

- We can't both win, but let's not both lose.

- Let's be satisfied with ...

- I'm prepared to ... if you will ...

- Let's both come away with something.

A manager is likely to face potential conflict not only with and between members in his or her function but possibly also with individuals or other teams outside of the group; these could include bosses, peers or subordinates. The conflict could be about a wide range of subjects from resource allocation, priorities, values, personality clash, misunderstandings, stress, role confusion or time management. The manager's style of dealing with conflict (or causing it) also stems from a number of influences some of them ingrained 'personality' issues and others of a more transitory and situational nature. That said, there are different circumstances in which the different ways of handling conflict are best utilised.

When to use the competing style

- When quick, decisive action is vital, e.g. in emergencies

- On important issues where unpopular courses of action need implementing, e.g during cost cutting exercises, enforcing unpopular rules, discipline

- On issues vital to company welfare, when you know you are right

- To protect yourself against people who might take advantage of non-competitive behaviour.

When to use the accommodating style

- When you realise that you are wrong, or to allow a better position to be heard, to learn from others, and to show that you are not unreasonable

- When the issue is much more important to the other person than to yourself; this satisfies the needs of others and, as a goodwill gesture, helps to maintain a co-operative relationship

- To build up social credits or 'Brownie points' for future issues which may be more important to you

- When continued competition would only damage your cause, or when you are outmatched and losing

- When preserving harmony and avoiding disruption are especially important

- As an aid in the managerial development of subordinates, by allowing them to experiment and learn from their own mistakes.

When to use the avoiding style

- When an issue is trivial, of only passing importance, or when other more important issues are pressing

- When you perceive no chance of satisfying your concerns, e.g. when you have low power or you are frustrated by something which would be very difficult to change (national policies, someone's personality, etc.)

- When the potential damage of confronting and tackling a conflict outweighs the benefits of its resolution

- To let people cool down, i.e. to reduce tensions to a productive level and to regain perspective and composure

- When gathering more information outweighs the advantage of an immediate decision

- When others can resolve the conflict more effectively

- When the issue seems tangential or symptomatic of another or more basic issue.

When to use the compromising style

- When there are two pieces of strong evidence to support apparently conflicting viewpoints

- When there is a strong argument on an insignificant topic which is an obstacle to major progress on the project as a whole

- To preserve harmony and avoid disruption of the team relationships.

- When continued competition would only damage your cause

- When you wish to encourage and support the other person as a development strategy.

When to use the collaborating style

- When your objective is to learn, e.g. by testing your own assumptions, or understanding the views of others

- To merge insights from people with different perspectives on a problem

- To work through hard feelings which have been interfering with an inter-personal relationship

- To gain commitment by incorporating others' concerns into a consensual decision

- To find an integrated solution when both sets of concerns are too important to be compromised.

ACTIVITY 10

You are chairing a meeting. You want to make sure that the meeting is effective and that contentious issues generate the minimum of conflict. What strategies would you adopt to ensure that the meeting runs smoothly?

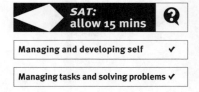

SAT:
allow 15 mins

Managing and developing self ✔

Managing tasks and solving problems ✔

Commentary

Here are some suggestions:

- Listen to whoever is speaking at any time, not only to what he or she is saying but also to the feeling behind it.
- Build on suggestions and comments that have been made.
- Ask clarifying questions on vague or unclear statements which may have been made.
- Avoid interrupting someone before they have finished making their point.
- Avoid emotional attacks as opposed to reasoned disagreements.
- Avoid putting up blocks on suggestions that others make on the basis of personal prejudice.
- Do not impose your solutions.
- Do not minimise or devalue the worth of others' suggestions.
- Do not knock others' experience, actions or hopes.
- If no one else does it, try to summarise what has happened at regular intervals.
- If no one else does it, try to draw in or evoke the more quiet members of the group.
- Bring people back to the central issue where you see attacking or defensive attitudes being adopted or where tangents are being followed.

Meetings as aids to decision making

Perhaps the most used, but least effective, decision-making or information-giving medium is 'the meeting'. Meetings take place all the time in organisations, whether they are between a few people in the immediate working area or between larger groups of people in offices or conference suites. If meetings go well, the advantages can be seen in improving communication, participation commitment and a sense of teamwork. If they do not go well, issues are not clearly presented, decision making is mismanaged or people are left feeling confused, unconsidered, manipulated or frustrated. The individual, team and organisational costs can be huge.

There are a number of different aspects of meetings that can cause difficulties:

- the physical setting of the meeting

- the process

- the timing

- the agenda.

Let us look at these issues in a little more detail.

Physical setting

The meeting place will be unsuitable if it is uncomfortable, too hot, too cold, too big, too small, too noisy, badly laid out or there are interruptions or distractions.

Process

Any of the following failures in the process can cause difficulties:

- The person running the meeting adopts a style which is unacceptable to those attending, or is inappropriate for the task.

- Some members are allowed to dominate the meeting, participation is not balanced and people feel ignored or unconsidered.

- Discussion is allowed to wander and no sense of progress is apparent.

- Decisions are steamrollered through and some people emerge as winners while others feel they have 'lost' a decision, but have also been maltreated in the process.

- There is either no record kept of what has been discussed or decided, or a variety of individual records are kept by members with resultant bias.

- The concentration is on the agenda and people's feelings are ignored.

- People speak at the same time and seem not to listen to each other.

- Some members have hidden agendas (i.e. they pursue their own purposes) which distracts from the main one.

Timing

Poor timing can also cause problems:

- The meeting is held at a time when people are tired or when it is convenient due to other pressures at work or at home.

- Insufficient notice is given of the date and time of the meeting.

- The length of time allowed for the meeting is inappropriate for the agenda to be dealt with.

The agenda

Problems due to the agenda include the following:

- The objectives of the meeting are not clear, not agreed or not accepted by those attending.

- The agenda is not regarded as sufficiently important, relevant or interesting to involve those attending.

- Priority items are not given sufficient time. Less significant items are given too much time. People stray from the point, irrelevancies are pursued.

- There is no visible agenda and so there is no sense of progress as items are dealt with.

- Summaries are lacking so the discussion wanders and lacks focus.

- Necessary information is lacking or relevant papers or materials are not available to the members.

- The status of the meeting is not clear, so members are not sure whether the purpose is to give information, gather or exchange opinions, or to make decisions or plan policy.

- The agenda is pursued too rigidly. Important issues that emerge during the meeting are suppressed, leaving members frustrated.

ACTIVITY 11

This activity is designed to develop your understanding of the function and meaning of an agenda. Put yourself in the position of having to organise a meeting for the students of your course.

The meeting has the main objective of analysing the effectiveness of the course. You want to discuss the advantages and disadvantages of the various methods of learning involved. But you also intend to arrange a series of social events for next term; you want ideas for a suitable programme and volunteers to help organise the activities.

In the following check-list, there are a number of questions related to the formation of an appropriate agenda. Given the above purpose of the meeting how would you answer each of the questions on the check-list?

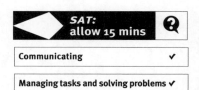

SAT:
allow 15 mins

| Communicating | ✔ |

| Managing tasks and solving problems ✔ |

Item	Comment
What topics need to be included in the main body of the agenda?	
What are the issues that your key participants will want included?	
What words and phrases do you need to use to avoid being vague?	
What is the most logical sequence of agenda topics?	
What items should be at the head of the sequence because of urgency and importance?	
What urgent, but not necessarily important, items can be delt with quickly first to allow time for the important, and often longer-term, items?	
Have you allowed for a brief item at the top of the agenda to check with participants for important issues they feel need to be addressed?	
What time do you need to allocate for each topic on the agenda?	
What time should be given to the topics sent in (or requested) by other participants?	
What specific points do you want to ensure are dealt with under each item?	

MANAGEMENT STYLES IN MEETINGS

The manager/leader needs to give adequate consideration to a number of issues in planning a meeting.

- What are the objectives of the meeting?

- Who will be there?

- How much time is available?

- What information is needed?

- Where are the physical arrangements?

- What tactics might be required to influence the meeting?

Seating positions, for example, can have a major influence on the interaction within a group or meeting. The relative positions and 'shape' of the group can reflect and reinforce communication styles, the degree of formality and the frequency of comments passing between individual members. For example, team members may find sitting around a table leads to a sense of formality, while sitting together in a circle with no 'barrier' between them is a more relaxed format.

Management styles might differ according to the degree of scope allowed to other people to influence the meeting's progress and outcome. A 'directive' style allows others little scope whereas a 'participant' style permits others room to influence members during a meeting. The *laissez-faire*, or 'abdication' style involves allowing a free rein to the others at the meeting.

When choosing a style, it is worth reflecting upon the effects that different approaches may have on goal achievement. We have already referred to the various management styles and approaches to leadership. These are equally important in meetings as they are in other activities.

There are several types of behaviour which help the group to remain in good working order, creating a good climate for achieving objectives and making decisions:

- harmonising

- sharing

- encouraging

- compromising

- listening to the words, yet hearing the music.

It is important during meetings to be aware of interaction processes as well as task activity: to be aware of the 'words and music' of face-to-face interaction.

Positive behaviour indicates warmth, agreement or releases tension and is vital to a successful meeting. It creates a positive task climate and facilitates individual and group goal achievement.

Negative behaviour indicates unfriendliness or creates tension, for example, by 'putting down' another person. The usual pattern is that a negative act produces an equally negative response from the recipient, leading to an escalation of negatives, which if not checked will mean the 'words are drowned by the music'.

The leader of the meeting should show positive behaviour, and avoid being hooked by a negative statement from someone else, however tempting the bait of conflict may be.

summary

This session has looked at the increasingly important role played by teams in business. It has considered how to develop effective teams and how to manage teams successfully. Key points include the following:

- The development of teams can be characterised by seven stages: formation, fight and flight, accommodation, development, integration, stagnation and disintegration.

- Formation, fight and flight, and accommodation are all group stages of development; beyond the development stage groups increasingly take on the characteristics of teams.

- Teams pull together to solve allocated tasks. Key characteristics include: members sharing objectives; members valuing and respecting the contributions of others; clear roles and responsibilities; and an acknowledgement that both 'results' and 'process' or 'methods' are important.

- Successful teams typically have from four to ten members. Between them, team members ought to have the skills and attributes to undertake key roles. Belbin identified eight important roles found in teams: chair, shapers, innovators, evaluators, organisers, entrepreneurs, team workers and finishers.

- In dealing with conflicts within teams there are five basic options: structural approach, perception approach, moralising approach appealing to people's values, law and order approach (i.e. wielding the stick) and attitude training.

▶ In dealing with conflicts with team members or other staff, a manager can adopt five styes: competing, accommodating, avoiding, collaborating and compromising. Each style has its merits depending on the circumstances of the situation.

▶ To run effective meetings, managers must pay attention to the physical setting, the process or conduct of the meeting, the timing of the meeting and the agenda.

Performance at work

Objectives

IDENTIFYING TRAINING NEEDS

PROVIDING TRAINING

REVIEWING TRAINING ACTIVITIES

INDIVIDUAL PERFORMANCE REVIEWS

DISCIPLINE AND GRIEVANCE

SUPPORT STRATEGIES

After participating in this session, you should be able to:

▶ describe ways of identifying training needs

▶ recognise potential solutions to identified training needs

▶ describe methods for monitoring training

▶ identify methods for reviewing the performance of individuals

▶ understand discipline and grievance procedures

▶ describe strategies to support employees in improving their performance.

In working through this session, you will practise the following BTEC common skills:

Managing and developing self	✔
Working with and relating to others	✔
Communicating	✔
Managing tasks and solving problems	✔
Applying numeracy	
Applying technology	
Applying design and creativity	

Identifying training needs

Training activity may place emphasis on a number of different factors:

- the development and acquisition of knowledge

- the development of skill

- the changing of attitude.

Defining the current position and identifying what is needed in the future in each of these areas is a complex and challenging task for managers. Every individual employed in the organisation ought to be covered in the assessment and identification of training and development. This includes research scientists, salesmen and saleswomen, accountants, typists and chief executives.

ASSESSING ORGANISATIONAL NEEDS

To start an effective process of human resource development, you would probably start by examining the organisation itself. What is currently happening? What is the starting point for assessing training requirements? To answer this, an audit of the organisation may be carried out. This can be done in a number of ways, and by a range of different people. It could be by training department staff or, where there is no specialist in-company training unit, by a group of managers. In any event, a manager should always be involved in the auditing of an organisation, even though he or she may not be involved in initiating it.

In general terms, an audit might include most of the following:

- organisational goals and objectives

- the organisational structure

- roles and tasks within the organisation

- organisational culture – its values, beliefs and ideologies

- compensation systems

- communication systems

- relationships inside and outside the organisation

- techniques and tools being used

- leadership (Who is co-ordinating things?).

This review provides the basic information from which you can go on to assess individual training needs.

ASSESSING INDIVIDUAL NEEDS

One starting point for analysing the training needs of individuals occurs when someone has obviously failed to meet agreed targets. Identification of a person's needs in this way is often:

- made by the person's immediate manager through some kind of appraisal process

- based on self-admission and faults

- based on past failings

- unrelated to the organisation's long-term plans

- identified without the person's agreement and commitment.

A different approach is to ask staff to identify their own needs. People often have a better awareness of their own needs; they might realise that they need training on a new technique or that they need updating in their field. Organisations that strive to meet the training needs as identified by the people for themselves will have a more motivated staff because the staff will be able to see tangible results.

However, these self-declared needs can also be a diversion. The individuals' interests might not be the same as those identified by their immediate managers. It is the manager's job to ensure that the self-declared needs of an individual do relate to the organisational needs.

A better approach is to identify and agree training needs as part of a joint process between an employee and his or her manager. If this does not happen, it is either because a manager does not have the appropriate awareness and skills, or because the company does not have an appropriate system.

USE OF APPRAISAL INTERVIEWS

In many organisations, training needs emerge from appraisal interviews. These are not always the productive and creative sessions they are intended to be. There might be a tendency for the boss to assume that failure to meet targets implies a failing in the individual, when it could be due to an ineffective system, outmoded equipment or another non-training related reason.

In any case, the fact that targets have not been met should not arise for the first time at an appraisal interview. If it does, it implies that there is an inadequate monitoring and control procedure, and the supervising manager should take steps to redress the situation.

Poor communication between an appraisee and an appraiser can also result in a lack of commitment by people to any training plans that are prepared. The extent to which this happens in otherwise 'staff-centred' organisations is quite surprising. It is important that any needs identified through an appraisal system are well documented; then they may be referred to during the following period or at the next appraisal.

In some organisations, training needs are identified by appraisal systems which concentrate on weaknesses or inadequacies, so the training is arranged to counteract these. This approach arises from the use of appraisals to look back rather than forward. In some situations, more detailed training needs may be recognised in general terms within appraisals, but will often need to be specified and quantified outside the appraisal interview.

A more sound approach might be to concentrate on the positive aspects of the previous year's performance, and plan training and development to build on the individual's strengths.

Most small organisations use informal methods for identifying training needs. At its simplest, the boss assumes he knows the problem and sends the employee for training. This approach can be ineffective because it does not gain the commitment of the employee to the training. Even a brief conversation between the manager and the individual would clarify better any training need and identify the objective.

TRAINING IS NOT ALWAYS THE BEST OPTION

Managers often use the word 'problem' when analysing individual, group or organisational needs. In other words, they have identified a weakness or deficiency and have to find a solution. The first thing to consider is what is actually causing the problem.

There are many dangers in assuming that a problem is always concerned with a weakness in knowledge, skills or attitude. There are many other possible causes of a problem. There may be a single cause or a range of causes of the problem.

At some point, the resolution of these contributory causes to the problem may involve some training, but in many cases the solution is more likely to be either the provision of more resources or the establishment of a new system.

ACTIVITY 1

Below you will find a list of many factors which can influence an individual's performance in a job or occupation. These factors range from national and international issues (less powerful influences?) through to the very personal factors (the most powerful factors?).

Measure yourself against these influences and carry out an analysis of the key factors which are currently having a negative effect on your performance. Which of these factors could be totally resolved through a training and development solution? Which factors could be resolved partially through a training and development solution? Which factors have a non-training solution?

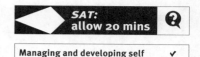

legislation – trade unions – technological innovation – the market place – general public – government – shareholders – social demands

organisational objectives – company structure – company technology – company values – organisational climate – leadership – company policies

level of responsibility – level of accountability – level of authority

other managers – payment – your boss – your subordinates – technology in your department – training – the role demanded – union pressure – specialists

your needs – your expectations – your ability – your personality – your experience – your attitude

Providing training

Where a training need emerges, an organisation is faced with a choice of actions:

- to design a custom-built training activity specifically to suit the needs of the individual

- to place the individual with the need on an already well-established internal training activity

- to send the individual with the need on an external training activity.

Because of the unique nature of each individual's training and development needs, it is difficult for a single organisation to provide all the facilities and training opportunities within its own walls. Only very large organisations are able to design and run cost-effective training activities for groups with similar needs, and only major organisations are able to employ sufficiently skilled trainers to run these programmes effectively. In most circumstances, learning is either carried out by the individual alone, as in distance learning, or in an external learning environment, such as a college or university.

Many different training solutions are available:

Custom-built courses

These may be designed by in-company training staff or external consultants to meet the needs of a group. These could include, for example, courses on new machinery or on new administrative procedures. This can often be the best way to resolve a group training need, but is usually only practicable where there are sufficient numbers of trainees (and back-up staff).

External courses

A massive range of courses exist which cover every conceivable subject. These courses are often the most popular and effective solution to training needs. Time and cost are the usual constraints here. Some courses can be expensive, or not completely appropriate. They can require substantial periods away from work or involve travelling and overnight accommodation which may not be suitable for some people, such as mothers with young children.

Open learning

There are many different vehicles for open learning currently on offer, most of them aimed at the acquisition of a qualification or, increasingly, a competence accreditation. While becoming increasingly popular as a training solution, there are some inherent problems in this approach, including the difficulties many people have with time management and motivation.

Education programmes

Management and business education programmes exist at all levels, certificate, diploma, degree – although they tend to be designed to cover a wide range of skills and knowledge and are, therefore, more suitable for staff at the beginning of their careers.

Secondment

Secondment offers an opportunity for an employee to gain a greater breadth of experience. It can be carried out within a company where opportunities exist or, with agreement, in other companies or organisations.

Coaching and instruction on-the-job

This is probably the most widely used form of training and development. Undertaken well, it is of immense benefit but this kind of hands-on training can be of a poor quality because of lack of time allocation, or inadequate instructor skills.

Programmed instruction and computer-based training

This can be a cost-effective way of acquiring specific skills and knowledge. But it is a lonely and often ineffective method, not because of the intrinsic technology, but because of lack of opportunity to practise skills and transfer learning to the real work situation.

SAT:
allow 15 mins

Managing and developing self ✓

ACTIVITY 2

Look through the list of training options above and identify those which you have undertaken at some stage in your life. Analyse the needs on which these options were based and identify to what extent the solutions were appropriate. Would any of the other forms of training have been preferable to you?

Commentary...

In many instances a combination of the above methods are used, particularly where a career development programme is being implemented. The degree to which one or other of these options is chosen as a central focus normally depends on:

- the training and development budget of the organisation

- the internal resources, in terms of facilities and expertise

- the time available to the trainee/learner

- the policy of the organisation.

Without doubt, the training policy of an organisation, if devised properly, should result in sufficient finance and time being allocated for the acquisition of skills and knowledge required for the effectiveness of the organisation. The only alternatives to this are a 'hire-and-fire' organisation or an inefficient organisation.

INTEGRATING INDIVIDUAL AND ORGANISATIONAL SOLUTIONS

In an ideal world, the training needs of the individual would match the long-term skill requirements of the organisation. Sadly, this does not always happen, so managers must resolve any conflict between these two sets of goals.

This presents managers with two issues to consider:

- the need of the organisation to acquire the skills it requires

- the satisfaction of the individuals' aspirations.

Effective management development and career planning can resolve the potential conflict between individual and organisation requirements. A sensitive appraisal system that focuses on the future rather than the past will help. On the few occasions where an individual's requirements do not match the organisation's plans, the choices for each party should be clear. Employees can either accept modified career plans or business opportunities or seek alternative activities.

PLANNING TRAINING AND DEVELOPMENT

A training plan describes the training and learning activities that will take place to achieve the learning objective. The **learning objective** is described in terms of what the learner needs to be able to do at the end of the learning activity; for example, one of the learning objectives for this session is that you should be able 'to recognise potential solutions to identified training needs'.

Once the learning objectives have been established, the training department must work out by what methods the learners can best carry out and complete the learning processes. In any organisation, the formulation of training plans and the training design normally involves both line managers and the training function.

The tasks of the training function are:

- to prepare and recommend training plans for individuals and groups

- to agree targets for performance standards

- to advise on expenditure

- to set up reference data for future assessment

- to recommend the distribution of training tasks between training department and line management

- to allocate tasks within the training department.

SAT:
allow 5 mins

Managing tasks and solving problems✔

ACTIVITY 3

Look at the list of tasks of the training department in the formulation of training plans. Try now to identify at least three additional tasks relating to training that ought to be the responsibility of line management.

Commentary...

The tasks of line managers in formulating training plans are:

- to provide data necessary to devise training plans, programmes and budgets

- to assess proposed training programmes

- to give approval to training plans and budgets

- to approve assessment methods

- to allocate personnel, finance, space, materials and equipment

- to approve responsibilities given to line managers
- to brief the people to be trained.

TIME CONSTRAINTS

If the analysis of training needs has taken place as part of the business planning process, it is likely that clear indicators of time constraints will be seen on two dimensions:

- the amount of time available for training activities off-the-job
- the most appropriate time to schedule training activities.

The time available for training varies from job to job. If there are many people doing the same tasks, they can cover for each other during the training activities. If they are specialists and cannot easily be replaced, it is more difficult to schedule their training.

It is also easier to schedule discrete learning events, e.g. workshops or seminars. The problem is to ensure that the training objectives are met within the agreed time-scale. More difficult is the planning of open-ended learning which continues until the objectives have been achieved.

Reviewing training activities

For managers, there is a need to install and monitor a range of systems for reviewing the activities of training and development in the organisation. For example, there are the so-called soft systems:

- **Regular meetings**, both formal and informal, may be held with individuals, small project groups, or the whole department of the organisation.

- **De-briefing** trainers immediately following a training activity is another excellent way of controlling effectiveness and improving performance, especially if the de-brief is conducted with the aid of other feedback such as end-of-course validation forms (often called 'happiness sheets').

- **Appraisal interviews** can be used to examine effectiveness and to identify ways of improving performance.

- **Benchmarking** (or checking on the standards, methods, and performances of competitors and other training providers) can also be a useful monitoring activity. This usually means sending someone to training and development conferences, seminars, and exhibitions to monitor trends and best practice. It can also be achieved through reading journals and text books, and through talking to company representatives and trainers.

VALIDATION AND EVALUATION

Let us consider the different terms we use in assessing training and development:

> **!?!** **Assessment of training effectiveness** describes the process of ascertaining whether training is efficient or effective in achieving prescribed objectives. It covers both validation and evaluation.
>
> **!?!** **Internal validation** is a series of tests and assessments designed to ascertain whether a training programme has achieved the behavioural objectives specified.

Internal validation measures

All training and development activities may be categorised in terms of knowledge, skill and attitude.

- A number of tests can be used to assess learners' **knowledge**: subjective tests, oral tests, objective tests or a combination of all of these.

- It is important to have assessors trained in the relevant **skill** areas so that they can standardise subjective judgements. For physical skills, a range of trainers' subjective assessments can be used along with rating scales and check-lists. For social or inter-personal skills, trainers' observation, categorised behaviour analysis or specific skill scoring can be used with different levels of reliability. For mental skills, it is difficult to isolate the particular competence you want to measure, but there are psychometric tests which can help.

- Trainers' subjective responses, together with the use of **attitude** scales do not avoid the enormous difficult of obtaining validity in this area. There is dispute about whether 4, 5 or 6 point scales are the most reliable, given the normal human tendency to rate almost everything somewhere in the middle.

> **\?/ External validation** comprises a series of tests and assessment designed to ascertain whether the behavioural objectives of an internally valid training activity were realistically based on an accurate initial identification of training needs in relation to the criteria of effectiveness adopted by the organisation.

External validation measures

When you come to measure the effects of training on the performance of a recently trained individual, you will be looking at the individual's increased range and scope of activities as well as the increased quality of performance. The ways of seeking this information include:

- comparison of actual performance against specified required standards

- on-the-job follow up, including self and supervisors opinions

- completion of questionnaires or rating forms

- assignments or projects

- discussion and review of the programme

- completion of action plans, which serve as a useful link between the training and the performance at work.

Evaluation

Evaluation refers to the assessment of the total value of the training activity in social as well as financial terms. This is important since financial information is often either too general, or too over-detailed to be of any real use. Evaluation differs from validation in that it attempts to measure the overall cost benefit of the training and not just the achievement of the specific training objectives. The term is also used in the general judgemental sense of continuous monitoring of an activity or of the training function as a whole.

Whether you are attempting to validate or to evaluate an item of training and development, there is a broad framework of assessment within which some pertinent questions may be asked:

- reactions of participants to the training activity

- identification of learning achieved

- changes in job behaviour

- wider effects on the organisation

- ultimate value of the activity.

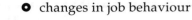

RECALL:
allow 10 mins

Describe the differences between:

- **internal validation**

- **external validation**

- **evaluation.**

SUBJECTIVE JUDGEMENTS

Some questions are about opinions where the answers can only be subjective. The questions are of a type, like: 'Did you enjoy the course?' or 'Was the training well presented?' If you want a little more detail from a subjective response, you could ask people to rate how they felt about the course on a scale of say 1 to 5 and then compare the accumulated results with those of other groups of trainees taking the same course. The results are still subjective but perhaps more informative than a simple response to the original blunt question. Of course, the more detailed and specific you can be in asking questions about attainment or performance against specific criteria, the more objective you will be able to be.

You could use a scale, called a Likert scale. Here is an example.

> Circle one number on the scale below:
>
> **How well did the course meet your expectations?**
>
> <u>Not at all</u>
> 1
> 2
> 3
> 4
> 5
> <u>Completely</u>

NORM-REFERENCED AND CRITERION-REFERENCED MEASUREMENTS

Many examination bodies are now switching from norm-referenced testing where all candidates' results are ranked – and a certain percentage deemed to have 'passed' – to criterion-referenced testing where the demonstration of a specific skill or competence is deemed to be the qualification for a 'pass' grade.

Traditionally schools, colleges and universities in the UK have used norm-referenced testing. They claim that their examiners' experience over many years enables them to standardise year-on-year to offset variations in the ability of the annual intake of students.

In UK industry, trainers have developed criterion-referencing testing to show that trainees can successfully carry out specific tasks after some training. In criterion-referenced testing, the learner, the manager, and the trainer are interested only in the fact that the individual can carry out a set task to the required standard. In other words, they are required to demonstrate their competence. In this sense, these tests should have a pass mark of 100 per cent: it is an all-or-nothing situation. Trainees either can demonstrate their competence or they cannot.

FORMATIVE AND SUMMATIVE ASSESSMENT

To obtain the most valuable results, you need to assess before, during and after every training activity.

- If you make an assessment before training takes place then you can make adjustments to the programme in the light of any lack of competence revealed by the assessment.

- If you carry out assessment during the training activity (**formative assessment**) you will be able to adapt the training so that it remains relevant to the learners.

- When you undertake assessment at the end of training (**summative assessment**) you are obtaining information about the learner's ability to perform at the end of the programme and something about the effect of the training programme itself.

When you use any measuring instrument, there are three basic criteria which you should attempt to satisfy: the instrument should be accurate, convenient and acceptable. This might seem obvious, but it is often ignored when constructing an assessment measure.

Subjective assessment – based upon personal opinion or judgement – is strengthened if two or more assessors take part. Objective assessment is more accurate and more effective, but more expensive to carry out. In today's world of competency-based training and development, the existence of NVQs has made assessment more objective through the accompanying definitions of units and elements of competence, performance criteria, and range statements.

You need to balance all these factors against administrative convenience. You are aiming to achieve the fairest system of assessment with the highest levels of accuracy, reliability, consistency and validity, that can be achieved with the resources allocated to do the job.

Validation techniques – though extremely useful in evaluating training – can be difficult to apply in some circumstances, especially where there is low morale or a poor business situation. In these circumstances, people may be suspicious of questionnaires, rating forms, and other documents, seeing them as a threat to their jobs. This may result in inaccurate answers and over-optimistic assessments.

COST EFFECTIVENESS

You can also take a cost-benefit view. Has the training added more value to the work of the organisation than it cost to run? If so, the training is now contributing to the profitability of the company.

You should check the full costs of training. In training terms, when someone attends an external course, the cost includes the course itself plus perhaps travelling and hotel expenses for the trainee. For an internal course run within an organisation, the real costs are indirect and include the salaries of the trainers, the cost of materials and equipment used on the course, and the administrative costs involved in setting up.

SUPERGEAR ENGINEERING

In Session three we met Supergear Engineering. With 100 employees, the company manufactures engineering parts to order. It has been extremely successful because of its high levels of technical expertise and flexibility, and expansion plans are gathering pace.

Judith Frampton, founder and owner of the company, is a qualified engineer with the technical knowledge to deal very effectively with customers, many of whom have an excellent relationship with her. In fact she maintains regular contact, in a sales role, with all her major customers even though she already has far too many responsibilities and has an enthusiastic and dedicated sales team. This causes problems because orders are often processed incorrectly when Judith agrees changes verbally with her customers but forgets to discuss the changes with the sales executive servicing the account. The production team acts on the original orders from the sales executive but then discovers that customers are disgruntled because they haven't received exactly what they wanted.

As well as complaints from customers about orders not being fulfilled correctly, some suppliers have been grumbling about late payment of invoices. At present there is only one PC in the sales department and most of the essential information concerning orders and payments is distributed in memos and reports. To cope with the expected expansion, Supergear intends to install a computer network that links the sales team with the production department and the accounts department.

ACTIVITY 4

This activity is designed to test your understanding of how training can be used effectively in business. You should consider how you might identify training needs, plan a training programme and monitor its effectiveness. First, read the case study above about Supergear Engineering.

Consider the issues that the company needs to address in order that the introduction of its new computer accounts system is successful.

Produce a brief report highlighting the issues that have a training solution. Separately list problems which may need to be tackled in other ways.

Develop a training plan for the sales, production and accounts staff that will be using the new system. Bear in mind that some staff will have little computer experience. Your plan should include the following features:

ASSIGNMENT:
allow 1 hour

Managing and developing self	✔
Communicating	✔
Managing tasks and solving problems	✔

(a) a review of the training needs of the staff;

(b) an outline of a one-day induction programme on the new system;

(c) proposals on how the company can test whether the training has been effective.

Use a separate sheet of paper to record your answer. Summarise your findings in the box below.

Individual performance reviews

The process of evaluating the effectiveness of human resources involves every individual employed in the organisation whether they be apprentices, shopfloor workers, supervisors, and managers. In evaluating the effectiveness of employees, managers can choose from a number of methods, ranging from informal discussions with the people themselves through to formal appraisal. In all these activities, the manager is trying to assess the employees' knowledge, skills, and attitude.

Managing tasks and solving problems ✓

ACTIVITY 5

List three aspects each of an employee's skills, knowledge, or attitude that the manager may wish to evaluate. For example, under skills, you may identify technical skill, or interpersonal skill.

Commentary...

You may have included some of the following:

Knowledge

- Systems
- Technology
- Techniques
- Environment
- Markets
- Legislation

Skills

- Technical
- Interpersonal
- Managerial

- Communication

- Innovation

Attitude

- Involvement

- Commitment

- Confidence/self-esteem

- Positivity

- Enthusiasm

There are a range of techniques available for assessing and monitoring individual performance:

- **appraisal systems**

- **personality and psychometric tests**

- **assessment centres.**

We shall now explore some of these techniques in a little more detail, beginning with the most well-used technique – appraisals.

APPRAISAL SYSTEMS

Performance appraisal is not a precise tool of management, but is widely used. If managers decide to implement an appraisal scheme they should spend time making sure they get it right. When an organisation tries to implement a poorly devised scheme – and the employees find it unacceptable – the backlash makes the subsequent implementation of a good scheme extremely difficult.

What are the objectives of appraisals? A manager needs to consult widely among employees to ensure agreement as to the purpose of an appraisal scheme, which could include: assessment, feedback, performance improvement and pay.

- For **assessment purposes**, job targets might be agreed for all personnel. One feature of the system could be to record the achievement or otherwise against these targets.

- **Feedback** of the views of managers will be important to people and the manner in which this is done should be spelled out in the system. People need to know how they are doing.

- If the system is designed to improve **performance**, it should clarify what rewards and penalties are available and how they will be brought into operation.

- If the scheme is to be linked to the **pay** or bonus structure, the relationship between additional pay awards and performance levels has to be spelled out.

In introducing a new scheme, starting at the top of the organisation is a good publicity tactic and allows for some minor amendments before going 'live' with the whole organisation.

When managers have decided whether they are measuring outcomes, behaviour or competencies they can decide on the measuring tools to use as part of the whole system, together with the performance criteria they will establish. Managers need to investigate a number of options including: self-completion diaries, observation, interviews and questionnaires.

Self-completion diaries

Although time-consuming for the busy person, these diaries provide insight as to the way their days are being spent. They might alternatively be of the critical-incident type to focus on the handling of important issues which arise daily.

Observation

Shadowing a person through a few days will reveal what is really happening, and whether there is a discrepancy between actual activity and reported activity.

Interviews

The most common element in any appraisal scheme is the interview, usually annual, at which the employee's work is analysed, the outcomes agreed and future objectives discussed. This aspect of appraisal schemes is consistently flawed and does not receive enough attention by organisations. Common problems include a failure to take account of performance over the full year, managers relying too much on subjective judgements and a procedure linked too closely to a pay settlement rather than performance review.

Questionnaires

A range of open and closed questions might reveal the appraisee's view of the work period and his or her performance. It might also be necessary to obtain the views of senior managers for an agreed assessment to be achieved.

Other factors can come into play. The management style of the organisation bears strongly upon the style of the scheme. Obviously a very bureaucratic organisation is not comfortable with a loose appraisal arrangement and, conversely, if managers work in a small, dynamic matrix, they need to make the appraisal scheme just as flexible as the organisation's other procedures.

Documentation will vary to match the requirements of the different jobs but in no case should the basic appraisal form exceed four pages. This is enough space to comment on current achievements, style and competence and to set targets for the following appraisal period.

SAT:
allow 10 mins

| Managing and developing self | ✔ |
| Communicating | ✔ |

ACTIVITY 6

Consider how you would feel about being appraised. What would some of your fears and anxieties be? Suggest some guiding principles for the effective operation of such schemes, that would reduce or eliminate these concerns.

Commentary...

To overcome the fear that an appraisal scheme may be used to discipline, or to terminate employment, the aims and objectives need to be clear and the implementation has to be seen to be correct and fair. If people are to be judged, the following issues should be considered:

- Overt agreement and commitment of people concerned in the appraisal needs to be established.

- There needs to be a clear definition of knowledge and skills required to do their existing jobs.

- There needs to be an identification of strengths to be built on for future roles and developments.

- There needs to be an identification of skills and abilities needed to balance the whole team.

- There needs to be an identification of inadequacies in performance that cannot be overlooked in the present or future jobs.

PERSONALITY AND PSYCHOMETRIC TESTS

A somewhat controversial means of assessing an individual is through the use of 'personality' and psychometric tests. Their development and application has now become an industry in its own right. A wide range of organisations are now using these types of tests, ranging from single hand-completed check-lists to complex computer-aided audits. Some of these tests have a firm basis in psychological theories and have been well researched and validated; others are extremely subjective.

Many of these tests begin their lives in the recruitment and selection process where they are ideally used as a conversation piece for candidate interviews. Unfortunately, many tests acquired a poor reputation following their use by ill-trained practitioners who used them instead of, rather than in addition to, good interview skills.

Many original tests are now extensively used for career counselling purposes and for problem solving in issues such as team development and conflict resolution. They are also used as a means of identifying training and development needs either as a discrete activity or in the context of a training and development workshop.

ASSESSMENT CENTRES

Assessment centres developed initially in the late 1970s as a means of improving the effectiveness of management recruitment and selection. A 'centre' is not necessarily an actual place, but the term is usually used to mean a bank of tests and assessment techniques that are combined over a short period of time (maybe two or three days) to cover a wide range of topics from analytical ability, interpersonal skills, practical dexterity, stress levels and so on. An individual is asked to take part in the tests and is assessed by 'experts' who usually offer the candidate feedback as well as presenting an overall evaluation to the client company.

The purpose of an assessment centre is to provide a series of tasks and activities which simulate the real work of a manager. Much evidence has been collected and collated in an attempt to prove the efficiency of such a system. However, there remains a strong doubt about the integrity of the process since it suffers from the same inherent criticism as written examinations – people confronted with real problems very often operate differently and less consistently.

INFORMAL METHODS

We have examined a number of formal methods of evaluating effectiveness of employees. There are, as we indicated earlier, a number of informal methods which are often used in smaller 'pioneering' organisations:

- observation of an person while on-the-job – useful for practical skills assessment particularly in manual jobs

- examination of a person's performance record – used to measure performance of salespeople and others who have individual output measures

- reaction to serious errors or performance weaknesses by an employee

- informal discussion with the person and/or other staff – usually carried out with people in supervisory or management roles.

ACTIVITY 7

SAT:
allow 20-40 mins

Communicating ✔

Managing tasks and solving problems ✔

If you have some personal experience, either as a manager or an employee, list the different methods of evaluating individual effectiveness which you have seen, or used, in the organisations you have worked in.

If you are a student, you could ask to interview two or three staff from the learning institution in which you are studying (including a manager), and ask them about the techniques used as a means of assessing them.

How successful do you consider these various approaches to have been?

Commentary...

Most small organisations use informal methods where, at its simplest, the boss assumes he knows the problem and sends the person for training (or sacks them). This approach is thought to be ineffective because it does not gain the commitment of the trainee to the training. Even a brief conversation between the manager and the individual would clarify the problem and identify the potential remedy. Larger organisations might have begun more formal methods only to find they conflict with local culture.

Discipline and grievance

So far in this module, we have examined the phenomenon of conflict from a perspective of positive management. However, it is necessary to acknowledge that, with all the best intentions, there may still be negative situations which emerge within companies. We referred to some of the means of dealing with conflict previously and we should now return to some of those in order to take a look at discipline and grievance.

In Session 5, we examined five possible approaches to dealing with conflict:

- structural approach

- perception approach

- moralising or missionary approach

- law and order approach

- attitude training approach.

Of these approaches, the one which relates most closely to the features of discipline and grievance is 'law and order'. This approach is 'aimed at behaviour where physical controls are brought in, or status and power is used to force people into controlled behaviour'.

DISCIPLINE

A disciplinary situation normally arises as a result of perceived misconduct on the part of an employee. We use the word 'perceived' because, until the apparent misdemeanour is thoroughly investigated, there is no certainty that there has in fact been misconduct. It would probably be taking it too far to suggest that, in industry and commerce, a person is innocent until proven guilty but, nevertheless, there are some safeguards that have to be undertaken which can reduce the possibility of a wrongful accusation or an inappropriate punishment.

There are several different types of misconduct:

- unreliability – lateness, absenteeism, or consistent failure to meet agreed commitments

- insubordination – insulting behaviour or the refusal to follow reasonable instructions

- offences connected to health and safety – not following safety procedures, causing accidents, or failure to avoid preventable health and safety hazards

- criminal offences – stealing, fraud, malicious damage or violent conduct

- malicious interference with plant and equipment – sabotage, or failure to follow procedures resulting in damaged equipment

- violence, harassment or unruly behaviour towards another employee

- incompetence – consistent failure to achieve required standards of performance.

If these situations do occur, then managers have a number of alternatives open to them dependent upon the degree of seriousness of the alleged offence. In the very first instance, the action to be taken should be a thorough investigation of all the circumstances surrounding the item of misconduct. This investigation should always include the employee and his or her trade union or personal representatives and should attempt to analyse and identify the actual cause of the behaviour. In many cases, after an investigation, the real cause of problems has been found to be very different to the original suspicion and has often led to misconduct being dealt with in a more helpful way than a disciplinary process.

SAT:
allow 10 mins

Managing tasks and solving problems ✔

ACTIVITY 8

Look through the list of types of misconduct given above and identify a number of reasons why some of this behaviour may have taken place without malicious intent being involved on the part of the employee.

For example, an employee may be consistently late because he or she has a sick spouse to look after, or an employee may be incompetent because he or she has not received adequate job training.

Now identify at least three more reasons why poor performance may occur and list appropriate actions that a manager may take in dealing with these causes.

Commentary...

You may have identified some of the following alternative causes or reasons for the misconduct or poor performance:

- misunderstandings
- personality clashes
- differences in perception of goals
- sub-standard training or preparation
- confusion over methods to be used
- lack of clarity about areas of responsibility
- lack of clarity about areas of authority
- frustration through any of the above
- competition for limited resources.

In the event of one or more of these causes being established, there are an number of actions that managers may need to take.

Retraining or coaching: where incompetence has been discovered as being the result of lack of skills and knowledge, training including one-to-one coaching could resolve the difficulty.

Counselling: where it is apparent that an individual has a specific difficulty with a situation as a result of a lack of understanding, a personal emotional problem or failure to think through the options, counselling may provide the answer.

Giving information: where there is a simple lack of clarity over procedures, responsibilities or authority, the presentation of good, clear information can often resolve a problem.

Giving advice: where a person has taken inappropriate action or decisions, the manager may simply need to offer some clear advice on what should be done.

Changing systems and procedures: where the cause of the difficulty has been shown to be a problem with systems or procedures and not related to the employees themselves, the manager may need to change, or recommend a change, in the situation in order to prevent further difficulties.

In some circumstances, the manager may have learnt enough from an investigation to come to the conclusion that alterations in recruitment and selection procedures need to be made in order to prevent staff being employed in the future who may run the risk of committing further 'offences'.

Having exhausted all the possibilities of dealing with the misdemeanour in a positive and constructive way, the manager may in fact reach the stage where disciplinary procedures have to be invoked. If this happens, there are some key guidelines to adopt:

- ensure that all staff have a copy of the organisation's disciplinary rules and procedures

- in the case of the procedure needing to be followed, first give a verbal warning which should be noted and recorded

- if the offence is repeated, give a first written warning, which should be noted and recorded

- if the offence is repeated once again, a second written warning (again noted and recorded) should be given in which dismissal is stated as being the next stage

- if the offence is repeated yet again, formal notice of dismissal is given.

At any stage during the disciplinary process, alternative actions may be adopted if the circumstances change or if new evidence relating to the case emerges. The manager, for example, may decide to suspend the individual for a period pending further investigation, or to transfer the individual to another department or job, either temporarily or permanently. This could involve demotion as a form of punishment, or as a means of placing someone in a position in which they are more capable of performing to an acceptable standard.

It is well worth noting that the above procedure applied to misconduct but there are cases of **gross misconduct** when the employee is likely to be instantly dismissed. It is important, in view of the above, for the company to specify what offences it regards as misconduct and what offences it regards as gross misconduct and to make sure its employees know what they are.

Misconduct could cover:

- lateness

- insubordination

- absenteeism.

Gross misconduct could cover:

- malicious damage

- falsification of expenses claims

- sexual harassment

- serious breaches of safe working practice.

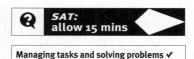

? SAT:
allow 15 mins

Managing tasks and solving problems ✔

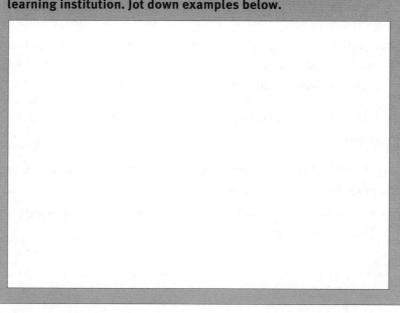

ACTIVITY 9

Now obtain a copy of your company's document which identifies forms of misconduct and see how it compares with the above list. If you are a student, ask to see the document which is used in your learning institution. Jot down examples below.

Unfair dismissal

Whatever the action decided by the manager, it is essential to carry out procedures properly. The result of not doing this can be a claim for 'unfair dismissal' by the person who has been disciplined.

Unfair dismissal usually occurs where disciplinary procedures have not been adequately followed, for example by not giving sufficient numbers of verbal or written warnings. Sometimes, the person claiming unfair dismissal will state that they were unaware that they were actually committing an offence, and this can place the onus on the employer to demonstrate clearly that published company rules and procedures were satisfactory and available.

Constructive dismissal

There is also a legal term called 'constructive dismissal' which can be invoked by employees if they leave a company of their own volition and subsequently claim that they were forced to resign on the basis of unfair pressure being exerted on them, through for example deliberate changes in job content or in their terms and conditions of employment.

To reduce the possibility of claims for unfair or constructive dismissals, there are some essential features of the disciplinary procedure which should always be adopted.

At each stage the individual:

- may be accompanied by a representative

- must be told of their right of appeal and to whom

- must be told of the complaint against him or her

- must be allowed to state his or her case

- must be told of the consequences of further offences

- must be given, in writing, details of the disciplinary action to be taken.

Records of the disciplinary action taken and the reasons for it must be kept by the organisation.

GRIEVANCES

> **!?!** A **grievance** is usually described as a situation where an employee believes that the employer has breached the agreed terms and conditions of employment and requests a formal investigation through a company's grievance procedure.

In the case of grievances, there are some less formal approaches to resolving problems that may be useful as a means of avoiding full grievance procedures. Let us consider the original list of approaches that may be used. The perception approach involves attempts to clarify misunderstandings and people are allowed to let off steam in controlled circumstances. The moralising approach is aimed at attitudes where an appeal is made to people's values and sense of fair play. It is only successful if the appeal is made to basic values which have not been abandoned.

However, if there becomes a need to invoke the grievance procedure, there are, once again, some basic procedures to adopt:

- Ensure that all staff have a copy of the organisation's grievance procedure.

- In the case of the procedure needing to be followed, first offer an informal hearing of the complaint in which the person with the complaint should be able to deal with his or her immediate manager. This hearing should be noted and recorded.

- If the complaint is not resolved to the complainant's satisfaction, offer a formal hearing with the immediate manager, which should also be noted and recorded.

- If the complaint is still not resolved to the complainant's satisfaction, offer a formal hearing with the next level of appeal in the organisation. This person will normally be the immediate manager's manager, and again this hearing, of course, should be noted and recorded.

- If the complaint is still not resolved to the complainant's satisfaction, there may be yet another level of appeal, (depending on the particular organisation's procedure) or there may be a 'failure to agree'.

- In the case of a 'failure to agree', all the available resources to action should be reviewed and a mutually agreeable option chosen.

As in the case of disciplinary situations, the failure to follow correct procedures in grievance can unfortunately lead to claims of unfair dismissal. To reduce the possibilities of this happening, the essential features of the grievance procedure should always be followed.

At each stage:

- the individual may be accompanied by a representative

- must be told of the next level of appeal, how to appeal and to whom

- must be allowed to state his or her complaint

- must be provided with detailed contrary evidence, if available

- if the complaint is resolved must be given, in writing, details of the agreed action to be taken

- records of the grievance discussions and reasons for it must be kept by the organisation.

Support strategies

It is possible to distinguish between six types of supporting and helping strategies which a manager may be able to offer to staff within the organisation:

- **counselling** – helping someone to explore a problem and alternative ways of dealing with it so that they can decide what to do about it, i.e. helping people to help themselves

- **coaching** – helping someone to acquire knowledge or skill; passing on facts and skills which improve someone's situation

- **giving advice** – offering someone your opinion of their best course of action based on your view of their situation

- **giving information** – lacking information can make someone powerless; giving a person the information he or she needs in a particular situation (e.g. about legal rights, or the whereabouts of particular agencies) can be enormously helpful

- **direct action** – doing something on behalf of someone else or acting to provide for another's immediate needs, e.g. typing a letter for someone, or asking for assistance from a student's boss

- **systems change** – working to influence and improve systems which are causing difficulty for people, i.e. working on organisational development rather than with the individual.

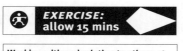

EXERCISE:
allow 15 mins

Working with and relating to others ✔

Managing tasks and solving problems ✔

ACTIVITY 10

Form into groups of four. Discuss in what circumstances you would use each type of supporting behaviour described above. Consider when each option might be appropriate. Summarise your conclusions in the box below.

Commentary...

Each one of these strategies make up a supportive manager's 'tool bag'. Although we have placed counselling and coaching at the top of the list, there is no ranking involved. Each one may be helpful in any particular support situation. What a manager needs to do is choose which approach or strategy best fits the situation that occurs.

Counselling is usually appropriate for dealing with work problems in which the employee actually has the answer, but cannot 'see the wood for the trees'. It is also useful for dealing with more personal problems that may be affecting work, although care has to be taken not to delve too deeply into potentially emotional issues without being properly prepared. In these circumstances, a referral to a professionally trained counsellor may be more advisable.

Coaching is more often reserved for instances where employees lack specific skills or knowledges, or where specific improvement in particular skills are required.

It should be noted that aspects of the other four strategies are never as clear cut and simple as to warrant one pure adulterated strategy. Even a committed and experienced counsellor comes across, from time to time, a situation where a simple piece of straight information is required.

Giving information within a counselling session is perfectly acceptable since the acquisition of the information may, in itself, enable the person to help himself/herself.

Giving advice is slightly different since it assumes the helper knows best. Obviously if a situation is encountered where the other person is apparently incapable of recognising the correct course of action, then providing advice may be appropriate and, as such, this may occur more frequently in coaching sessions.

Direct action is often the final resort for a manager if the other person appears incompetent or incapable of carrying out a task alone. It might also be appropriate where the outstanding task is such an easy one to accomplish that its completion by the helper would not detract from the person's learning. Direct action may be something which needs to take place where the other person does not have the status, stature or resources to do it him/herself.

Finally, **systems change** is quite a complex strategy since it is normally only appropriate where the manager is able to take an overview of an organisational situation in which there are obstacles being presented to progress. In these situations, it may be that the manager is in a privileged position to take action to remove the obstacles so as to enable people to make progress. This may involve discussion with the person's boss (if it is not the manager him/herself) or colleagues.

So each of the six helping strategies are useful 'tools' for the manager and some of them may be used simultaneously to deal with a particular situation.

COUNSELLING AS THE MAIN STRATEGY

Having stated that there is no ranking in the six available helping strategies, we can make one exception to this rule: counselling is the most effective strategy to use in the widest range of situations if it is used properly.

ACTIVITY 11

What do you think might be some of the advantages of counselling over the other available strategies in a work situation?

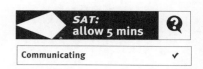

SAT:
allow 5 mins

Communicating ✓

Commentary...

To explore the reasons why counselling, if carried out properly, is always one of the most powerful tools available to the manager, we should return again to our simple definitions of the techniques: 'Helping people to help themselves'. If someone has been taken through the process of building a relationship of equality, trust and respect with the manager, exploring feelings, options and alternative courses of action, and then developing and agreeing a solution or plan, then it normally follows that the person will have greater commitment to the solution or plan than if it had been arrived at through advice or straight direction. In other words, the full involvement of the individual in the realisation of a solution does engender total commitment, motivation and enthusiasm for the outcome. The solution is not someone else's, but rather has emanated from, and is the property of, the individual.

There are other advantages to counselling such as:

- the development of a sense of self-esteem and the building of a closer – and more trusting – relationship between the person and the manager

- the probability is that not only have all other possible alternative solutions been explored and discarded, but also any partially useful alternatives have been identified as contingencies

- counselling is an **empowering process** and as such, it is the one tool that enables the integrity of both the staff member or trainee and the manager to remain intact.

summary

▶ In assessing training needs, you need to take into account both the needs of the organisation as well as the aspirations of the individual. In reviewing unsatisfactory performance, look for the reasons for poor work rather than assume that training offers the only remedy.

▶ Training solutions include custom-built courses, external courses, open learning, education programmes, secondment, coaching, on-the-job instruction and computer-based training. The preferred solution depends upon the resources and facilities of the organisation, the type of training need being identified, and the time available in which to undertake training.

▶ In evaluating training, senior management must consider internal measures (whether the training achieved the specified learning objectives), external measures (whether the training resulted in improved performance at work), and its general cost effectiveness (whether it added value to the company or organisation).

▶ Several techniques are available for assessing and monitoring the performance of individuals. Common examples are appraisal interviews, personality and psychometric tests, and assessment centres.

▶ Misconduct by employees may arise from a number of factors. Managers may take a number of actions to resolve problems, these include retraining, coaching, counselling, giving advice or information, changing systems and procedures.

▶ A further option – and one that would be used for all instances of gross misconduct – is to institute disciplinary procedures. It is important that organisations follow established disciplinary procedures if they are to avoid claims for unfair dismissal.

▶ Managers can adopt a range of support strategies designed to help their staff improve their performance. Counselling is – above all others – the most effective strategy to use in the widest range of situations, if it is used properly.

Managing Activities

Work planning and organisation

STRATEGIES AND PLANS

PLANNING TOOLS

EFFECTIVENESS AND
EFFICIENCY MEASURES

ORGANISATIONAL ANALYSIS
TECHNIQUES

METHOD STUDY

Objectives

After participating in this session, you should be able to:

▶ explain a number of organisational strategies and approaches to planning

▶ describe three planning techniques

▶ define sources of information for measuring effectiveness and efficiency

▶ describe and use key organisational analysis techniques

▶ identify the basic principles and methods of method study.

In working through this session, you will practise the following BTEC common skills:

Managing and developing self	✔
Working with and relating to others	✔
Communicating	✔
Managing tasks and solving problems	✔
Applying numeracy	✔
Applying technology	
Applying design and creativity	

Strategies and plans

Many businesses operate a **traditional strategy** in their approach to planning, mainly because their activities are relatively predictable and regular. With an agreed strategy, a detailed plan can be produced with short-, medium- and long-term goals, with details of what has to happen, who is involved, when it should happen, how it should happen, where it should happen, and why.

In traditional organisations, this may be the end of the business planning process, and the point where the people in the business just get on with their jobs. However, for many businesses, the 'complete' traditional strategy may not be appropriate. Some smaller businesses may not have the systems, management and information database necessary to carry out the key tasks within the planning process. These types of organisations often use so-called **emergent strategies** which enable them to:

- react to changing circumstances

- develop a direction without extensive prior planning.

In the hard, practical world of business, strategies for success are mostly a combination of the traditional and the emergent.

Two other forms of strategy are strategic disturbance and the military model.

Strategic disturbance

This strategy regards the traditional approach of establishing mission statements as irrelevant. Instead, comprehensive and integral control systems are seen as more important. They allow organisations to adapt to disturbances in the market place. In this approach, organisations are regarded as systems – an interdependent set of parts – and controls are needed to keep the system in balance.

The military model

Some corporate strategy models have been derived directly from military models in which, to survive, you have to learn to fight by the rules of the game. In smaller businesses, the strategy may be likened to a guerrilla fighter; plans for survival and growth have to be adapted on a day-to-day basis.

In a dynamic framework with ongoing business planning and emergent strategies, the implementation of the plans – both through people and through physical things – is an integral part of the planning process. It requires constant feedback on performance and progress. This leads to the important stage of monitoring and review where, at regular intervals, overall progress towards the planned objectives is considered. Alterations to the plan may be initiated. The original objectives, and even the mission statement, may be altered. The business planning process in these circumstances is a fully cyclical activity.

When examining the nature of planning, the work of Bill and Roy Richardson (*Business Planning,* 2nd edn, 1992, Pitman Publishing) is worthy of note. He puts forward a comprehensive approach to planning with his 'All the Aces' approach. This idea is based on the acronym, ACES-ACES, which are the first letters of his planning system.

All the Aces

- Aspirations planning

- Contingency planning

- External future planning

- Second-nature responsiveness planning

- Administration planning

- Creative innovation planning

- Efficiency/productivity planning

- Shock event planning

To highlight this approach, let us look at each element closely.

Aspirations planning

Many people are involved with an organisation, either as employees or, less directly, as customers, suppliers or shareholders. Each individual has different goals and desired outcomes. The organisation has to decide how it matches the aspirations of these 'stakeholders' with its own objectives.

Contingency planning

This type of planning recognises that the future may not always be as envisaged at the initial planning stage. Contingency planning seeks to minimise costs and the impact of unplanned events.

Extended future planning

This is necessary where you may have projects with long-term future payback, such as the building of a new property or the acquisition of or merger with another business. In Richardson's view, 'extended future planning' covers corporate planning, which is a commonly used phrase to describe the process of planning the growth and development targets of businesses.

Second-nature responsiveness planning

Here you adopt a responsive strategy that says: 'We are happy to make necessary adjustments to satisfy customers.'

Administration planning

This involves the total co-ordination and control of plans and planning to enhance the total organisational effort. Administration planning is concerned with ensuring that events occur in the agreed sequence.

Creative innovation planning

Richardson states: 'This type of planning is responsible for the success demonstrated by the firm in creating and implementing new and improved ways of operating and in producing and distributing new and better products and services.'

Efficiency/productivity planning

Here the aim is to make the best of available resources, so that costs are pruned to a minimum.

Shock-event planning

There needs to be a responsive structure and strategy to ensure that unforeseen events are contained.

Managing tasks and solving problems ✓

ACTIVITY 1

Imagine you are a manager in a medium-sized confectionery business. From this perspective, invent one example of an issue, or situation, which may have to be considered under each one of the eight aces. For example, under aspirations planning, the company may have to consider the implications of a manufacturing director who wants to diversify the product range.

Commentary...

Of the many situations that could be considered, here are a few that you may have identified.

Aspirations planning: career hopes of young graduates; demands from major customers for a total quality philosophy to be adopted.

Contingency planning: planning an alternative supply of milk against the possibility of the company's present suppliers going out of business or increasing prices exorbitantly.

Extended future planning: the organisational implications of the company establishing a new head office in the Midlands.

Second-nature responsiveness planning: being prepared to design and develop new packaging for a major customer; developing new accounts systems demanded by customers.

Administration planning: briefing of all managers on the contents of the business plan and the ramifications of new procedures.

Creative innovation planning: running training events to assist in the development of quality improvement teams; training managers in effective meeting skills.

Efficiency/productivity planning: carrying out development activities to improve efficiency rather than using expensive external consultants.

Shock-event planning: making plans for how the company should respond if one of its products becomes the subject of a food poisoning scare.

Planning tools

We now look at three more basic tools for planning:

- Gantt charts

- critical path analysis (CPA)

- programme evaluation and review techniques (PERT).

All these tools can be used in forward or reverse mode, i.e. they can be used to schedule forward from a given date to find the overall completion time or back from a given end time to determine the necessary start time. They are appropriate, and useful, techniques for production planning. In the areas of jobbing or batch production, the tools can be limited in the degree of complexity that can be handled. Computer packages can handle more complex tasks, but these tools need not be computer-based. In any case, computer-based tools can reduce the 'visibility' of what is happening operationally – an important element to ensure that the manager still feels in control.

It should be noted that the aim of this module is to provide an appreciation of the strengths and weaknesses of these techniques rather than a complete background.

GANTT CHARTS

At the start of the century an objective planning method for projects was developed by Henry Gantt. In its basic form (figure 1.1), the horizontal divisions represent time and the vertical rows items to be scheduled. Lines, bars, brackets, shading and other devices can mark the start, duration and end of a schedule. The purpose of a Gantt chart is to clarify – and thus improve understanding – and serve as a focus for discussion.

In manufacturing, charts are used in the following situations:

- The number of work-centres is low. Its use is precluded where the numbers are large due to queuing effects and the need to keep the chart dynamic. This, in itself, becomes too big a task to make it worthwhile.

- Job duration is measured in days and weeks rather than hours. Otherwise again, it becomes too difficult to reflect the dynamics of the system.

- Routings are short. Otherwise the effects of queuing will add a random element into each stage, making the chart unworkable.

There are a large number of reservations with the Gantt technique. Most concern its ability to provide a control function as the complexity of the work increases. It cannot account for hold-ups, for plans only ever being 'best estimates' or for plans being undermined by Murphy's Law (anything that can go wrong, will go wrong).

Schedule for jobs	M	T	W	Th	F	S	Su
Wages		●	●				
Purchases			●	●	●		
Revenue				●	●	●	

FIGURE 1.1: *A simple Gantt chart – an example chart for an accounts clerk.*

The major shortcoming of a Gantt chart is that it does not provide a method of determining how resources may be optimally allocated. For example, if manpower could be shifted from one activity to another, the second activity might be completed in a shorter time with the first taking longer. Would this benefit the company overall? This kind of 'what-if?' scenario is not feasible under Gantt. Also, there is no correlation between activities and cost.

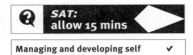

SAT:
allow 15 mins

Managing and developing self ✔

ACTIVITY 2

Construct a Gantt chart to display your own personal schedule through one term of this course. Your headings across the page should be in terms of weeks, while your headings down the page could include reading, completing assignments, attending workshops, producing project reports, liaison with tutor.

CRITICAL PATH ANALYSIS (CPA)

The development of this technique is variously attributed. CPA was developed in the 1950s as a method for improving planning and control of a project to construct a plant for Du Pont Corporation. It was credited at the time as having made substantial savings in time and cost. Its use is now widespread. (The technique has been variously attributed to the Catalytic Construction Company, Du Pont Consulting, J. E. Kelly of Remington-Rand and M. R. Walker of Du Pont.)

The central focus of this technique is to identify specific activities that will hold up a whole process or project if they are themselves held up. This vulnerable chain of activities is known as the **critical path**. The process is started by determining the following:

- ● earliest start time (EST) for the process or project

- ● earliest finish time (EFT) for the process or project.

The earliest finish time (EFT) is given by the earliest start time (EST), plus the overall activity duration (DUR) encompassing all activities.

It is also possible to work backwards in the process once all the activities have been charted. From this, it is possible to calculate the latest start time (LST) for each activity and latest finish time (LFT) for each activity. The latest finish time (LFT) is that time by which the activity must be completed to avoid holding up subsequent activities. The LST is therefore given by the LFT, minus the activity duration.

In plotting a critical path, an analyst identifies all the activities required to complete a particular task.

Each activity is represented by a node, containing information about the activity's start and finish times and duration; in figure 1.2, ACT is the name or code for the activity.

EST	EFT
ACT	DUR
LST	LFT

FIGURE 1.2: *The node in a critical path analysis diagram.*

Next, the analyst would determine the sequence of activities and construct a precedence relationship. The interrelationship of activities, i.e. which activities need to be completed before others can be undertaken, is shown by arrows between the nodes.

Once information on the sequence and duration of individual activities has been established, a critical path can be identified which links the LFTs of all the activities, thus enabling accurate scheduling and planning.

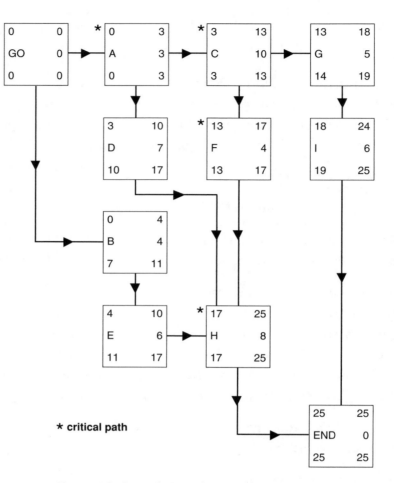

FIGURE 1.3: *A sample critical path analysis diagram.*

PROGRAMME EVALUATION AND REVIEW TECHNIQUES (PERT)

PERT was developed in 1958 by Booz Allen & Hamilton Inc. under contract to the US Navy Special Projects Division for use in the Polaris project. It aims to rectify some of the weaknesses of CPA.

CPA only considers single point values for the start and finish times of activities. But it is unlikely that the 'crystal-ball gazing' that takes place in project planning will yield values with such a high degree of certainty that there will be no errors. To take account of the inherent variability in activity time, a distribution is used to characterise the probability of activities finishing within a given margin before/after the estimated duration time.

The following steps are required in developing a PERT analysis. The first steps follow the same procedure needed to carry out a critical path analysis.

Step 1: Identify each activity to be carried out

This simple process requires that every activity in the process or project is listed. It is important, however, that care is taken to ensure that each activity is identified in a relatively constant level of detail. For example, in constructing a warehouse, an activity such as 'install lock on front door' would not be shown in the same PERT chart as 'erect side walls'. In PERT terminology they are at different levels of indenture, and such a mixture of large and small activities would be inappropriate.

As an example, we are going to illustrate the process of testing a new prototype. The activities are listed below.

A: Design

B: Build prototype

C: Evaluate equipment

D: Test prototype

E: Write equipment report

F: Write methods report

G: Write final report

Step 2: Determine the sequence of activities and construct a table reflecting the precedence relationships

The person constructing the PERT analysis must consider the interrelationships of activities and present them in visual form. In our example, the precedence table is as shown in table 1.1.

Activity	Activity designation	Immediate predecessors	Expected duration
Design	A	–	21
Build prototype	B	A	5
Evaluate equipment	C	A	7
Test prototype	D	B	2
Write equipment report	E	D	5
Write methods report	F	C,D	8
Write final report	G	E,F	2

TABLE 1.1: *Precedence table*

Step 3: Determine critical path

An analyst would calculate the critical path and expected completion time for the overall task and using the above figures, this would result in the network diagram in figure 1.4.

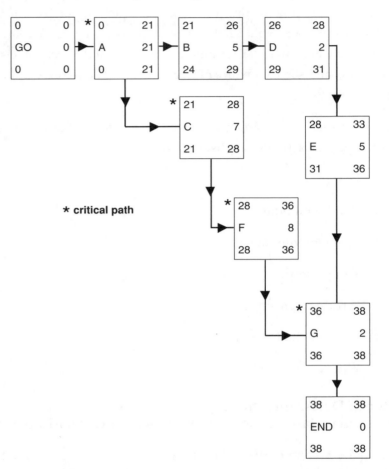

FIGURE 1.4: *Critical path analysis for testing a prototype.*

The critical path for this network, i.e. the maximum time through the network on activities with no float time is:

GO → A → C → F → G → END

Step 4: Calculate probability estimates

In PERT, the expected duration is a weighted average of three estimated times: the optimistic time *(O)*, the most likely time *(M)*, and the pessimistic time *(P)*. These three estimated times are combined into a single workable time value, known as the expected time.

$$\text{expected time} = \frac{O+4M+P}{6}$$

To describe the variation or dispersion in the activity times in a PERT network, we use the variance of the activity times (i.e. the square of the standard deviation). This is determined by:

$$\text{variance} = \left(\frac{P-O}{6}\right)^2$$

Table 1.2 shows the estimated times, expected time and variance for each node in our network.

Activity	Code	Time Estimates			Expected times	Variance
		Optimist (O)	Most likely (M)	Pessimist (P)	$\frac{O+4M+P}{6}$	$\left(\frac{P-O}{6}\right)^2$
Design	*A	10	22	28	21	9
Build protoype	B	4	4	10	5	1
Evaluate equipment	*C	4	6	14	7	2.78
Test prototype	D	1	2	3	2	0.11
Write reports	E	1	5	9	5	1.78
Write methods report	*F	7	8	9	8	0.11
Write final report	*G	2	2	2	2	0

∗ critical path

TABLE 1.2: *Estimated times, expected times and variance for activities in PERT example*

From the CPA diagram, we can calculate that the critical path involves activities A, C, F and G, with an expected total time of 38 weeks. Table 1.2 shows the computed variance for each activity. If the activity times on the critical path are statistically independent, the standard deviation of the earliest finish time is given by the formula:

Standard deviation of earliest finish time with four activities on critical path

$$= \sqrt{\text{variance (act.A)}+\text{var(act.C)}+\text{var(act.F)}+\text{var(act.G)}}$$

In our example, this standard deviation =

$$= \sqrt{9+2.78+0.11+0}$$

$$= \sqrt{11.89}$$

$$= 3.45$$

Suppose you would like to know the chance of the project being completed in 40 weeks. PERT assumes that the distribution of the total project time is a normal distribution, as shown in figure 1.5. Here we have shown the expected earliest finish time (38 weeks) and indicated the completion time in which we are now interested (40 weeks). We know the standard deviation of the critical path is 3.45 weeks. Thus, the distance from the mean to 40 weeks is:

$$\frac{40-38}{3.45} = 0.58 \quad \text{standard deviations}$$

Statistical tables show the area under a normal curve, and these tables give the area from the left-hand tail to a point 0.58 standard deviations above the mean, 0.719. In our example, therefore, there is a 72 per cent chance that the project will be completed in less than 40 weeks.

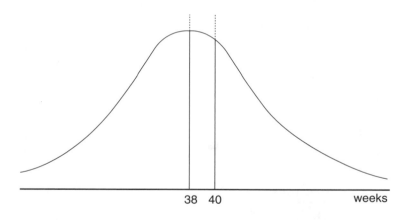

38 40   weeks

FIGURE 1.5: *Normal distribution of project finish times.*

The use of PERT techniques provides analysts with a range of useful information. In our example, it shows the following:

- The expected project completion time is 38 weeks.

- There is a better than 70 per cent chance of finishing the project within 40 weeks. The chances of meeting other deadlines can also be determined by this method.

- Activities A, C, F and G are on the critical path – any fall behind on these activities will affect the whole project.

- Activities not on the critical path (B, D and E) can fall behind by varying amounts (their slack times) without causing the project to be late.

- The earliest starting and finishing times are known for all the activities in the project.

ACTIVITY 3

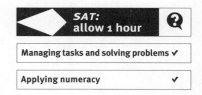
You are requested by Mano plc to provide estimates for the inspection and cleaning of chemical storage tanks, and the replacement of valves and corroded pipework.

Mano plc has identified the activities that need to be undertaken. Table 1.3 lists these activities, their immediate predecessors, expected duration and cost. In addition, you estimate that the daily fixed costs associated with the inspection and overhaul (which have to be met over and above the cost of specific activities) is £2,000 for each day of the project.

On behalf of Mano plc, advise a suitable project completion time (using critical path analysis) and supply a cost estimate. Support your advice with suitable diagrams and calculations.

Activity	Description	Immediate predecessor(s)	Normal duration (days)	Normal cost (£)
A	Drain tanks/pipework	–	4	3,000
B	Erect scaffolding	–	5	8,000
C	Inspect tanks	A,B	3	3,500
D	Inspect pipework	A,B	6	5,500
E	Clean tanks	C	7	3,500
F	Remove defective pipework	D	3	4,500
G	Remove defective valves	D	1	2,500
H	Replace pipework	F	5	4,000
I	Replace valves	G	2	2,000
J	Pressure testing/safety checks	E,H,I	2	3,000
K	Remove scaffolding	J	3	1,500
L	Clean area	J	2	2,500

TABLE 1.3: *Activities and costs for undertaking inspection and overhaul of chemical storage tanks*

Commentary...

The network illustrating this task, and showing the critical path, is drawn in figure 1.6.

The critical path is:

GO → B → D → F → H → J → K → END

This shows an estimated project completion time of 24 days. On this basis, you can provide a cost estimate.

Daily costs (24 x £2,000)	£48,000
Normal costs (A+B+C+D+E+F+G+H+I+J+K+L)	£43,500
Total cost	£91,500

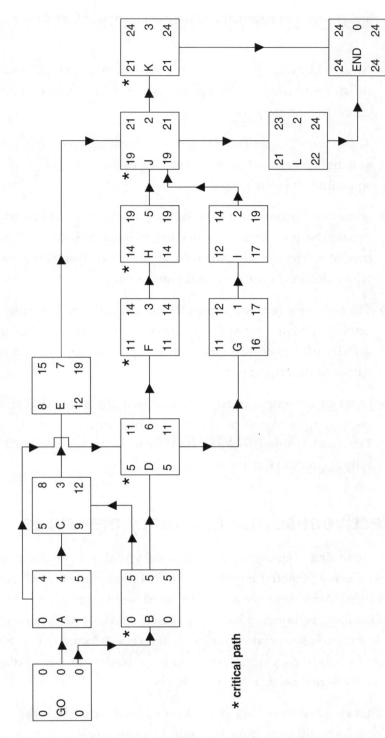

FIGURE 1.6: *The critical path analysis chart for undertaking the inspection and overhaul of Mano plc's chemical storage tanks.*

There are a number of potential weaknesses inherent in both CPA and PERT:

- All activities must be clearly identified as having finite start and finishing points, this is not always true in some complex processes and projects.

- The nature of organisational activities is usually very dynamic and using solid planning techniques such as these can, sometimes, be restricting.

- Some of the activities in these techniques may not have clearly predictable outcomes, they may have several or none at all. It, therefore, becomes difficult to construct the analysis before the whole process or project is actually in operation.

- The technique concentrates on the critical path and the critical activities. What is more likely to happen, in practice, is that an activity off the critical path is held up, changing the entire nature of the critical path.

- Most of the current applications of CPA and PERT are computer based and tend to be complex in their operation. Time and a sound background in mathematics is needed to fully appreciate the use of these techniques.

Effectiveness and efficiency measures

When analysing effectiveness and efficiency within organisations, there are many potential sources of information, some more reliable than others. Many questions need to be asked about every aspect of an organisation's activities. Interviews, discussions, observations of people and processes, and examination of factual information are all helpful in building up a picture of an organisation, of where it is now, and where it needs to go in the future.

The following activities look at the kind of information that can be obtained from different sources within business organisations and show some of the effectiveness and efficiency measures that can be constructed.

ORGANISATIONAL SOURCES

ACTIVITY 4

Some sources of organisational information are listed below together with examples of the data and performance measures that can be extracted from these sources. Try to add at least two more examples in each category.

Organisational sources	Examples
Business Plan	Organisational Objectives Business Strategies
Human resource inventory	Number of employees Age range
Indicators of organisational health	Labour turnover Absenteeism
Efficiency index	Cost of Labour Cost of material

Commentary...

Your list of examples may include the following suggestions:

- **Business plan:** new or changed systems and structures; financial estimates and constraints; aspirations for new organisational cultures.

- **Human resource inventory:** male/female mix; organisational chart; skills inventory; training records; career plans; appraisal records.

- **Indicators of organisational health:** productivity; accidents; sickness; customer complaints.

- **Efficiency indexes:** quality of materials; equipment utilisation; wastage, downtime; late deliveries.

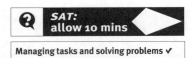

SAT:
allow 10 mins

Managing tasks and solving problems ✔

JOB SOURCES

ACTIVITY 5

Some types of information relate to the particular job or activity under review. Some sources are listed below, together with examples of data and measures that can be extracted. Following the pattern of the last activity, try to add at least two more examples in each category.

Job sources	Examples
Documentation	Performance standards
	Professional journals
Operational analyses	Waste figures
	Late deliveries
Questioning	Of senior managers
	Of supervisors

Commentary...

You may have suggested some of the following:

- ◉ **Review documentation** to obtain: job descriptions; comparisons of statistics from other industries, using government reports, academic research, trade association data.

- ◉ **Analyse operational problems**, to show: downtime reports; repairs; quality control.

- ◉ **Obtain further information by questioning:** job-holders and/or peers and colleagues.

INDIVIDUAL SOURCES

Finally, a great deal of information can be obtained from individual employees.

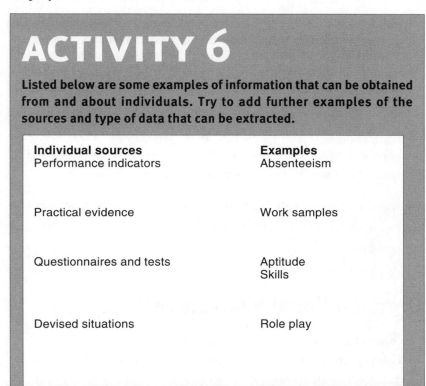

ACTIVITY 6

Listed below are some examples of information that can be obtained from and about individuals. Try to add further examples of the sources and type of data that can be extracted.

Individual sources	Examples
Performance indicators	Absenteeism
Practical evidence	Work samples
Questionnaires and tests	Aptitude Skills
Devised situations	Role play

Commentary...

You may have suggested some of the following:

- **Performance indicators:** productivity; accidents; sickness; grievances; waste; late deliveries; quality; downtime; repairs; customer complaints.

- **Practical evidence:** work observations of specific task problems; interviews; performance appraisal; work diaries; critical incident analysis; and/or coaching.

- **Questionnaires and tests:** job knowledge; skills; achievement; attitude; personality.

- **Devised situations:** case-studies; in-tray exercises (a technique for assessing competence at dealing with day-to-day problems); assessment centres.

Extracting useful and reliable information is not always straightforward. Business plans are not always clearly written, and are open to different interpretations. Organisation charts can also be misleading; there are organisation outlines that are documented, ones that are described by the employees, and those that are actually being operated, and all three may be different. Statistical information can be more reliable although statistics can be interpreted differently. Job descriptions sometimes bear little resemblance to the actual job being performed and individuals' views on job problems may vary greatly.

The type of information that you are looking for needs to be clearly defined in advance. Prepare questions to elicit the data you need. Open questions, like 'What are the strengths and weaknesses in your department?', may be useful to begin a discussion. Provide greater focus by asking closed questions like, 'Do you operate this piece of equipment in the way prescribed in the operating manual?'

To acquire accurate information, it is essential to check and cross-check, and always sift evidence for opinions, assertions and judgements.

Organisational analysis techniques

We now examine the frameworks which are commonly used to analyse organisational development (OD) strategies. OD is the term used to describe the processes of changing the culture, climate, values, attitudes, structures and systems in an organisation.

At the outset, any strategy needs to be placed in the context of the business as a whole: where it is now, and where it wants to be. To define the starting point for an organisational development strategy, it is necessary to carry out some form of diagnostic survey, particularly with regard to the definition of the current culture and levels of competence. This work can, in itself, be very beneficial. The feedback to participants can also lay the foundations for involving people in the change process.

With a structured approach to planning, it is possible to complete an organisational development route map. This shows the steps to be taken in changing the organisation. It might detail specific measures such as corporate awareness and communication programmes, objective setting, performance indicators, and team building programmes.

The strategy must be flexible so that it can be changed as the plan takes place. Irrelevant items can be dropped and new items included in the light of experience. A typical plan may be based on the questions 'Where are we now?' and 'Where do we want to be?'

JOHN SPENSER'S DEPARTMENT STORES

In John Spenser's Department Stores, business consultants have carried out an organisational development survey of the business. They have recommended that certain things need to change.

The company's staff development system of moving people around jobs in one store is not working successfully because there are few vacancies. Management wants to give people a broader experience of the business, so the consultants recommended a national staff development system in which people can be seconded to different stores within the group. The consultants also found that staff in some stores are working more effectively in teams; as there is a general need to adopt more participative styles in all stores, they decided to focus team-building activities in the weaker stores.

They found the management structure to be top-heavy; some functions overlapped, whereas the plan called for flatter, and more clearly responsive, structures. There is a staff appraisal system in operation which supposedly measures the performance of individuals against set objectives, but it is in disrepute because of inconsistent styles. A review of the appraisal system has been undertaken. Career development and succession planning is one area where the current arrangements work well and suit the objectives of the business.

The consultants discovered that employees' perception and awareness of the business differed according to their geographical location and their particular manager. For the full implementation of a total quality initiative, it is considered essential that communications are improved. In the future, internal communications should emphasise issues about where the business is moving and how it is performing. It has therefore been decided to implement a team-briefing system across all stores.

The above case study illustrates a number of areas to focus on when asking our two key questions: 'Where are we now?' and 'Where do we want to be?'. This type of format is shown below.

	Where are we now?	Where do we want to be?
Staff development systems		
Skills development and team building		
Management structure and controls		
Objectives setting		
Measures of performance		
Career development		
Succession planning		
Corporate awareness		
Communication programmes		

An alternative way of looking at all the factors at work in the organisation is to divide these into hard and soft structures. This approach has been used by **Peters and Waterman** (*In Search of Excellence,* Harper & Row, 1982) who developed the 7S framework.

The three hard elements are:

- structure

- strategy

- systems.

The four soft elements are:

- shared values

- staff

- style

- skills.

We shall now look at the important techniques of internal organisational analysis and external organisational analysis.

INTERNAL ANALYSIS

The first technique is concerned with the internal organisation, and it involves a thorough analysis of the following items:

- **Structure and roles**
  What is the current structure?
  Who does what within it?

- **Relationships**
  How well do individuals and departments work together?

- **Rewards**
  How appropriate and fair are the financial and non-financial rewards?

- **Systems and procedures**
  What systems and procedures are currently in operation?

- **Resources**
  What finance, plant, equipment and labour is available?

- **Skills and knowledge**

  What is the current expertise of the entire work-force?

- **Leadership**

  What is the current strength and style of leadership in all areas?

EXTERNAL ANALYSIS

In a broad external analysis (sometimes referred to as **environmental scanning**) many organisations use an approach called PESTLE. These letters stand for: political, economic, sociological, technological, legal and environmental.

- **Political**

  What are the current and potential influences from political pressures?

- **Economic**

  How does the local, national and world economy impact on us?

- **Sociological**

  What are the ways in which changes in society affect us?

- **Technological**

  How does new and emerging technology affect our business?

- **Legal**

  How does local, national and world legislation affect us?

- **Environmental**

  What are the local, national and world environmental issues?

STRENGTHS, WEAKNESSES, OPPORTUNITIES, THREATS (SWOT)

SWOT analysis is a very widely used tool of business and marketing planners. It simply asks the planners to consider all the data accumulated in both the external environmental and the internal organisational analyses. The first two items – strengths and weaknesses – are a summary of the conclusions reached under the internal analysis; the second two items – opportunities and threats – are a summary of the conclusions reached under PESTLE analysis. SWOT analysis may be used in a variety of different business situations, e.g. for examining a product range, a particular company department, a system of administration or a company policy.

ORGANISATIONAL ANALYSIS
TECHNIQUES

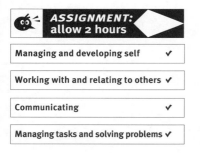

ASSIGNMENT:
allow 2 hours

Managing and developing self	✓
Working with and relating to others	✓
Communicating	✓
Managing tasks and solving problems	✓

ACTIVITY 7

Preferably, form into groups of four to carry out this assignment.

This activity is designed to let you practise the use of organisational analysis tools. Use PESTLE and SWOT analysis to look at a contemporary business. Choose a business that either interests you or one that the group is familiar with. You could also choose a company that is a 'household name' where you might find it easier to obtain background information to carry out the analysis.

For example, if you choose British Gas, write to the company for copies of its latest annual reports. Use libraries to search for recent articles on the gas industry and the wider energy market. Monitor the business press, such as *The Economist* and *The Financial Times*. Obtain any recent reports from OFGAS, the industry regulator.

Analyse the company's strengths, weaknesses, opportunities and threats. Produce a two-page report on your findings. Use a separate sheet of paper to record your answer. Summarise your main findings in the box below.

Method study

Method study examines and analyses the way work is organised by gathering, on a systematic basis, information about the working process. It breaks down work into different tasks, and it attempts to find the most effective method of working.

Its objectives are to:

- improve efficiency
- reduce or eliminate waste
- improve workplace or department layout
- improve working conditions
- improve material handling
- improve the use of machines and equipment
- reduce employee fatigue.

A central issue of method study is to examine critically existing and proposed ways of doing work. To accomplish this, a number of primary questions are asked:

- **Purpose**
  What is achieved?
  Is it necessary?

- **Place**
  Where is it done?
  Why there?

- **Sequence**
  When is it done?
  Why then?

- **Person**
  Who does it?
  Why them?

- **Means**
  How is it done?
  Why is it done that way?

SAT:
allow 10 mins

Managing tasks and solving problems ✔

ACTIVITY 8

Identify a job which is done at work, in the home or at college and apply the primary questions of method study to it. Take, for example, a task like redecorating your home. Use the five method study questions, to examine your options. Summarise your answers below.

Commentary...

The method study questions are designed to reach the heart of the issue. In the decorating example, it questions whether the job needs to be done, whether the job is best done by you, other members of your household or an outside decorator, and addresses the way you might go about the task.

You might find that once you have asked the primary questions, you wanted to go on to ask a second set of questions:

- **Purpose**
  What else could/should be done?

- **Place**
  Where else could/should it be done?

- **Sequence**
  When could/should it be done?

- **Person**
  Who else could/should do it?

- **Means**
  How else could/should it be done?

Jobs can be changed and reorganised in a number of different ways, e.g. by:

- improving the work-place layout

- improving the design of plant and equipment

- changing the sequence of operations

- changing the mix of materials involved in the process

- reducing wastage of materials and skills

- eliminating unnecessary fatigue.

Method study engineers use charts to record the facts about a job clearly and concisely, e.g.:

- process charts – simple and two-handed

- flow process charts

- flow diagrams

- multi-purpose charts.

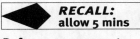

RECALL:
allow 5 mins

Before we move on to explore the application of these charts, state the five basic questions that comprise method study.

PROCESS CHARTS

In process charts, various symbols are used to designate particular activities:

- Operation, O

- Transport, →

- Delay, D

- Storage, △

- Inspection, □

A simple process chart presents a picture of the sequence of operations in a process. An **operation** is an action that takes a material, a component or a service a stage further towards completion by:

- changing its shape

- changing its composition

- adding material to it

- taking material from it.

A **transport** is a movement. A **delay** is an interruption to the process. An **inspection** is something that either accepts the previous operation or rejects it because of defects in quality or quantity. It does not assist in the completion of the product or service.

Figure 1.7 identifies work done, using O for operations, and inspections using □ . It starts with a delivery point, then follows and identifies all operations and inspections until it reaches completion.

9.00	9.30	10.00	10.30	10.45	11.00	11.30	12.00
O	□	O	□	O	□	O
work done	inspec- tion	work done	inspec- tion	work done	inspec- tion	work done

FIGURE 1.7: *A simple process chart.*

This does not examine in any detail the type of work done, nor does it identify any delay or transport, but it does show the amount of time spent working as opposed to inspecting. A completed process chart should show the way a job is completed and the sequence of operations.

THE TWO-HANDED PROCESS CHART

This chart identifies all the hand motions performed by a worker. It also identifies transport, operation, and delay. The two-handed process chart is useful for analysing simple, repetitive mechanical tasks, particularly in a factory environment. It might also be used in office contexts, for repetitive keyboard work and clerical tasks.

The purpose of the chart is to identify hand activities and should always start with hands moving from an idle position. The left-hand activities are shown in relationship to the right-hand, showing simultaneous activities as they occur.

Left hand		Right hand	
Activity	**Symbol**	**Symbol**	**Activity**
to bolt	→	→	to 1st washer
obtain bolt	O	O	obtain washer
hold bolt	D	←	washer to bolt
	D	O	fit washer
	D	→	to 2nd washer
	D	O	obtain washer
	D	←	washer to bolt
	D	O	fit washer
	D	→	to nut
	D	O	obtain nut
	D	←	nut to bolt
	D	O	fit nut
	D	O	tighten
assembly to bolt	←	→	hand to rest
assembly in box	O	D	hand idle
hand to rest	←	D	
hand idle	D	D	
Total: O 2 D 12 → 3			Total: O 7 D 3 → 7

FIGURE 1.8: *The two-handed process chart showing the activity of assembling a nut, bolt and two washers.*

FLOW PROCESS CHART

The purpose of flowcharting is to break down any process into its component steps, presenting a clear picture of what does, and should, happen. Once a flowchart is complete, a number of things should be clear, including:

- the order in which tasks or activities are done

- all the activities needed to complete a task

- the information required at each stage

- the documents referred to

- decision points.

Constructing a flowchart sounds easy, but it is not. It is surprising how often people disagree about what should be done and in what order. Often such differences of view remain hidden until someone tries to draw up a flowchart. It will usually be necessary to consult many people to define the complete process. During this consultation process, grey areas can be clarified and the definitive procedure agreed. There are special conventions about how flowcharts are presented. Whichever style you use, it is in the construction of the flowchart that the most value lies.

Figure 1.9 gives an example using the process of problem solving.

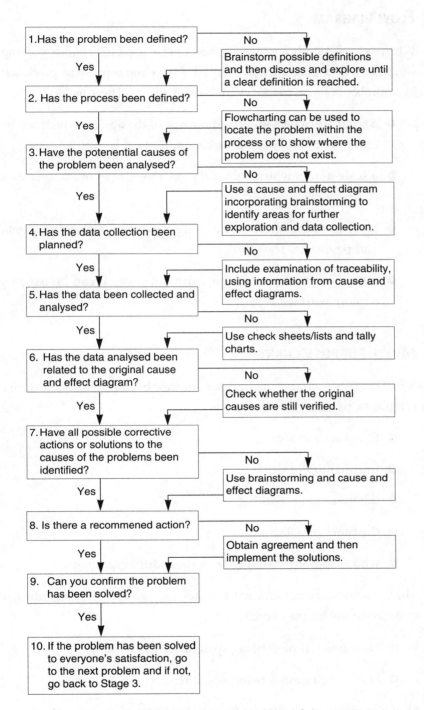

FIGURE 1.9: *A flowchart describing the problem-solving process.*

FLOW DIAGRAM

When a method study engineer wishes either to explore or plan a working situation, a flow diagram may be used. Such diagrams can be produced in a number of forms to test a variety of situations. These include:

- a template, which is cut to the shape of the design, which can be manipulated to test the various options of layout

- a scale model which shows the relative size of machinery and components

- a string diagram which shows the distance which components and people are travelling

- a two- or three-dimensional drawing which can be used to explore working layouts.

MULTI-PURPOSE CHART

Multi-purpose charts are more complex because they show the relationships between:

- the quality of work

- the quantity of work

- the time spent working

- the times of delay

- who is responsible for each of these different things.

These factors are set against a time-scale so that two important questions may be answered:

- How much time is being spent actually working?

- How much time is being wasted?

So, for example, a chart could be designed to show the path of raw material, arriving at a factory, through to conversion to a finished product, showing all the operational stages. The chart would show where the material is being processed, the flow path it follows through the factory, the storage points, and, ultimately, its dispatch from the factory loading bay. Any unnecessary delays can be identified. The drawing, for example, shows the movement of the material within the factory which might indicate that machinery or storage sites are located inefficiently.

Alternatively, a chart could show the pattern of work and inactivity over a set time period. It could, for example, be used to consider the situation of a typist being summoned to a manager's office for dictation through to the completed letter being posted.

OTHER APPROACHES

Method study engineers are always developing new approaches and techniques. These often have their own particular jargon:

- **Ergonomics** concerns the relationship between a task and a specific individual, in terms of their physical size, shape, strength, and dexterity.

- **Simo-motion** refers to a situation where two parts of the body have to act together. The detailed examination of simultaneous movements is often done by film which are projected one frame at a time, with each movement being measured by a 'wink' counter.

- **Therblig** is a system of eighteen symbols with different names and colours, used to illustrate work patterns in a graph. It was named after the man who invented it, Gilbreth (backwards).

- **Methods-time-measurement (MTM)** is a form of synthetic time standards which was developed in the 1940s and is now used throughout the world in various forms.

ACTIVITY 9

Using a simple (or two-handed) process chart, illustrate a particular task that you have to perform regularly. This could be work-related, or something to do with your studies, or even a social task.

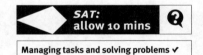
SAT:
allow 10 mins

Managing tasks and solving problems ✔

Commentary...

You may have discovered some ways that the particular task you analysed could be improved. If you have, you should consider the implications for this particular approach in the workplace. In the past, method study has had a mixed reception from employees, mainly because there have been many situations in which it has resulted in lost jobs, reduced pay and extra time pressure.

There are still many pitfalls to avoid in implementing the results of a method study investigation. The implementation may be improved by:

- recognising that people who have been carrying out jobs for a long time, have social and psychological attachments to them

- involving people in the process and consulting them on proposed changes

- seeking suggestions for improving jobs from the people doing them, and rewarding them for their ideas

- demonstrating to employees that any savings made will have a beneficial impact on their situations as well as for the company.

summary

This session has examined a number of tools and approaches which can be used to plan business activities, develop organisational strategies and analyse work tasks.

▶ Richardson's 'All the Aces' approach emphasises key areas for planning: aspirations, contingency, extended future, second-nature responsiveness, administration, creative innovation, efficiency/productivity, and shock event.

▶ Gantt charts, critical path analysis (CPA) and programme evaluation and review techniques (PERT) offer ways of scheduling a range of activities that make up a complex task.

▶ SWOT analysis can be used to develop business strategies by assessing both internal and external factors. The acronym stands for strengths, weaknesses, opportunities, threats.

▶ PESTLE analysis addresses the external factors that affect organisations under the headings: political, economic, sociological, technological, legal and environmental.

▶ Method study is used to examine critically the way in which work is organised. It examines the purpose, place, sequence, staffing and means of carrying out tasks.

▶ Tools used by method study engineers include simple and two-handed process charts, flow process charts, flow diagrams and multi-purpose charts.

Communications

Objectives

GIVING ORDERS

INSTRUCTION

TRAINING AND
DEVELOPMENT STYLES

TEAM BRIEFING

REPORTS

PRESENTATIONS

After participating in this session, you should be able to:

▶ recognise the factors which influence the style of giving orders

▶ explain the stages and styles of instruction

▶ recognise the principles and main ingredients of team briefing

▶ describe the purpose and structure of effective reports

▶ describe the purposes and key stages of presentations.

In working through this session, you will practise the following BTEC common skills:

Managing and developing self	✔
Working with and relating to others	
Communicating	✔
Managing tasks and solving problems	✔
Applying numeracy	
Applying technology	
Applying design and creativity	

Giving orders

You don't lead by pointing and telling people some place to go. You lead by going to that place and making a case.

Ken Kesey

There are many ways of giving orders. One extreme is the 'dictator' type of manager who is dominating, makes quick decisions, overrules anyone who dissents and, as a consequence, ends up with poor decisions. At the other extreme you might find the 'country club' type of manager who ensures that everyone feels good, but little action is taken or progress made.

Observers have researched the behaviour of groups in great detail, and these two extremes illustrate the basic dilemma facing managers:

- Should they have more concern for the **group process** (the social interaction)?

or

- Should they pursue the **tasks** on the agenda (and obtain results even if a few staff feel left out or antagonised)?

In the first section of this module, we examined in some depth whether managers should focus on tasks or on people. We came to the conclusion that, as a management style, neither extreme is usually very productive, although each end of the spectrum can be used in different circumstances. In the context of giving orders, this **task/group process split** is worth exploring in more detail.

There is a need for balance to be maintained between concern for the task and group process. One way of examining this issue is to consider the matrix shown in figure 2.1.

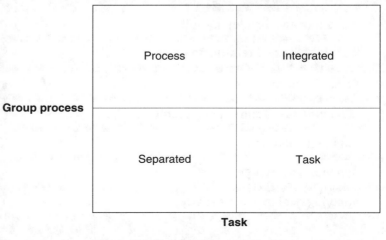

FIGURE 2.1: *Task/group process matrix.*

The four quadrants illustrate various styles of working with people. Each has different benefits:

- The **task** style is good for making progress, avoiding going over old ground and keeping to time-scales. This is most appropriate where quick and pragmatic decisions are required, and where the social formalities are either unimportant, or are already at a high degree of effectiveness.

- The **process** style is good for drawing people in, encouraging quieter people and 'fishing' for ideas. This is useful in the early stages of policy or strategy formulation, where the involvement and commitment of everyone is, at least initially, more important than making progress with the task itself.

- The **separated** style is good for attention to detail, record keeping and complying with existing rules and procedures. This style is really only suitable for relatively unimportant activities which do not require either lengthy involvement, or detailed technical analysis.

- The **integrated** style is good for summarising and team spirit, consolidating progress made. This could be said to be the ideal style, but it can be time-consuming unless the group of people within the communication process are long-standing colleagues, and there are some high levels of trust.

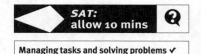

SAT:
allow 10 mins

Managing tasks and solving problems ✔

ACTIVITY 1

Look at the task and group process diagram in figure 2.1 and answer the following questions.

1. Which quadrant would you select as the most effective for leading or changing a group of people in an organisation?

2. How would a very 'process' oriented manager appear to a very 'task' conscious group (or vice versa)?

3. How would you supply the counterbalance to ensure an overall range of styles for the group?

Commentary...

Most management experts conclude that there is no one best style. Each style is appropriate to different situations or different stages of the decision-making process. The effective manager needs to be aware of this process, to be able to adopt behaviours appropriate for each style, and to respond to staff with suitable behaviour at different stages of the decision-making process.

Most people tend to describe people with opposite skills to themselves in rather negative terms. The 'task' manager probably thinks of the 'process' manager as wishy-washy and ineffective. The 'process' manager might see the 'task' manager as insensitive and pushy. Neither is likely to see the other as caring and concerned or effective and result-oriented.

The effective manager must consider both task and process elements to reach good solutions.

The task elements include:

- the technical expertise concerned with the problem

- the skills of focusing on the problem

- considering alternative courses of action

- summarising progress so far

- progressing towards the achievement of the solution.

The process elements ensure that staff:

- are motivated to contribute to their maximum ability

- feel their contributions are listened to and built on

- share a sense of common purpose in finding a solution

- sense that their contributions and effort are recognised.

A style may be described as the pattern of behaviour adopted by the manager during group communication. Styles differ according to the degree of scope allowed to other people to influence progress and outcome.

A 'directive' style allows others little scope for intervention whereas a 'participant' style permits others room to influence. The *laissez-faire*, or 'abdication', style involves allowing a free rein to the others.

In the following diagram – a version of the autocratic/democratic continuum featured in Section 1, Session 1 – you can see the continuum of styles available. They range from tells – a total use of authority by the manager – to joins, where there is freedom for action by the others.

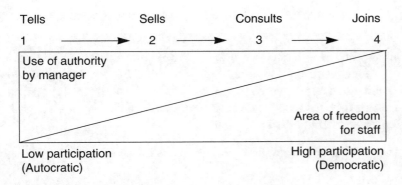

FIGURE 2.2: *The autocratic/democratic continuum.*

The style may be varied according to the needs of the situation. A highly authoritarian pattern (with low participation in decision making) may be appropriate in emergencies or when it is otherwise essential that all staff do the same thing. In such cases, staff can achieve the necessary objective most readily by acting in unity, even though the action taken may not be theoretically the 'best' option. No organisation, however, is continually in a crisis situation – although a few managers do appear to attempt to run things by continual panic. In a less pressured situation, it is possible to enable staff to contribute their skills and experience in order to make a 'better' position.

When choosing a style, it is worth reflecting therefore upon the effects that different approaches may have upon goal achievement.

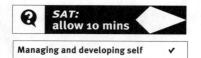

ACTIVITY 2

There are nine sets of four words below. Rank the four words in each set across the page in order, assigning a 4 to the word which best describes your behaviour, a 3 to the next best, a 2 to the next best and a 1 to the word which is least descriptive of your behaviour. Be sure to assign a different rank number to each of the four words; do not allow ties.

You may find it hard to choose the words that best describe your behaviour because there are no right or wrong answers. Different behaviours described in the inventory are equally good.

	A	B	C	D
1	forceful	negotiating	testing	sharing
2	decisive	teaching	probing	unifying
3	expert	convincing	enquiring	co-operative
4	resolute	inspirational	questioning	giving
5	authoritative	compelling	participative	approving
6	commanding	influential	searching	collaborating
7	direct	persuasive	verifying	impartial
8	showing	manoeuvring	analytical	supportive
9	prescriptive	strategical	exploring	compromising
	2,3,4,5,7,8	1,3,6,7,8,9	2,3,4,5,8,9	1,3,6,7,8,9

To obtain a profile of your style, total the scores in each column, but only for the words numbered below the list. So, for column A you would add up your scores for all the words except for the first, sixth and ninth words; for column B you would leave out the second, fourth and fifth and so on.

The four columns represent four styles as follows:

A = tell   B = sell   C = consult   D = join

Make a note of your 'strongest' style (the column in which you scored the most). Also note your 'weakest' style (the column you scored the least).

Commentary...

This profile is based on the work of **R. Tannebaum** and **W. Schmit** (*Harvard Business Review*, March/April, 1958). They established the classic range of leadership styles from autocratic (telling) to democratic (sharing) discussed earlier.

The main point to emphasise is that you need to be aware of the range of styles, and realise that no one style is 'best'. What matters is to choose the right style for the right solution. In an emergency telling would be appropriate, but for developing a new policy joining would seem more suitable.

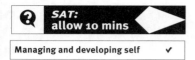

Managing and developing self   ✔

ACTIVITY 3

To compare your own personal style with the styles of managers in industry, you need to compare your scores with theirs. You can do this using figure 2.3.

	Tell		Sell		Consult		Join
100%	20		21		21		21
	17						
			19		19		19
80%					18		18
			18				17
	15						
					16		
60%			17				16
	14						15
			16		15		
	13						
40%			15				
	12		14		14		14
	11				13		13
20%	10						
							11
			12		10		
	8						9
0%							

FIGURE 2.3: *Assessing management communication styles against other managers.*

To use this table, shade in each column up to your score line using the numbers inside the columns on the table. Notice that these numbers are not all at the same level for each style.

You can then read off an approximation of how much you use each style compared with other managers. These are percentiles not percentages; this means that they show the percentage of other middle managers in industry and commerce who have responded to the management style words in a similar way to yourself.

To compare yourself on the telling style for example, read across from your score line to the per cent column. Note if it is above or below 50 per cent. If you scored 12, the nearest mark is 40 per cent. This means that you only use this style as much as 40 per cent of managers (or, put another way, 60 per cent of managers tend to use this style more than you do).

If you scored, say, 16 on telling, the nearest mark is 80 per cent. If you scored 16, therefore, you use this style more than 80 per cent of managers (or only 20 per cent use this style more than you do).

Note the percentage marks for each of your styles. If one of your percentage marks is noticeably higher than the others, this is the style you will tend to use most, particularly if you are under pressure or stress.

Make a note of the possible negative effects your preferred style might have on any group that you might be asked to lead.

Commentary...

For each of the four styles, the strengths and weaknesses are as follows:

- **Telling** is good for action, but risks missing opportunities for gaining commitment; you might be seen as a poor listener or, at worst, as an insensitive autocrat.

- **Selling** is good to avoid looking like an autocrat, but too much selling can look like telling under another name. Selling is based on the benefits of the solution, not its technical features.

- **Consulting** is good for gaining ideas as few managers have all the answers, but do not fall into the trap of paying lip service to consultation; colleagues and staff might say: 'Oh, she pretends to ask our views but she's made up her mind already.'

- **Joining** is very useful for gaining commitment to a task that could be done in a number of ways. Problems can arise if someone produces an idea that the manager does not agree with, or if the staff suspect that the manager is trying to avoid taking the lead.

Notice as well that if any of your percentage scores were well below the others, this is probably the style that you tend to avoid, particularly if you feel under pressure or threatened.

Instruction

Most people, at some time in their life, are asked to pass on skills, information or ideas, to someone who may be new to the job. You may be asked to do this formally, at a certain time of the day, against a written schedule, or informally, when it suits both you and the trainee best. In either case, there are some important issues to consider. First, there is the sequence in which the instruction is carried out. Consider the stages of instruction shown in table 2.1.

Stage	Task	Elements
1	Analyse the task to be learnt	Knowledge Skill Safety elements Key points
2	Set learning objectives	
3	Prepare instruction	Stages for learning Appropriate materials Aids and equipment
4	Prepare the learner	Introduction Assess previous experience Put at ease Correct positioning
5	Demonstrate	The whole task Then, step by step
6	Practise	Learner tries the steps Errors corrected Appropriate questions Praise and encourage Check understanding Practise the whole task
7	Follow up	Allow time to gain proficiency Extra instruction if necessary

TABLE 2.1: *Stages in practical instruction*

Let us examine these key stages in more detail.

ANALYSE

It is not helpful to offer instruction in a particular activity if you do not know exactly what the task entails. You should make quite sure that you are familiar with all aspects before proceeding to the next stage.

SET LEARNING OBJECTIVES

It is important to have clear definitions of objectives when embarking on, and planning, a learning activity. In this way, you can determine whether you are making any progress. These objectives need to be defined in as much detail as possible, but in any event they should contain the following elements:

- **Terminal behaviour** – a clear statement of what the learner should be able to do at the end of the instruction.

- **Standard of performance** – a clear statement of how well the learner should be able to perform this terminal behaviour.

○ **Conditions of performance** – a clear statement of the circumstances and conditions under which the learner should be able to perform this behaviour.

In other words, when planning and designing learning activities you must have clear and well-defined objectives. You need to be particularly accurate in your definition of the skill, knowledge and aptitude that are required as a central core.

PREPARE INSTRUCTION AND PREPARE THE LEARNER

If you are to instruct someone in a complete job or a complicated task, then it is advisable to develop a clear instructional plan for your own use. You need to:

○ break the task into skills and knowledge

○ identify clear 'chunks' of learning which can be easily digested by the learner

○ identify the best method of teaching each element

○ ensure all the necessary equipment is available

○ determine how long each part will take.

You also need to prepare the learner for the instruction by:

○ setting the learner at ease and making sure he or she is comfortable

○ checking out his or her previous experience

○ setting the particular task in context of the whole job or process

○ introducing the task in outline

○ checking if the learner has any concerns or questions.

DEMONSTRATE AND PRACTISE

Depending upon the complexity of the task, the instructor either begins the session with an overall demonstration of the task, or encourages the learner to 'have a go'. The emphasis in most progressive instruction is towards a hands-on, learner-centred approach. The instructor should continue by either demonstrating or helping the learner through each stage, while always encouraging questions. Errors are corrected, and after several stages of the task have been completed relatively successfully, the learner should be encouraged to undertake a group of stages in one go.

Instruction should continue, with praise and encouragement at all times, until the learner is capable of carrying out the whole task without error or hesitation.

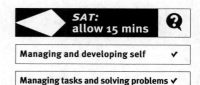

ACTIVITY 4

Taking account of the points made above, design a programme of instruction for a job you are familiar with, at work or at home. Set out the main elements of the programme in the box below.

FOLLOW UP

The instructor may have to consider whether safety requirements demand that the learner should continue to be supervised while he or she practises. In many cases, the learner may be left to develop experience with just an occasional check on progress. In any event, it is important to review the whole exercise at a date not too far into the future.

Training and development styles

Four types of instruction style have been identified by **Richard Brostrom**. He suggests that each type has a set of behaviours and approaches that are directly linked to particular personality traits. His styles are also indicative of attitudes towards training and development, and to some extent they typify aspects of traditional and modern approaches.

Behaviourists believe that new behaviour can be shaped by well-designed training programmes. They are trainer-centred; they design training activities which engineer a reinforcement schedule that systematically encourages learners to progress towards predetermined end behaviours. They tell trainees what to do and how to do it. They issue handouts, procedural instructions and check-lists. They expect their trainees to listen, to take note and then to do as they have been instructed. Their aim is for their trainees (they are unlikely to use the word 'learner') to behave in a consistent and uniform manner.

Structuralists believe that the mind is like a computer, and the teacher is a programmer who organises the contents of the training and feeds it bit by bit to the learners. This type of trainer 'keeps people awake' while simultaneously entering data. They are also trainer-centred since they have clear end requirements and are concerned with direction, planning, organising, presenting and evaluating. Their training sessions are immaculately planned, and time is strictly controlled while the training, principally of knowledge or procedures, is broken up into digestible 'chunks' or lessons. These instructors are very concerned to cover the planned timetable and may become more concerned with the methods of training than with the outcomes. In other words, they may be more concerned about how they have performed rather than about what people have learned.

Functionalists believe people learn best by doing, and that they will perform best if they are doing what they want to do. Trainees must be willing and motivated by the training process otherwise it is useless to try to teach them anything. Functionalists believe that 'on-the-job' performance is the true test; they are very learner-centred, ensuring that all learning is based on reality, involvement, feedback and achievement. These instructors are very keen to have people doing things and are unlikely to provide lengthy demonstrations. They are more likely to arrange for their trainees to have access to machinery or equipment so that they can 'have a go'.

Humanists believe that learning is a self-directed discovery; that people 'unfold if others do not inhibit the process'. Essentially learner-centred, these instructors base all their activities on freedom, spontaneity, experience, feelings and a clear equality with the learners. This style works well for people who are already experienced learners and who are able to manage their own learning. For learners who prefer more structure, this style might appear to be rather vague, and they may become confused and even distressed by the apparent lack of direction or poor control of the trainer.

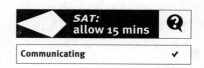

SAT:
allow 15 mins

Communicating ✓

ACTIVITY 5

Reflect for a moment on your own personal experience of learning. Identify occasions when you have experienced each of the four styles outlined above. Comment on whether each style was appropriate to the occasion when it was used.

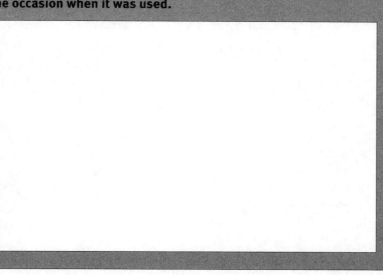

Commentary...

You may have experienced these four styles at some of the following occasions or types of training event:

- **Behaviourist:** formal lessons, lectures, pep talks.

- **Structuralist:** job instruction, training for new procedures.

- **Functionalist:** practise on new equipment, fault-finding and problem solving training, use of simulators.

- **Humanist:** group discussions, one-to-one coaching on the job, personal development programmes.

Each of these teaching styles could be appropriate for particular types of instruction. For example, the behaviourist or structuralist style is more likely to be effective for teaching technical tasks. This is especially true if health and safety concerns mean that it is absolutely critical that clearly defined procedures are followed. These styles lend themselves to formal training events carried out away from the job and are essentially trainer-centred.

The humanist or functionalist styles, which are learner-centred, are more likely to be appropriate in the management or support of personal development programmes, where the learners, to a large extent, manage their own learning, often on an individual basis.

Wherever possible, therefore, it is clearly best if instructors with appropriate styles are selected to deliver or support training activities according to the type of activity and the particular training or learning objectives.

RECALL:
allow 10 mins

Briefly describe the four Brostrom styles of training and instructing:

- **behaviourist**

- **structuralist**

- **functionalist**

- **humanist.**

Team briefing

Team briefing is an effective method of ensuring that essential data is cascaded throughout an organisation. It allows, within a space of 24 or 48 hours, everyone to receive the same messages. It is an excellent vehicle for passing on success stories and achievements, as well as for prompting staff with suggestions and areas for work improvement.

Team briefing is based on six principles:

1. Face-to-face presentations by managers and supervisors to their own staff are important. Rather than issuing instructions and communications by memo or electronic mail, they allow question and answer sessions which are vital to understanding and ensure that the message is clearly understood.

2. Briefing small teams of 4–15 people encourages constructive comment and questions. Where work teams have a common identity, it is easy to ensure that what is communicated is relevant. If you are a manager of over 25 people, try not to brief them all in one session.

3. The person doing the briefing must be the person who is responsible for the results of the team or group, and each manager should be held responsible for ensuring that the briefing succeeds in their own immediate area or responsibility.

4. The regularity of briefings is important. The effectiveness of briefing is lost if the time between them is too great.

5. It is very important that people being briefed find the information relevant, since poor and irrelevant briefings can affect morale and the group's will to work. As a rule of thumb, two-thirds of the information in a typical brief should be local with one-third concerned with the organisation as a whole.

6. Monitoring should be carried out by managers on other managers' briefings to ensure that preparation has been adequate, that information is correct and relevant and that the messages have been received.

There are usually two elements to a team brief:

- the core brief, passing on information that has originated at senior management level

- the local brief, primarily concerned with your own area of work.

The technique of team briefing is only effective if the information being passed on is seen as relevant to the group of people being briefed and, therefore, it is important that most of the brief is prepared by you. This means that you can inject the local flavour to the information. The core brief will have been already prepared by senior management and will be duplicated. The individual manager needs to consider the information that is to be conveyed and make an assessment:

- What exactly are the key points in the core brief?

- Why is it happening, or why is the company doing this?

- How will it affect my team?

When you brief, you should make your commitment to management decisions very clear even if, privately, you disagree with a decision.

Figure 2.4 shows an example of a briefing form.

Core brief	Name of Briefer: Date and Time:
Items and key points	Notes for briefers giving examples and responses to possible questions

Local brief	Name of Briefer: Date and Time:
Items and key points	Notes for briefers giving examples and responses to possible questions

FIGURE 2.4 *Briefing form.*

THE CONTENTS OF THE TEAM BRIEFING

Items included on the agenda for briefing might be:

- policy

- progress

- people

- points for action.

ACTIVITY 6

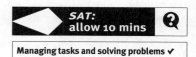

**SAT:
allow 10 mins**

Managing tasks and solving problems ✔

List at least three examples of items that might be dealt with under each of the four 'P's described above. For example, you could consider:

- policy: opening of a distribution centre in Thailand

- progress: new product development

- people: induction procedures

- points for action: car parking.

Commentary...

Examples of topics which might be covered under the four headings include:

- **policy:** expansion plans; capital investment programme; project reports.

- **progress:** product sales; financial results; cost comparisons.

- **people:** overtime levels; absenteeism; selection procedure.

- **points for action:** heating and ventilation; accident record; materials shortage.

KEY FEATURES OF TEAM BRIEFING

Briefings should be short – as the name suggests, ideally they should be brief! There should be no discussion of the points, merely questions and answers. Plenty of examples and illustrations should be used.

Questions should be handled sensibly. They need to be encouraged, but if they are irrelevant they should be dealt with afterwards. Equally, if you do not know the answer to a question say so, and make a note, always being sure that you provide an answer within three days.

Make absolutely sure that you have a clear understanding of the briefing contents, especially the items on the core brief. Also make sure that the team members have a clear understanding of all the items, by asking them questions.

Feedback from the team needs to be handled sensitively because, while you want to encourage interest and involvement, you do not want to be drawn into a discussion. If comments or suggestions are made, then arrange to discuss the suggestions with the person later. Note the names of absentees from the briefing and brief them when they return. If you are away or you cannot provide a brief for some reason, ensure that a deputy takes your place.

When you commence a team briefing, try not to begin by introducing complex and emotive subjects, or a major change, as this will associate team briefings with bad news.

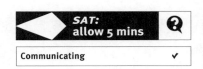

ACTIVITY 7

Read through the key points of team briefing again, and suggest at least three things you would do at the beginning, during the brief, and at the end.

Commentary...

At the beginning:

- have your briefing notes available

- welcome the team

- tell the team they can ask questions after each item

- tell them what you are going to cover

- appear positive and confident

- be on time

- make sure everyone is comfortable

- look at the team and not at your notes.

During the briefing:

- use your own words

- use practical examples and not generalisations

- relate any core items to your department

- encourage questions

- beware of 'red herrings'

- check understanding by asking questions
- keep to the time allowed
- finish on a positive note.

At the end of the briefing:

- summarise all the main points covered
- tell the team the date and time of the next briefing.

Remember that team briefing is not:

- a general discussion
- a grievance session
- a discipline session
- a negotiation.

Team briefing is a regular explanation of what is happening and where the organisation is going.

Reports

Most organisations expect their managers to produce reports on a regular basis. These may relate to new developments, industrial relations problems, technical concerns or recruitment difficulties. The manager may also produce reports for customers on new products or market research. When faced with this key managerial task, there are some important principles which should be followed.

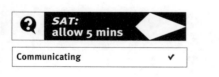

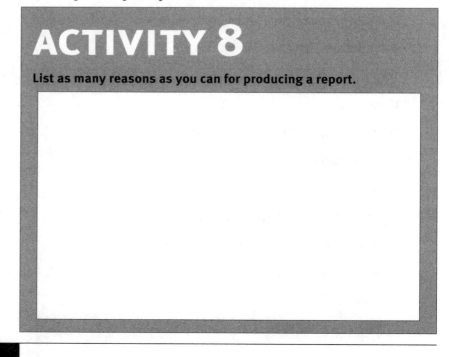

ACTIVITY 8

List as many reasons as you can for producing a report.

Commentary...

You may have listed some of the following purposes of reports:

- ○ to inform

- ○ to put on the record

- ○ to clarify

- ○ to gain agreement

- ○ to ensure that action is taken.

The purpose of each report determines the priorities you should give to various aspects of your material; for example, to put the matter on the record requires a rather 'legal' style, to gain agreement you need to be more persuasive, and to ensure action you have to convince your readers, and also demonstrate the potential outcome if no action is taken.

REPORT STRUCTURES

A report should be the minimum length consistent with presenting all the facts and should have the main points clearly signposted. Busy managers tend to read only the main points anyway, unless they disagree with your findings or stand to lose if your recommendations are accepted.

The following items should form part of the report:

- ○ title page

- ○ acknowledgements

- ○ table of contents

- ○ summary

- ○ introduction

- ○ main body, conclusions and recommendations

- ○ bibliography

- ○ appendices.

The **title page** should show the title of the report, the author's name, the organisation (if appropriate) and the matter to which it relates. The title should arouse interest while clearly indicating the subject matter.

You should always **acknowledge** all those people who have helped, not only as a matter of courtesy but also to let the readers see how successful you have been in persuading others to lend their interest and support.

The **table of contents** should list not only all the main sections and subsections but also any appendices, major figures, diagrams, illustrations, as applicable.

The **summary** should not exceed one or two pages in length. It should state the objective of the report, indicate the main approach and summarise the conclusions and recommendations.

Although the format and content may vary, the **introduction** provides an opportunity to make readers aware of background information about the organisation and about the circumstances in which the report came to be written. Any constraints inhibiting the author's work could be mentioned as may the reasons for the choice of the particular subject selected, its precise limits and any relevant information not covered elsewhere in the report.

In the preparation of the **main body** of the report, you have wide latitude in selecting the manner and format by which to demonstrate clearly:

- the precise nature of the work undertaken and methodology used

- the knowledge and understanding of matters covered

- the application of this new knowledge and skill to meet a practical situation

- the ability to communicate effectively.

In planning the sections, chapters, etc., a clear, logical order must be followed, leading step by step from the gathering of data (both theoretical and practical), via analysis, evaluation and discussion of that data to arrive at conclusions and subsequent recommendations. It is usually best to group together conclusions and recommendations in a separate section rather than scatter them throughout the report.

The analysis, evaluation and discussion of the data should involve consideration of the facts, a discussion of the options with arguments for and against each, leading to **conclusions** about what should be done. Presenting a lot of information to your readers and leaving them to analyse it for themselves is not good enough. You know more about the subject of the investigation than they do, so tell them what you think should be done. Naturally, they want to know how you reach your conclusions and what your line of argument is, in order to assess your proposals.

In forming **recommendations**, which are in effect the actions you may wish others to take, care should be taken to ensure they are clear, crisp, concise, and unmistakable; also, take care to show that cost considerations have been taken into account. The wording should be such as to require no questions from the reader to elicit exactly what is meant.

If appropriate, you should include a **bibliography** listing the reading done in preparation for the report showing for each publication the author's name, title, date and publisher.

Where a table, diagram, copy document or other self-contained material is too bulky to fit comfortably within the text it is better to show it on a separate sheet as an **appendix**. All appendices should be numbered in sequence. You must exercise judgement on the amount of material to include (and how it is presented) where the work involves large quantities of raw data. If you do include appendices you must ensure that they are referred to and/or explained within the text. Including the data, and leaving the readers to work out what it is for, is not enough.

ACTIVITY 9

Imagine that your new managing director has just been appointed from an American subsidiary. New to the UK, she wants a report about the press coverage of business affairs.

Compile a concise report based upon the coverage of business matters in three daily newspapers. Choose a tabloid, a broadsheet such as *The Times*, and *The Financial Times*, and review their business reporting over a one-week period. Compare the amount and depth of coverage. In your report, sketch out a typical reader profile of each paper. Consider using statistics to indicate the amount of coverage given to different topics in the paper. Finish by suggesting some ways in which a company might use the media to raise its profile.

Write a two-page report on separate sheets of paper. Use the box below to summarise your findings.

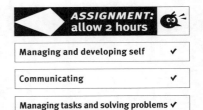

ASSIGNMENT:
allow 2 hours

Managing and developing self	✔
Communicating	✔
Managing tasks and solving problems	✔

Presentations

There are a number of reasons for making presentations:

- Presentations enable managers to raise the profile of particular topics. They focus attention on problems. This helps to ensure that the problem (and potential solutions) are considered comprehensively by those concerned.

- If everyone affected by a particular problem or issue is at a presentation, they have the opportunity to influence decisions and they may become more committed to the eventual solution.

- Presentations give managers the opportunity to sell their work both to potential opponents and to potential customers.

- Presentations may be required not just for decision-making purposes but also for information-giving purposes.

There are three stages to any presentation: preparation, the meeting itself and the follow-up.

PREPARATION

There are five main steps in the preparation stage:

1 Decide clearly what you want out of the presentation.

2 Attempt to look at the presentation from the other people's or customers' points of view and anticipate problems which may arise in their minds.

3 Ensure that your presentation is logical and of the right length. In practice, this means briefly outlining the process which you went through, culminating in a solution.

4 Try to list all the possible questions which may be asked at the presentation (including the awkward ones) and be able to provide answers.

5 Decide which visual aids might be appropriate; the presentation needs to be professional but not necessarily too formal. In deciding what to use, remember that there are visual aids which can be useful as prompts.

THE PRESENTATION

In the presentation meeting itself there are some key points to remember:

- You may be nervous; this is normal and can help to sharpen reflexes.

- First impressions are strongest, so make sure the meeting room is set up as you want it with everything in its right place. Also ensure that the opening sentences or phrases are punchy.

- Tell your audience what you are going to cover, then make your presentation and, finally, summarise what you have said.

- Be enthusiastic (unless, for example, it's about closing the company).

- Be natural.

- Accept questions.

- Speak clearly.

- Look at your audience.

- Use gestures moderately (avoid excessive use of pointing fingers and thumping the table).

- Try to avoid mannerisms (jingling keys, 'um', 'er', 'OK?', 'do you see?', 'understand?').

THE FOLLOW-UP

You may need to follow up a presentation. For example, this may be necessary to assure yourself of the commitment to action by decision makers. The follow-up can be discussed, negotiated and agreed, during, or at the end of, the presentation itself, or it can be carried out as a completely separate exercise.

Finally, it is important for the presenter to have identified some clear criteria on which the success or otherwise of the presentation is to be measured. This means being very clear personally of the objectives for the presentation. Ask yourself: 'What would I like the audience to be able to do as a result of the presentation?'

summary

Effective management of both people and activities requires good communication skills. In this session, we have looked at some of the techniques and styles for giving orders, training, briefing, writing reports and making presentations.

▶ Managers tend to have a preferred style for giving orders. Styles range from the autocratic issuing of orders to more participative approaches that involve others in decision making. It is important to recognise that different situations call for different styles.

▶ In planning training activities: analyse the task to be learnt, set clear learning objectives, prepare beforehand, put the learner at ease, demonstrate the required skills, provide opportunities to practise, and follow up to see if objectives have been met.

▶ Effective briefing requires face-to-face sessions, small groups and opportunities for questions. Briefers must have a full understanding of their briefs. Material needs to be relevant to the audience.

▶ Reports should be concise – a minimum length consistent with presenting all the facts. The style of the report should be determined by its purpose.

▶ Presentations allow managers to sell their work both to colleagues and customers and to bring people together to tackle common problems. Presentation skills need to be honed together with thorough preparation and effective follow up.

Identifying constraints and meeting objectives

EXTERNAL INFLUENCECS

REGULATORY CONTROLS

NEGOTIATING

MANAGERIAL ROLES

CO-ORDINATNG ACTIVITIES

Objectives

After participating in this session, you should be able to:

▶ consider the impact of external influences

▶ identify a number of regulatory controls which impact upon the management of activities

▶ describe negotiation techniques which can be used to control resources

▶ recognise that role interpretations can influence effective management and resource allocation

▶ understand ways of co-ordinating activities.

In working through this session, you will practise the following BTEC common skills:

Managing and developing self	✔
Working with and relating to others	✔
Communicating	✔
Managing tasks and solving problems	✔
Applying numeracy	
Applying technology	
Applying design and creativity	

External influences

There are many external factors that can influence and change organisations. These can have a significant effect on managers, acting as constraints in the way they plan and manage activities. As discussed in Section 2, Session 1, these influences may be categorised under the 'PESTLE' headings:

- political

- economic

- social

- technological

- legislative

- environmental.

Many of the forces associated with these external influences are outside a manager's control, but it is a necessity to acknowledge and respond to them for both company and personal survival. Before considering this topic further, undertake Activity 1 to review some of the factors which limit a manager's scope for action.

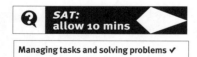

SAT:
allow 10 mins

Managing tasks and solving problems ✔

ACTIVITY 1

For each of the six external influence headings (PESTLE), list two examples of factors which might impact on business.

Commentary...

You may have identified some of the following examples of external influences.

Political

Political changes can be national, as in the case, for example, of major moves towards nationalising or privatising certain industries. Under these circumstances the role, or very existence, of certain types of manager is threatened. Newly privatised companies will expect their managers to adopt more entrepreneurial behaviour and develop the necessary private sector skills.

Political changes can also be on an international scale as is the case, for example, of recent Middle East conflicts. Here, threats forced companies to question export programmes. Chrysler, for instance, put an embargo on exporting car components to Iran when it became clear that there was some danger of the company not being paid.

Economic

Once again, the influence of economics may be felt at national or international level. A simple example is the case of interest rates fluctuating, and having a marked effect on the financial transactions of a business. Currency speculation can influence business strategy and affect investment decisions. On a larger scale, it may also determine whether a company opens a new factory or office in certain countries.

Sociological

Sociological pressures on business are often subtle but nonetheless profound, in that they can have a significant effect on culture and style within a business. Equal opportunity, for example, has become a major social issue as well as a legislative one in the last 20 years, and changed people's behaviour in a wide range of industries. It has impacted on recruitment and career development policies, and led to severe reappraisal by many managers of their role and behaviour in the workplace.

Technological

It is here, that it could be argued, that most of the major changes have occurred in recent years. Information technology, advanced manufacturing processes, very short lead times in product development, personal computers and new design mechanisms have affected nearly every industry. The effect on managers has been massive; they have had to cope with smaller numbers of employees (and of managers themselves) and increasingly complex systems and procedures. Many first-line supervisors are now expected to operate within a computer network as well as supervise the few employees that are left on the shop floor. The speed and size of technological change shows no sign of slowing down and will have significant effects on businesses for the foreseeable future.

Legislative

Reference has already been made to the influence that equal opportunity legislation has had on industry. However, there are many other legislative instruments that exert tremendous pressures on managers, both from internal sources – our own Parliament – and from external sources – the European Union. Internally, there have been major pieces of new law, such as the Health and Safety at Work Act (1974) which produced major changes in business emphasising the responsibility for health and safety of management. The European Union has produced many social and industrial directives which UK businesses have had, albeit somewhat reluctantly, to adopt.

Environmental

It is argued that the environmental lobby will increasingly be a major influence in the world of industry and commerce. Recently, environmental legislation has been introduced, tightening pollution control and control of hazardous substances, but there have been more subtle influences on the world of work, such as no-smoking or healthy eating campaigns. Excessive noise on the factory floor has led to the requirement for new ways of working and redesigned plant and machinery. The environment issue has seriously affected the existence of whole businesses, as in the case of the move from glass to disposable bottles, or in the production of asbestos.

The impact of these external factors may be quite considerable in the future. Many respected management experts have formulated radical perspectives on the future shape of business organisations and the role of managers. There is a growing belief that changes will demand from managers improvement in the following basic skills and attributes:

- influencing, persuading and negotiating skills

- facilitation skills

- integrity

- total commitment to the objective

- access to formal power holders

- access to organisational information

- knowledge of, and skill in using, change strategies.

These are the basic attributes. There are other more specific skills often associated with the manager as a change agent; these are to do with the change interventions that may be needed at any stage of the work process and each manager can have a significant effect on the successful adoption of these change attributes from a perspective of leadership.

Regulatory controls

We now consider one of the external influences – the legislative factor – in more detail. There are many regulatory controls which may affect the management of activities. Here we deal specifically with health and safety legislation and product liability and intellectual property rights as particular examples, and then identify further examples of legal controls which also impinge on managers.

HEALTH AND SAFETY OBLIGATIONS

All managers have moral and legal responsibilities for health and safety. Much of the legal framework is described under the Health and Safety at Work Act (1974) together with a wide range of codes of practice.

Broadly speaking, the Health and Safety at Work Act (1974) indicates the main work hazards by outlining the areas employers must consider in safeguarding their employees from unnecessary risk. The potential problems areas can be summarised as:

- machinery that is not adequately guarded or has not been installed or maintained correctly

- unsafe ancillary equipment, including hand tools

- unsafe systems of working

- unsafe arrangements for the handling, storage and transport of any goods

- poor access and egress

- lack of information, instruction, training and supervision

- a poorly maintained and/or unhealthy working environment.

The Act also requires employers to have a written safety policy, which deals with the organisation and arrangements for implementing the policy. This written policy explains the company's code of practice on health and safety matters. It needs to be seen and understood by all employees. However, it must be emphasised that the written word does not prevent accidents. It is the implementation and application of the policy that prevents accidents.

ACTIVITY 2

If you are required to draw up a health and safety policy for a company, what main aspects would you incorporate?

Commentary...

The effective safety policy is the one that is carried out, not simply the one that is written down. It should reflect the following principles:

- There is a clear commitment to health and safety at senior management/director level, and a clear statement of the company's objectives and values in relation to health and safety.

- Adequate resources have been allocated and priorities set for the identification, assessment, and control or elimination of hazards.

- The uniqueness and special needs of the company are reflected.

- Management responsibilities for health and safety rank equally with responsibilities for sales, finance and so on.

- The relationship between the safety adviser and line management is clear.

- The nominated safety officer or adviser is not burdened with disproportionate or unrealistic responsibility, and the control of safety issues remains a line management responsibility.

- There is an effective information system which helps to identify and assess problems and provide information for those who need it.

- Understandable and practical standards and goals are set at all levels in the organisation: strategic at director level, and operational at other levels. Ways to let people know whether or not these standards/goals are met are agreed.

- Reference is made to the support needed by all personnel to achieve the objectives of the safety policy, i.e. expert advice, information, training and facilities.

- Employees are encouraged/required to co-operate in the safety effort and provision is made for consultation and involvement.

- Provision is made for monitoring, evaluation and revision of the policy by management.

PRODUCT LIABILITY

The main purpose of the Consumer Protection Act (1987) was to remove the need for a consumer to prove negligence on the part of a manufacturer if one of their products had caused injury. The Act stated that this general safety requirement applied to anyone who supplied goods – 'goods' are defined as consumer goods (except crops, water, food, aircraft, motor vehicles, controlled drugs and tobacco). In order to define goods as safe, a comprehensive range of standards have been introduced and continue to be developed.

Liability under the Act extends to components and raw materials, so that if a product contains a defect in a particular component both the manufacture of the finished product and the component manufacturer may be liable.

Printed matter is not covered except in the case of warnings or instructions for a product. Similarly, a design consultant is not liable for a mistake in a design which causes a product to be defective: the producer of the product itself would be liable. Computer software is often supplied as an intrinsic part of a product, and in some cases can cause personal injury (e.g. airline navigation systems or production line robots). Again, liability in such cases is imposed on the producer of the product.

An injured person can take action against producers, importers and/or own-branders:

- ● Producers are usually the manufacturers or in the case of raw materials, the persons who mined or otherwise obtained it.

- ● Importers includes importers into the European Union and not only into the United Kingdom. Where goods are imported into another member state and subsequently sold in the UK, liability rests with the first importer not the UK importer.

- ● 'Own-branders' are suppliers who put their own brand name on the product and give the impression that they are the producers.

Other suppliers such as wholesalers and retailers are not liable unless they fail to identify the producer, importer or own-brander if asked to do so.

ACTIVITY 3

The implications of the Consumer Protection Act (1987) for businesses are quite serious. Businesses must closely examine all their procedures if they are to obtain a 'clean bill of health' under the Act.

Preferably, form into small groups. Devise a short list of the advisable precautions an organisation needs to take if the potential for legal action against it is to be minimised.

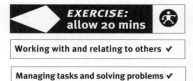

**EXERCISE:
allow 20 mins**

Working with and relating to others ✔

Managing tasks and solving problems ✔

Commentary...

To avoid the problem areas caused by the Act, an organisation needs to consider a number of issues:

- Review procedures and check that each stage of production of goods (design, manufacture, presentation and marketing) ensures that only safe products reach the customer.

- Check whether existing or proposed safety standards (whether approved or not) are applicable and to what extent the firm's products are or could be made to meet the standard.

- Consider the implications of a quality assurance system such as the ISO9000 series (BS5750) in order to document procedures and systems for ensuring quality of production.

- Assess whether the company's insurance cover is adequate, including product liability insurance.

- Review any contractual arrangements with suppliers, customers or others with whom the business has relevant contracts (a business cannot contract out of any liability under the Act, but might seek an indemnity from others in the event of liability).

- Decide whether the records kept by the business are adequate, bearing in mind the working life of the product, the 10-year potential liability for product liability claims, and the possible need to identify suppliers of defective products to the business in defending a product liability action.

In the absence of action on the above points, a manufacturer, an importer or an 'own-brander' may find themselves facing legal action. In this case, there are only six possible defences:

1 the company did not supply the product

2 the state of scientific/technical knowledge at the time the product was supplied was insufficient

3 the defect was caused by compliance with the law

4 the defect was not in the product at the time it was supplied

5 the supplier is no longer in business

6 the defect was due to faulty design of the finished product (in the case of action against a component producer).

INTELLECTUAL PROPERTY RIGHTS

Patents, registered designs, registered trade marks, service marks and copyright give legal recognition to the ownership of new ideas or brand names. They give the proprietor the right to stop other people exploiting his or her 'intellectual' property. These rights may be sold or licensed to others or may be used to safeguard investment in new ventures. Equally, it is possible to waive rights so that ideas and designs may be developed and exploited by anybody.

The Patent Office is responsible for granting patents, registered designs and registered trade and service marks. Since all these rights are essentially territorial, the UK Patent Office grants rights that are effective only in the UK, although the European Patent Convention and the Patent Co-operation Treaty also provide methods of obtaining patent rights in the UK.

\?/ Patents are a monopoly right to the exclusive use of an invention which can last for a maximum of 20 years. A patent must be concerned with the composition, construction, or manufacture of an article, or with an industrial process, rather than artistic creations, mathematical methods or business schemes.

\?/ Registered designs allow monopoly right for the outward appearance of an article of manufacture which lasts for an initial five years but which can be extended in five-yearly terms up to a maximum of 25 years. Not all designs are registerable, such as purely functional designs or where the design of a part is determined by the shape of the whole.

\?/ Copyright is an automatic right to the creators of certain kinds of material such as original literary, dramatic, musical and artistic works. This also includes computer programs. UK copyrights do not lapse until 50 years after the death of the creator.

\?/ Registered trade and service marks provide the exclusive right to use a trade or service symbol and the right to take action against others who might be infringing the registration. These marks may be kept in force indefinitely but renewal fees have to be paid at regular intervals. Registration lasts initially for seven years and renewal fees are payable every subsequent 14 years.

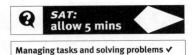

SAT:
allow 5 mins

Managing tasks and solving problems ✓

ACTIVITY 4

Give two examples of each of the following:

- **o** patents

- **o** registered designs

- **o** copyright

- **o** registered trade and service marks.

Commentary...

Patents: Drug formulations, the Black & Decker Workmate

Registered design: The Russell Hobbs electric kettle, designer swimwear, fabric patterns

Copyright: *A Brief History of Time* by Stephen Hawkins, *Cats* by Andrew Lloyd-Webber

Registered trade and service marks: the Texas star, McDonald's sign, the Abbey National logo.

Negotiating

Powerful individuals in any organisation can help or hinder the achievement of an objective. We now begin to concentrate on some of the detailed tactics involved in winning them over. These strategies aim to utilise your power and/or negate theirs. Some of the tactics apply to face-to-face situations, others deal with people at arm's length; some are for immediate effect, others for longer-term results.

At the outset, it is important to emphasise that not all success arises from the exertion of power. At the start of a game of chess both players have the same pieces and an equal time in which to make their moves. The winner is the one whose strategy (plans and determination) and tactics (moves and counter-moves) are more effective.

Let us consider some of these negotiating and influencing strategies. Take the following examples of an action designed to achieve a result:

- A chef shouts at the new staff in the restaurant kitchen to speed up.

- The government imposes sanctions on a foreign government to try to force it to change policies.

- A supervisor forces everyone to do as they are told by threatening to terminate their employment.

Obviously, the characteristic these examples have in common is that all the strategies are based on the exertion of pressure. For simplicity, we call these **'push strategies'**.

This approach often relies on threats. Examples of 'push' behaviour include:

- using **assertiveness** – this is not aggression, but might include checking up on subordinates' work, giving orders, or enforcing the rules

- using **sanctions** – a senior member of staff might prevent pay rises, threaten job security or withhold promotions

- **blocking** – a supervisor might cease to co-operate or refuse requests for overtime.

These strategies are very often extremely successful; they can force employees to change their behaviour. However, this change in behaviour might not mean a change in attitude. So, push strategies might be suitable for you to adopt if you are not particularly concerned with long-term attitudes (although attitudes might change when behaviour has been modified).

Push strategies do have their drawbacks. There is the potential for unpredictable response or negative after-effects. Employees might resent the treatment and fight back, even when they are in an extremely weak position and unlikely to be successful. In this case, the results are likely to be short-lived.

There are alternative strategies which are more likely to have a longer lasting effect, e.g.:

- offering a holiday for two in Australia to the company representative who chalks up the highest level of sales

- the government making extensive financial credits available to a foreign government on the release of political prisoners

- the rapid promotion of outstanding performers in the military services.

These **'pull strategies'** use positive forces rather than threats to influence behaviour. These 'carrots' might include opportunities for recognition, achievement and advancement. Money, bonuses or other tangible rewards are visible factors of pull strategies; the invisible pulls are, for example, charisma or personality of a leader.

Such pull strategies place obvious reliance on one's ability and/or authority to offer rewards, but they also involve other types of power, for example, personality power which usually has to be built up over a lengthy period.

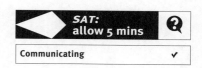

ACTIVITY 5

Identify one case when you have used a push strategy and another case when you have used a pull strategy.

Commentary...

Two possible examples on a personal level are:

- **Push strategy:** 'If you won't help me with my assignment, I won't go down the pub with you on Saturday.'

- **Pull strategy:** 'If you'll lend me those two compact discs, I'll let you borrow my car this evening.'

Obviously, these are examples outside of the working environment, but you can easily translate these verbal strategies to a business situation.

There are a number of different types of strategy which can be used in negotiating with colleagues and staff:

- persuasion strategies

- prevention strategies

- preparatory strategies

- multiple strategies.

PERSUASION STRATEGIES

Both pull and push strategies can be effective in persuading people to do what you want, but what sort of strategy do you use in order to achieve a long-term change in a person's attitudes, values or beliefs? The factors for this purpose would include:

- logic

- compromise

- exchange of views

- give and take

- argument

- negotiation.

You can regard all these as persuasion strategies. Where these rely on reasoning or logical argument to impel someone into or out of a course of action, then there is no hint of push or pull.

Very often, however, persuasion involves a combination of push and pull strategies – give and take. This is particularly appropriate when all parties have power and there is a need to maintain some sort of working relationship afterwards; everyone can come away with some positive outcome – perhaps an equitable sharing of computers, for example. Whereas push and pull strategies often need reinforcement to maintain the change in behaviour, persuasion strategies do not; all parties should come away satisfied.

The selection of strategy depends on many factors, but a major determinant will always be the degree and type of power that you wield. So, what strategies can you use if you do not have sufficient power?

PREVENTIVE STRATEGIES

One strategy is to adopt prevention or delaying tactics. For example, you might wish to delay consideration of an issue or the implementation of a proposal. You might decide to prevent a topic being raised at a meeting by keeping it off the agenda or by surrounding it with really contentious issues. A manager, for example, may not wish to 'loan' two of his staff to another department for a week.

There are many variations on this theme which are very effective, but only in the short term and only as a holding measure while you assemble your forces (or gain more power). By their very nature, employing such strategies means that you are potentially confronting someone with greater authority than you. They might also have the long-term negative effect of indicating that you never do anything constructive; in other words, you lose credibility in your organisation.

Taking steps to prevent things from happening is rather negative and, generally speaking, not recommended. Such actions might be interpreted as those of a desperate person. However, there might be times when you think you have no other option. But, tread carefully with this strategy.

PREPARATORY STRATEGIES

On many occasions, it might be a good idea to employ strategies which guarantee a sympathetic hearing for our ideas. Some activities can pave the way and create the right environment:

- acting in a friendly manner prior to asking for something

- praising someone before setting them a challenging task

- waiting for the right moment to ask for something.

While you might not exercise such cynical strategies yourself, you need to be aware of the times when others are doing so.

When managers can control the environment they sometimes gain the upper hand. They might hold a meeting in their own office, select who will and who will not attend, arrange the seating, order the agenda items, give information to allies and disarm opponents beforehand, etc.

MULTIPLE STRATEGIES

In practice, a manager may use multiple strategies to obtain results from subordinates by offering recognition, more pay or promotion for a good job, together with the threat of disciplinary action for getting it wrong. This is the carrot and the stick, pull and push approach.

If you are developing your influencing style, remember to ring the changes. You might prefer one strategy because it gives good results but your selection of strategy will be affected by a number of other issues.

Factors influencing the choice of strategy by a manager could include:

- the nature of the manager's goals or objectives

- the position and status of the person being influenced

- the contextual setting

- the power base of the manager

- the other people involved, their power levels, goals and strategies.

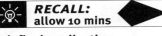

RECALL:
allow 10 mins

Briefly describe the principles of each of the following change strategies:

- **persuasion strategies**

- **prevention strategies**

- **preparatory strategies.**

Managerial roles

The roles that people play in an organisation are only partly determined by the formal job they do. By role, we are referring to 'how the occupant of a particular position in an organisation expects, or is expected, to behave'. People may have the same job status, but the way they do the job differs from one person to another. This difference comes from the range of influences and expectations that are operating on the person. The balance between the factors determines how people do their jobs and carry out their roles. To examine this, we can ask a number of useful questions.

What does the organisation expect?

This information may be defined in one or more of the following:

- job description

- contract or letter of confirmation

- priorities

- standards.

What do people expect of themselves?

This information may be obtained from examining a number of issues:

- beliefs about what should be done

- experience, abilities

- interests

- ambitions.

What do others expect of people?

This information may be obtained by examining some of the following issues:

- their previous experience of people in role

- relationships

- concerns/interests

- their own roles.

There is a constant balancing of the different demands and expectations put on people, and from this balancing act comes the role that people play within an organisation. A role is not a static thing like a job description, but is something that can change as new understanding, skills and relationships are developed. One of the key skills of any person in an organisation is finding the balance, finding the role.

SAT:
allow 30 mins

Working with and relating to others ✔

Managing tasks and solving problems ✔

ACTIVITY 6

Reflect for a moment on your own role, whether you are a full-time student or employed in an organisation. Are you clear what your role is in relation to the different expectations – of the organisation, of yourself, of others – described above?

Talk to your boss and colleagues, or, if you are a student, to your tutor and your fellow students to clarify what they expect of you, and what they think the organisation expects of you.

Commentary...

Overall, your role may present a formal function, recognised and supported by the organisation, with a person designated to manage it and a department established to co-ordinate and/or administer it.

On the other hand, it might be an informal arrangement where everybody contributes to activities as and when the need arises. Done well, this latter type of function can be highly effective, but it is essential that it is clearly negotiated and agreed by all parties, and directed and supported by the organisation.

ROLE DESIGNATIONS

A role designation, or job title, may or may not tell you exactly what a person actually does. In some cases, the job titles tell us more about the place in the organisational hierarchy and level of authority than about what people actually do. These role designations give an indication of the sorts of jobs held by individuals:

- marketing director

- personnel officer

- part-time canteen officer

- systems analyst

- beauty consultant.

Apart from the job titles which are reasonably descriptive, the designations outlined above do not offer much of a clue as to what people do.

A manager needs to ensure that there is a good fit between his or her behaviour and the organisational expectation. The person, together with his or her personal and professional ability and style, needs to match the organisational policies and management style; the better the fit, the more harmonious and effective the professional relationship is likely to be.

In examining role designation, we can consider three aspects: role, culture, and person.

- **Role** refers to the repertoire of behaviours and attitudes generally expected of a person holding a position in an organisation.

- **Culture** refers broadly to the sort of organisation within which the role is located: its history, management styles, values, rituals and typical modes of behaviour.

- **Person** refers to the role occupant's personality, skills and aptitudes, hopes, aspirations and enthusiasms, knowledge and abilities.

When the role occupant has achieved a good fit with the organisation the relationship is considered to be congruent.

This perspective of 'role–person–culture' points to two major requirements for successful managers, they must:

- possess professional management skills

- be able to manage complex social roles.

To be successful, managers have to manage the issue of congruence, or best fit. They need to develop effective and flexible approaches to gain legitimacy and influence.

There is no single role model. A number of types of role have emerged from management and business research, but you must not think that any one is preferable to the others. In practice, a manager in an organisation might find it necessary to vary the role adopted from time to time in order to achieve his or her aims more effectively.

REACTIVE AND PRO-ACTIVE ROLES

The terms 'reactive' and 'pro-active' effectively describe approaches to the job rather than the roles.

Managers who are reactive will stick to the roles and boundaries defined for them. They will do what they are asked to do, but they will not take risks and 'interfere' in anything beyond. They are unlikely to involve themselves in informal or improper activities. These managers may stay in a reactive mode of operation either because they are unaware of the potential influence they could have or because they are afraid of 'rocking the boat'.

A pro-active stance necessitates pushing the boundaries, building new relationships and initiating changes.

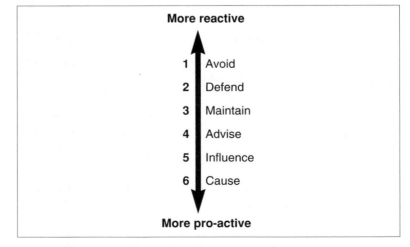

FIGURE 3.1: *Management roles.*

A number of roles may be adopted, as shown in figure 3.1. If we take each of the six types of role in turn, we can explore the possible activities of the manager within each role.

Avoid

At best, a person operating in an 'avoid' role responds to demands of other people in the organisation; they might provide information, resources and administrative support. At worst, they simply hide away and keep busy with operations and administrative tasks.

Defend

This slightly less negative role is still some way from being pro-active. A defensive person responds to demands within certain limits, but actively seek ways of deflecting the views of others who want to change or 'rock the boat' by, for example, pushing for a reallocation of resources.

Maintain

The 'maintainer' comes close to being pro-active, but the focus is on developing methods to improve and maintain existing practices. A high emphasis is placed on improving established systems, procedures and operational activities.

Advise

When requested, advice may be offered to others in the organisation concerned about a potential organisational difficulty. When the manager has identified trouble looming he or she may work with other managers to deal with the oncoming problem.

Influence

This role is significantly pro-active, actively seeking out the holders of power and the holders of information within the organisation. The influencer may take a push stance in which a more active and directive approach is assumed, or a pull stance in which a more persuasive and negotiating approach is assumed.

Cause

This is the most pro-active role taken on by the person. It is also a very rare role, since an individual needs self-confidence and expertise, together with a high degree of credibility within the organisation. Occasionally, he or she may assume a more overt role and set up meetings, courses or workshops to explore the reformist values. The person may also seek to influence individuals at one-to-one informal and formal meetings.

SAT:
allow 15 mins

Managing and developing self ✔

ACTIVITY 7

Consider your own role in your company (or as a student within a learning institution) and identify which of the six roles we have just discussed fits you closest. Do you believe that the use of this role influences in any way the organisation and how resources are used? If not, why not? How could you be more effective?

BOUNDARY MANAGEMENT

Any manager has a particular set of responsibilities. Outside this boundary, all the other activities in the organisation take place, e.g. production, marketing, research and development, personnel and finance.

Boundary management refers to the way in which any function (or manager's job and area of responsibility) relates to the other elements in its environment. These exchanges include how the function:

- acquires its resources and delivers its services

- exercises influence

- builds relationships and activates its image

- protects its integrity, territory and technological core from environmental pressure and threat

- co-ordinates activities with other units, roles and organisations.

In more simple terms, the exchanges refer to the relationship between the manager and the rest of the organisation. Erosion of this boundary can occur for a number of reasons:

- lack of support for the function from senior management

- no overall management of the function and no direction through a company policy

- management of the function that is too narrow and does not meet the operational needs of the organisation, forcing individual managers to make their own arrangements.

ACTIVITY 8

Construct for yourself a role map. With you in the centre, the role map should show all the people with whom you interact during the normal course of your work, or study.

Your role map should identify people to whom you report, with the arrows pointing away from you, and people who come to you, with the arrows pointing in towards you. Use people's names rather than their job titles, because it is with individual people that you interact.

The role map should help you to understand the concept of the role set; the people who are affected by the role you choose to play and who also influence your choice of role.

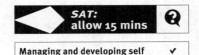

SAT:
allow 15 mins

Managing and developing self   ✔

Co-ordinating activities

Henri Fayol (*Administration Industrielle et Generale*, 1916), an experienced general manager of a French mining and metallurgical company, undertook an analytical study of the management process in which he identified five elements: planning, organising, command, co-ordination and control.

Fayol defined co-ordination as the need 'to keep all activities in balance and in suitable combination'. Though Fayol was writing at the beginning of the century, the importance of co-ordination as a function of management has endured.

Looked at strategically, businesses have three kinds of resources: human, physical and financial. The human resources include all the employees of the organisation: directors, managers, sales representatives, secretaries. The physical resources encompass buildings, equipment, materials, transport, etc.; financial resources include both the money available for capital investment and current expenditure.

These resources need to be linked together in order to achieve business objectives and maintain a company's longer-term survival.

One way in which company indicates that activities do not function independently but mesh together is the organisation chart. These charts illustrate the groupings of responsibilities and the specific authority relationships that arise between the groups.

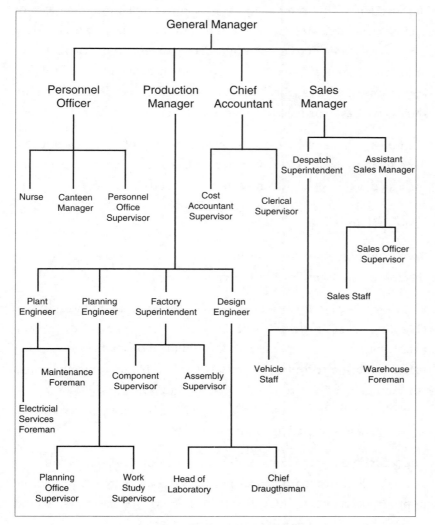

FIGURE 3.2: *A company organisation chart.*

Figure 3.2 shows an organisational chart for a medium-sized manufacturing company, which has identified the functions to be carried out and indicated how these functions are linked together. It also produces job descriptions to clarify individual responsibilities and to ensure that there is no overlapping of duties.

In these ways, organisations aim to achieve a balance between the work which has to be performed. They define individual responsibilities, providing (in the terms we used earlier) role descriptions and designation, and they set out functional responsibilities, i.e. they set the boundaries between different functions.

In Section 1, we looked at the stages in organisational development. Particularly relevant here is the move from the pioneer phase to the scientific phase. You should recall that pioneer organisations are very often successful until there is pressure for change – a growth in size is one pressure. This pressure puts a strain on existing management systems. As firms develop – and move to the scientific phase – they find they need new systems procedures, standardisation, specialisation, a clear management hierarchy and formal communications systems. In other words, they need to co-ordinate their activities in order to survive and develop.

A number of examples of the interrelationship of activities and the need to attain balance occur through this module. Specific examples include discipline, health and safety and product liability.

Discipline

Two particular lessons can be drawn from the management of discipline cases (see Section 1, Session 6).

The first relates to the need for a measured response to indiscipline. Organisations are faced with a number of potential discipline problems, ranging from unreliability and insubordination to criminal offences. The appropriate responses range from counselling and retraining to a system of warnings culminating in dismissal. The important point here is the need to provide a balanced organisational response to unacceptable employee activity.

The second point highlights the interrelationship between recruitment and selection procedures and performance at work. A pro-active approach to reducing discipline cases is to try to ensure that 'round pegs' are employed to fill 'round holes'.

Health and Safety at Work Act (1974)

This Act is an external constraint on company behaviour. The Act brought the need for a new function, the safety officer (or a manager with responsibility for safety) and it forces firms to define or redefine working relationships and plan work to ensure safety.

The Act requires that companies develop a safety policy reflecting certain principles, including:

- adequate resources are allocated and priorities set for the identification, assessment and control or elimination of hazards

- management responsibility for health and safety rank equally with responsibility for sales and finance

- non-line responsibilities are defined and the relationships between safety advisor, other specialists and line managers are made clear

- the nominated safety officer is not burdened with disproportionate or unrealistic responsibility.

These principles direct a company's attention to the need to define properly the interrelationships and balance between them. It requires the co-ordination of the company's human, physical and financial resources.

Product Liability Act (1987)

Following the Health and Safety at Work Act, we looked briefly at another external constraint.

Here we will briefly highlight one issue that the Act requires organisations to consider: 'The review of procedures to check that all stages of the production of goods (design, manufacture, presentation and marketing) help to ensure that only safe products meet the customer.' This requirement shows that functions do not operate independently and in isolation but have a bearing on each other – there is a need to co-ordinate them.

Planning and co-ordinating techniques

In different parts of this book, we feature three techniques of work planning which help to co-ordinate and balance work being carried out. In Section 2, Session 1, we examined critical path analysis (CPA) and method study.

The central focus of CPA is to identify specific activities that hold up a whole process or project if they themselves are held up. In other words, CPA identifies the interrelationship of specific activities within a chain of work and looks to co-ordinate the sequence in which they are carried out.

Method study is similar in one sense to CPA, in that it looks at the working process. It asks critical questions about work – its purpose, where it is carried out, its sequence, who does it and how it is done. It deals in detail with the relationship of tasks – e.g. operation, transport and inspection – with the intention of improving the production and working methods.

In the final session of the book, we study value analysis. This is concerned with the provision of a product or service which is acceptable to a customer at the least possible production cost. In the majority of cases, it is carried out by multi-function teams drawn from various departments within the company. The key point, from a co-ordination point of view, is the need to bring together experts from different disciplines in order to achieve effective results.

SAT:
allow 30 mins

| Communicating | ✔ |
| Managing tasks and solving problems | ✔ |

ACTIVITY 9

Identify the means by which your company co-ordinates its resources. If you are not currently employed, arrange an interview at a local company to discuss how they achieve co-ordination.

Write a 150-word report, summarising the main points in the box below.

Commentary...

While we cannot comment specifically on how the company you chose achieves co-ordination, we can make a number of general observations.

- It is likely that your company, unless it employs a very small number of people, has produced an organisation chart and job descriptions.

- Unless the company you looked at is medium-sized or large, and particularly concerned with manufacture, assembly or one-off projects, you probably found it did not use the techniques of critical path analysis, method study or value analysis.

- You may have discovered the use of co-ordinators for some activities, possibly the co-ordination of sales teams. (Some educational establishments, for example, use co-ordinators with responsibilities for particular areas of study, such as open learning.)

- Lastly, you may have found that the company utilises teams and particularly committees to ensure resources are co-ordinated.

summary

This session has consider some of the constraints on management action. It has discussed how managers can operate effectively within these constraints.

▶ Managers need to be fully aware of external factors which might constrain their scope for action.

▶ The regulatory framework is one important example of an external constraint which impacts on management activities. More generally, managers can assess the external environment using PESTLE (political, economic, social, technological, legislative, environmental) techniques.

▶ Within an organisation, conflicting demands and priorities mean that managers need good negotiating skills to achieve their objectives.

▶ Negotiating approaches include push strategies (largely relying on threats) and pull strategies (based on rewards). More sophisticated strategies involve persuasion, prevention and preparation.

▶ The role a manager adopts is influenced by three sets of expectations: the expectations of their employers, the expectations of the individual, and those of colleagues.

▶ Managers should be aware of the role they are adopting and how their responsibilities relate to and map with the rest of their organisation.

▶ Few jobs are self-contained. In business, it is important to co-ordinate activities effectively. A clear understanding of organisational responsibilities, together with planning tools such as method study, provides the basis for effective operations.

Review and monitoring

ESTABLISHING
PERFORMANCE STANDARDS

REVIEWING PERFORMANCE
STANDARDS

COMPETENCES

VALUE ANALYSIS

AUDITING

SYSTEMS ANALYSIS

THE IMPACT OF NEW
TECHNOLOGY

Objectives

After participating in this session, you should be able to:

- describe the issues involved in product or service specification

- describe the range of activities to be considered when reviewing standards

- explain what competence is and how it is accredited

- describe and use the process of value analysis

- explain the objectives, components and skills of auditing

- describe four approaches to systems analysis

- describe the uses of a number of new technologies.

In working through this session, you will practise the following BTEC common skills:

Managing and developing self	✔
Working with and relating to others	✔
Communicating	✔
Managing tasks and solving problems	✔
Applying numeracy	
Applying technology	
Applying design and creativity	

Establishing performance standards

The development and setting of clear and unambiguous standards for products or services has evolved over a long period of time. These days, it is commonplace for standards to be recorded in the form of product or service specifications.

Specifications are important because they provide the basis for the achievement of quality standards. There are different approaches that may be adopted depending on whether products are being produced for established customers or whether products and services are being developed for new (and potentially unknown) customers.

WHERE THERE IS AN ESTABLISHED CUSTOMER

Where there is an established business relationship, the specification for a new product or service is usually discussed and negotiated between the supplier and the customer before any order for supply is placed or accepted. The main advantage for the supplier in clearly defining the specification is that this should guarantee that realistic requirements are set which are both within the technical and resource capabilities of the organisation and at a realistic price that will make a profit for the business. The advantage for customers is that they can ensure that the specifications meet their needs to an agreed quality standard.

In most organisations, it has been traditional for the salesman and the buyer to agree the sales contract between them. In establishing the details of the specification, however, it may be necessary to involve a number of different people from other functions as well. So, for example, suppliers may want to involve their technical and production staff, to advise on design and manufacturing matters as they have specialised knowledge about the company's production capabilities.

Customers may also decide to involve their own technical and production staff – the people who will use the purchased items and should be able to talk about the real needs better than the buyer alone could. In this way, the supplier acquires a good knowledge of the customer's processes, the use to which the products will be put, and the capabilities of the customer in using the products.

It is important that specifications should be clear and understood by both parties. If there is any doubt on either side, there may be trouble later on as perceptions and interpretations of the required quality standards may differ.

Where the customer is unknown

When companies develop new product lines, they obviously cannot work with actual customers – there is no product. Instead, company departments must work together to anticipate the basic requirements of potential customers. In these situations, the customer could be said to be potentially everyone. However, most companies apply traditional marketing techniques to identify the potential market segments at which to target their new (or adapted) products and services.

Specifications can then be drawn up. These specifications are as important as those drawn up for established customers as they will be used as a basis for communication with prospective customers. For example, a company might promote its products in catalogues or data sheets. These would contain a certain amount of technical detail, depending on the nature of the product. Likely uses for the products would be anticipated and included in the publicity material.

In some cases, potential customers might also want to test the products to establish that they do meet the published standards. This independent confirmation of product conformity can be useful to a company in promoting the product.

When a company chooses to publish product standards or technical specifications, it can apply to an independent certification body for product approval. This independent body will carry out checks and tests to assess that the product is in conformity with the published specification, and then issue a certificate or mark of conformity. The most commonly known of these independent conformity marks is the BSI 'Kitemark'.

Independent standards have been in existence for many years. They apply to specific products or services to show that they meet the requirements of some widely accepted and published standards body. Most of these bodies produce marks such as the BSI 'Kitemark' and they will arrange tests through NATLAS accredited laboratories.

Designing to standards

Many of the quality systems, procedures and standards which should be used in an organisation will stem from the planning and design stage of the operation. Each department should be clearly focused not only on the customer's requirements for delivery and service schedules but also on product and service capability and specification standards.

The design function is critical to the setting of standards by an organisation. It involves several activities:

- Advising and working with customers, helping to identify their specific requirements, e.g. a clothing supply company might work with a major building society to design new staff uniforms.

- Assessing the technical feasibility of manufacturing a product or providing a service to the required standards, including an assessment of economic feasibility. This requires exhaustive market research in order to make a judgement on the potential sales.

- Translating the required product or service features and characteristics into clear design standards and specifications, including drawings. This is necessary in the case of products in engineering or plastics, for example.

- Specifying packaging requirements and special instructions for handling, storage and transportation or, in the case of services, specifying support services and resources, including after-sales activities.

Design considerations need to be taken into account during early negotiations with a customer, since customers may know their own requirements but they may want advice on how they actually may be met. Some customers rely totally on their suppliers to advise them on design aspects. At the other end of the scale, some customers know precisely what they want, and provide the supplier with detailed specifications and drawings. Usually though, the customer and supplier form a long-term relationship and work together. In this way, potential problems can be foreseen and overcome.

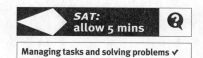

ACTIVITY 1

In determining the clear specification for a product at the design stage, what are the main factors that need to be considered by the designer? Imagine, for example, that you were just about to embark upon designing a new car or a new television set.

Commentary...

There are several factors that designers should always consider at a very early stage:

- technical feasibility

- quality control issues

- good communications.

Technical feasibility requires a careful assessment of whether the product or service is actually within the capability of the organisation, i.e. it assesses whether it is technically possible for the quality standard specified to be achieved. The assessment considers whether, given the company resources of machinery, equipment, buildings and people, production can be achieved economically and within the time-scale discussed with the customer.

Designers need to consider **quality control issues**. They need to assess the suitability of the product or service for economic quality control and conformance to specification. This is a necessary part of any design specification since it is important to recognise when there is an element of non-conformance.

There is no point in designing a product or service if it cannot be checked during its development, manufacture or preparation to see if it is complying with its specification.

Good communications are important so that everyone involved in the eventual production and selling of the product or service has clear specifications, setting out the main features and characteristics of service.

A great deal of time may be saved if attention is given at the design stage to developing a very clear specification not only for the product or service itself, but also for the purchasing requirements, production or work methods, and the quality control methods to be used to discover whether agreed standards are being met.

PRODUCT SPECIFICATIONS

Every business must find out exactly what their customers want. This is often expressed by the customer in terms of the required performance of the product or service concerned.

Once firms have established customers' requirements, they have to identify the features of the product or service that affect its ability to meet these requirements. Usually these are specified in two main ways:

- in physical terms – dimensions, weight, colour, shape, finish.

- in performance terms – strength, durability, behaviour under certain conditions.

At this point, workable specifications can be drawn up:

- product specifications including drawings to cover all characteristics

- details of work methods to be used for every stage of manufacture

- purchase specifications so that the right materials and components can be bought in

- quality control methods giving details of tasks and inspections

- specifications for the design and development process itself.

SERVICE SPECIFICATIONS

A service may be described as a set of standards for the individual provider of the service to follow. Guarantees are often provided against which the user or customer may be able to take action of some kind should the service be unacceptable. The guarantees may be couched in terms of time, cost, accuracy or performance.

These standards are often contained in documents such as British Rail's *Passenger Charter* or the National Health Service's *Patients' Charter*. Even the government has issued its own *Citizens' Charter*. These 'charters' are really only copying the principle of service contracts or service agreements that many smaller organisations have been supplying to their customers for years.

Some companies are now also beginning to define and agree standards for ancillary services such as invoice speed, response to complaints, replacement of faulty goods, or speed of delivery.

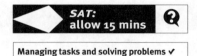

SAT:
allow 15 mins

Managing tasks and solving problems ✓

ACTIVITY 2

If you are employed, examine one of your company's products or services. List the specifications and standards attached to it. Are there any other standards that you think should be attached to it?

If you are a student, examine and list the specifications that may be attached to a service provided by the learning establishment in which you are operating.

Commentary...

Look at your list and check whether all these specifications are actually up-to-date and, more importantly, whether everyone in the organisation adheres to them in normal operations. Are they documented? If so, is everyone aware of the documents and do they have easy access to them?

Reviewing performance standards

Performance standards have a large impact on a business. They constrain not only managers, but all other employees in some way: through working to technical specifications, designing publicity materials to agreed standards, responding to complaints within a given time and so on. Performance standards, to a greater or lesser extent, circumscribe the way in which individuals work.

In any organisation, the job of employees is to translate all the specifications into reality efficiently and consistently. This, of course, can only be achieved if people know precisely what is expected of them and if they have adequate resources to enable them to achieve the required standards.

It is important that details of making the product or providing the service are worked out at the same time as the controls necessary to see that products or services meet the standards laid down. In other words, a business needs to pay as much attention to 'how it will provide a service' as it does to specifying 'what service it will provide'.

So, for example, a business might have to manage and set standards for the following tasks:

- obtain specifications from design/development

- plan production resources

- order materials

- install machinery

- train people

- schedule work

- devise quality procedures

- check quality of trial output

- carry out capability studies, if not done previously

- do trial runs to check process methods, test product samples

- produce products or services to required quality standard

- carry out regular control checks

- handle transport and store items to preserve quality

- keep records

- carry out regular reviews periodically and audit the system.

SAT:
allow 5 mins

Managing tasks and solving problems ✓

ACTIVITY 3

The manager of a production area in an effective organisation would have advance notice of future production needs. This will enable the manager to organise, for example, the scheduling of trial runs and the delivery of raw materials at the right time.

List two more activities that the production manager will need to organise.

Commentary...

Other kinds of activities or tasks the manager needs to organise include:

- adequate resourcing of equipment, material, and people

- training of people for new skills

- need for capability studies.

We have stressed that the required features and characteristics of each product should be clearly specified. These specifications are normally divided into two categories: variables and attributes.

> !?! **Variables** are characteristics that can be measured and have identified tolerance levels. Variables such as dimensions and weights can be directly measured.
>
> !?! **Attributes** are characteristics which are not measured quantitatively, either because they cannot be, or because it is not convenient to do so. In the specification it is important to establish two facts for each attribute. The first is the level below which the customer will not accept the product or service, a minimum acceptable quality standard, and the second is an acceptable quality level (AQL).

For each product or service characteristic that has been specified, you need some means of assessing whether or not the standard has been met. The assessment or control techniques should be in writing. This is often termed a control plan or an inspection and test plan.

If an organisation is registered as having achieved ISO9000/BS5750 or is moving towards accreditation, it is likely to have a reasonable range of testing, sampling, inspection and monitoring systems in place. ISO9000/BS5750 only requires fairly infrequent audits from external auditors. In practice, the frequency of the more specific tests and checks to be carried out varies according to:

- the potential for variance of materials, components or human performance

- the size of the task in terms of amounts of materials, components or frequency of the task

- the criticality of the potential faults, failures or defects in the materials, components or human performance.

There is a strong emphasis on performance controls in ISO9000/BS5750 and if used effectively these can provide valuable data. Such controls include:

- contract reviews between the manufacturer and customers

- purchasing controls

- inspection and test results

- identified non-conformance of material, product or system

- segregation of non-conforming items

- internal audits.

Corrective action procedures are also given strong emphasis.

Although ISO9000/BS5750 provides useful guidance, the systems it outlines are oriented towards controlling products. Companies should also take steps to control the production process itself. If the process is not right, then the resulting product will never be right.

Any activity in an organisation may be considered as a process, for example:

- taking an order from a customer

- placing an order with a supplier

- sending an invoice

- delivering a specific service to a customer

- assembling a product

- making up a load for despatch

- dealing with an enquiry or complaint.

All processes may be reviewed for their ability to meet the requirements of the customer and their own internal company standards. The ways in which these processes may be assessed can include measurement, testing, inspection, sampling, observing. Initially, it is essential that the organisation defines the process being investigated as clearly as possible.

SAT:
allow 10 mins

Managing tasks and solving problems ✓

ACTIVITY 4

Students on this course are required to undertake assignments. This can be regarded as a process. List below the stages of this process. What controls may be exercised to ensure quality?

Commentary...

For **process**, you may have included:

- understanding the question

- doing research/interviewing people/background reading

- producing a preliminary draft

- modifying the preliminary draft

- word processing

- handing to tutor.

For **controls**, you may have:

- checking your facts

- spell checking

- tutor observation.

Whenever a problem surfaces – and this may not be until a production operator, quality control inspector or even a customer spots it – it is vital to investigate how and why it occurred, until the real causes are exposed. This may mean crossing departmental boundaries, until all the possible factors causing or influencing the problem are established.

Once the whole picture or scope of the process is established, separate strands can be investigated in turn. Each of these can also be viewed as a process. Different people will be involved depending on which process is suspected as faulty. The problem has to be identified and defined very precisely. This might sound obvious, but does in fact require considerable skill. For example, the problem is usually seen differently by different people, so the first step is to decide which is the real problem.

As **John Oakland** (*Total Quality Management: the route to improving performance,* 2nd edn, Butterworth Heinemann, 1994) says: 'The question that many companies are continuously asking themselves is: "Have we done the job correctly?".' He suggests that this is not quality control, it is detection (post production) of a bad product or service before it hits the customer. The natural tendency is to rush into detection mode. Instead, it is necessary to ask a different question: 'Are we capable of doing the job correctly?'

Corrective action

Prevention should be the key principle rather than detection. But in the real world, no organisation has the ideal or perfect system for prevention of errors and non-conformance. All businesses have to take a significant amount of corrective action:

- At the simplest level, the inspector may take the corrective action required or alert a supervisor that output is not meeting the quality standard so that the problem can be investigated and further corrective action taken.

- On each occasion, a record should be kept of the problem and the corrective action, so that steps can be taken to ensure that the problem does not arise again.

- Every employee in an organisation has a key role in taking corrective action since problems, errors, failures and non-conformance accrue across the range of functions and stages of production or delivery.

Competences

> **\?/ Competence** is the ability to perform activities within an occupation to the standards expected in employment. The concept also embodies the ability to transfer skills and knowledge to new situations within the occupational area and beyond to related occupations.

Competence is the ability to perform a task to a given standard. It is the description of something that a person who works in a specific occupation should be able to do. It is an action, behaviour or outcome that a person who works in a specific occupation should be able to demonstrate.

A competence should:

- make sense to the workers, trainees, and trainers

- be related to what actually happens in the workplace

- be an activity which has an outcome

- be demonstrable

- be observable

- be assessable

- be transferable.

In 1986, the National Council for Vocational Qualifications (NCVQ) was established to achieve reform and rationalisation of the vocational qualification system in the UK. The council's aims are to:

- improve vocational qualifications by basing them on standards of competence required in employment

- establish a framework of National Vocational Qualifications (NVQs) which is comprehensible, comprehensive, and facilitates access, progression, and continued learning.

The NCVQ method is to accredit existing competences and to develop new qualifications where none exist at present. It seeks to ensure that qualifications awarded by relevant bodies are in line with the standards of competence demanded by employers. Qualifications are currently accredited at five levels of competence. It is intended that a competence-based system will ultimately encompass all professional qualifications.

The competences are established by representatives from industry who form Industry Lead Bodies – one for each of the key industries in the UK. For example, the lead body for management is an organisation called the Management Charter Initiative (MCI).

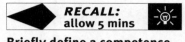

RECALL:
allow 5 mins

Briefly define a competence, and list its various attributes.

A system for accrediting competences has been set up. Lead bodies may themselves apply for approval as accreditors in a particular industry. They are then able to accredit people against established NCVQ standards. Any person wishing to be accredited – and so gain credit towards a vocational qualification – usually has to provide a portfolio of achievements and be observed carrying out tasks associated with the competency to the required standard. The process is illustrated in figure 4.1.

```
┌─────────────────────────────────────────────────┐
│                       Unit                        │
│                     Element                       │
│               Performance criteria                │
└─────────────────────────────────────────────────┘
                          │
                          ▼
   Determine the form and amount of evidence to be collected through a
                 combination of the following methods
                          │
                          ▼
┌──────────────────────────┬──────────────────────────┐
│ Performance evidence     │ Supplementary evidence   │
├──────────────────────────┼──────────────────────────┤
│ ● Natural observation in │ ● Multiple choice tests  │
│   the workplace          │ ● Computer assisted      │
│ ● Extracted examples     │   learning tests         │
│ ● Simulations            │ ● Open written answers   │
│ ● Competency tests,      │   (short responses, long │
│   skills tests, projects │   essays, etc.)          │
│   and assignments        │ ● Oral questioning       │
└──────────────────────────┴──────────────────────────┘
                          │
                          ▼
┌─────────────────────────────────────────────────┐
│         Evidence from prior achievements          │
│ (reports, designs, computer programs, certificates,│
│              testimonials etc.)                   │
└─────────────────────────────────────────────────┘
                          │
                          ▼
┌─────────────────────────────────────────────────┐
│              Portfolio assessed                   │
│            Accreditation verified                 │
└─────────────────────────────────────────────────┘
```

FIGURE 4.1: *Competence assessment: the accreditation process for NVQs.*

Each competency is usually defined in terms of:

- units – the overall task

- elements – the sub-tasks

- performance criteria – the observable measures of performance of competence.

Here is a simple example of how this works in practice. In the Hotel and Catering industry, a unit could be:

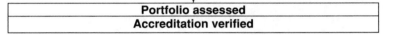

PREPARING SHELLFISH

Elements describe the smaller tasks within the unit; for example, in the unit above, elements could be:

1. Preparing and cooking frozen or fresh shellfish
2. Finishing shellfish for service

Performance criteria are the points that you would look for to say someone was competent. For example, in the first element above, performance criteria could be:

a) Work area prepared and free from obstruction.

b) Clean equipment of correct type and size assembled and prepared for use.

c) Ingredients are of correct quantity and type for amount to be prepared.

d) Shellfish selected is of correct quality. Free from abnormal odour, of correct colour, undamaged and intact.

e) Shellfish washed in clean, fresh, cold water and rinsed well. Excess water removed.

f) Shellfish cooked by appropriate methods.

g) Served immediately or stored appropriately.

ACTIVITY 5

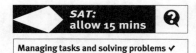

SAT:
allow 15 mins

Managing tasks and solving problems ✔

Take a simple task with which you are familiar, either in your working situation or in social life, and carry out a simple analysis of it in terms of elements and performance criteria.

Commentary...

If the task you selected was a large one, you would have had the problem of trying to define what is a unit and what is an element. This is one of the common difficulties facing the Industry Lead Bodies when developing competences.

In addition to this, the bodies are faced with another definition problem: that of describing the various circumstances in which the unit and elements would have to be performed in, for the person performing to be deemed competent.

In your task, you may have faced this problem as well. To overcome this concern, all competences are now accompanied by a **range statement** which is simply a description of all the relevant circumstances under which the unit may have to be performed. It also incorporates all the different materials, and equipment that may have to be used.

One of the key advantages of a competency system is that it makes life easier for trainers in devising their instruction plans or training sessions, because they have clear definitions of the skills required.

There are many other benefits of competency-based training and assessment:

- Structured training leads to efficiency and effectiveness.

- It offers systematic skill development.

- It requires greater flexibility and multi-skilling.

- Recognition of individual achievement is made possible.

- It allows more effective use of staff within budgets.

- It demonstrates competence to existing or potential customers.

- It provides access to staff skill profiles, which helps planning.

- It helps to justify rewards.

- It provides a basis for training plans.

- It enables accurate assessment of skills.

Value analysis

Before we explore the technique of value analysis, let us examine what the word 'value' actually represents. It can be argued that there are usually two types of value within a product or service: esteem value and use value.

- **Esteem value** is directly connected to the status, image or level of regard attached to owning the product or receiving the service.

- **Use value** is related to the function of the product or service – its ability to perform or deliver its specific purpose.

Value analysis is concerned with both of these definitions, although use value is by far the biggest component.

Ray Wild (*Production and Operations Management*, Cassell 1989) has defined value analysis as 'a functionally oriented scientific method for improving product value by relating the elements of product worth to their corresponding elements of cost in order to accomplish the required function at the least cost in resources'. A slightly less complex description of the technique would be that it is an organised approach to achieve the same performance, or better, at a lower cost without affecting quality.

Value analysis is a common-sense approach to product and service design or re-design. It comprises the following stages:

1. Collect information to determine the key function of the product or service.

2. Develop alternative methods of achieving the required function, usually by means of new designs for the product or service.

3. Cost and evaluate these alternative designs.

4. Recommend the most cost-effective design, and implement it.

INFORMATION COLLECTION

This first stage has to be undertaken from a customer's perspective. The customer's requirements are the main base of information:

- What does the customer want the product or service to do?

- What appearance does the customer require of the product or service?

- How much esteem is associated with possession of the product or receipt of the service?

- Is price an important consideration for the customer?

- How concerned is the customer about the replacement, exchange or disposal costs of the product or service?

SAT:
allow 15 mins

Managing tasks and solving problems✔

ACTIVITY 6

From a personal point of view, select a product which you possess or a service which you use and, as a customer, answer the five questions from the first stage of value analysis:

1 What do you want the product or service to do?

2 What appearance do you require of the product or service?

3 How much esteem do you attach to possession of the product or receipt of the service?

4 Is price an important factor in your decision to buy?

5 How concerned are you about replacement, exchange or disposal costs of the product or service?

Commentary...

You may like to reflect on whether you think that your answers to the above questions would be typical for other customers of the product or service you considered. In value analysis, these considerations will have to be taken into account, and a marketing or sales representative would at this stage of the analysis try to obtain a clear picture of customer requirements. They would want to know the spread of opinion.

DEVELOPING ALTERNATIVE METHODS

The second stage, developing alternative methods of achieving the required function, is a speculative and creative phase, but one where certain procedures may be followed. In looking for cost savings, you might consider designs which:

- eliminate parts, materials or operations

- simplify parts, materials or operations

- substitute alternative materials

- use standard parts, materials or operations

- relax tolerances or standards

- eliminate unnecessary design features

- change the design to make manufacture or service delivery more efficient

- buy in cheaper parts, materials or operations

- use prefabricated or prefinished parts

- rationalise product ranges

- eliminate waste.

COSTING AND EVALUATION

In the third stage, the alternative designs must be considered on a financial basis. All aspects of the alternative design should be costed using information from purchasing, production, service delivery and accounts. Adopt the discipline of examining thoroughly every possible alternative without eliminating any before complete analysis. Key questions should be asked at this stage:

- Which areas of the product or service appear to offer the largest savings?

- What percentage of costs are associated with bought-in items or services?

- What percentage of cost is associated with labour?

- What percentage of cost is associated with materials?

The main objective of value analysis is to increase profit and cost effectiveness by means of a critical examination of areas of high cost.

MAKING RECOMMENDATIONS

The final stage of value analysis, recommendation and implementation of the most cost-effective design, should then go ahead. In some cases, firms use a pilot or trial service period as the first part of the implementation phase. If the analysis has been carried out properly, the result should not be an inferior product or service but rather a product or service whose value and cost relationship has been improved, and one which provides the necessary function with the essential qualities at a minimum cost.

Value analysis can of course be carried out by individuals, or by a group of individuals, each working on a separate part of the analysis. However, practice has shown that the most effective way is through the use of teams whose members can be drawn from various functions within the organisation.

Auditing

> **\!?\!** The dictionary definition of **audit** is an 'official, searching examination'. Financial audits are required to check the accounting procedures of a company. The term **'quality audit'** is usually used to refer to searching checks on the way tasks and activities are organised.

There are several possible reasons for auditing, e.g.:

- to establish, from objective evidence, whether a procedure is under control, i.e. to check the proper procedure is being followed, it does work, and there are no hints that all is not as it should be

- to determine if a system as implemented is effective in helping the company to meet its quality objectives

- to provide factual evidence on which to base improvements.

Many organisations, if they are within the national standards system such as ISO9000/BS5750, are already subject to regular audits of their quality systems by external auditing agencies. However, leaving the maintenance of systems to external bodies is not good business practice and there should always be a regular system of in-company checks.

A quality audit:

- must have a procedure which should be followed systematically – the procedure defines what is to be examined, how and where

- needs to be carried out by someone who knows how the quality system should operate, and who is astute and independent enough to see what is actually happening.

So, let us examine in a little more detail the components of an audit of procedures and systems, including the issue of objective evidence and auditor skills.

PROCEDURE

A procedure is a document which details the purpose and scope of an activity and specifies how it is to be properly carried out; it usually contains the following elements:

- purpose, i.e. what activity does it control

- scope, i.e. who does it apply to, by function, department, etc.

- references

- definitions

- procedure description, including who does what, how, when, where and why

- documentation, i.e. what documents to use, records to keep, etc.

On reading a procedure, you should be able to see clearly what needs to be done, without ambiguity, over-complication or omission. It is preferable for all the procedures to follow a common format. It makes them easier to follow, and easier to check and audit.

CARRYING OUT AN AUDIT

There are seven main stages:

1. Produce a schedule.

2. Warn the people involved and agree the programme.

3. Review the current documentation including previous audit reports.

4. Develop a checklist.

5. Carry out the audit.

6. Complete a report including corrective action requests.

7. Follow up.

A sample document, typical of those which may be used in auditing procedures, is shown in figure 4.2. It is an overall systems review and audit form on which a system is audited, corrective action recommended and implemented (and signed for) and any follow-up action also recorded.

AUDIT REPORT

A. THE REPORT:

Signed (Auditor):

Date:

B. CORRECTIVE ACTION TAKEN:

Signed (Person responsible for correction):

Re-audit date:

C. FOLLOW–UP ACTION:

Signed (Manager):

Date:

Signed (Auditor):

Date:

FIGURE 4.2: *Systems review and audit form.*

ACTIVITY 7

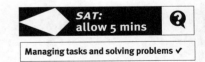

SAT: allow 5 mins

Managing tasks and solving problems ✔

Describe two ways in which objective evidence may be found in an audit.

Commentary...

Objective evidence can be found by:

- examining documents, records and test results

- observing what is done

- taking measurements if appropriate

- interviews with people – these, however, should only be accepted as objective evidence if they can be verified, e.g. by reference to records.

AUDITOR SKILLS

An audit is a systematic and independent examination intended to maintain or improve the performance of tasks and activities. Auditors must stifle their natural inclinations; they must avoid drawing conclusions, must not interpret what they see nor make allowances for production or other pressures. They must avoid all subjective interpretation. The two most important skills needed by auditors are impartiality and objectivity.

The auditor has to find out what actually happens, not what should happen – not what people say happens, but what actually happens. He or she can only do this by seeking out objective evidence through asking questions:

- Was the document completed as specified?

- Was the temperature specified reached?

- Did the envelope contain all the documents specified?

- Was the check or test done as and when specified?

- Did copies of the document reach the people identified in the procedure?

More open and subjective questions may be asked if the auditor is seeking for ways in which the quality system can be improved, where it may be quite valid to ask questions like:

- Should it be done this way or is there a better way?

- Does this procedure actually provide enough information? Is it clear, unambiguous, complete, not over-complex?

- Would it not be better if the operators did this, rather than rely on the supervisor?

- Why is this procedure not followed?

Further skills needed by auditors include being logical, precise, literate and constructive. They need to demonstrate:

- an understanding of the requirements of the system

- clear and concise report writing on findings

- ideas for recommending corrective action

- ideas for recommending improvements to the system.

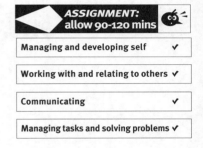

ASSIGNMENT: allow 90-120 mins	
Managing and developing self	✔
Working with and relating to others	✔
Communicating	✔
Managing tasks and solving problems	✔

ACTIVITY 8

This assignment is designed to practise the skills of auditing including effective questioning technique.

Conduct a small study of an observable service standard. You might, for example, choose queuing times – at McDonald's, at a bank or at a railway ticket office. You might choose a company you work for or with whom have good contacts. For the service that forms the basis of your study, find the answers to the following questions:

- Are there established standards of service?

- Who has set the particular standard?

- What is it?

- How is it measured?

- How is it checked and how frequently?

- What corrective action is taken if the standard is not being met?

Using the headings on the report form shown in figure 4.2, make separate notes on the specific questions you ask of various people, together with the answers you receive. Explain how you would propose to undertake a fuller study of service standards in this organisation.

Write your answer on separate sheets of paper and summarise your findings below in the box below.

Systems analysis

Systems can comprise human, technological, psychological, information systems and many others.

Significant changes have occurred in technology over the last two decades which have made the task of those who develop the systems more complex. Twenty years ago, systems were developed using established knowledge procedures. Design effort was labour intensive without too many problems. Then, technology had a time constant of approximately five years. Today, the picture has altered dramatically. Now, large and multi-disciplined project teams – difficult in themselves to constitute, organise and manage – are engaged in the design of systems which may involve highly interactive hardware and software.

This broad scenario presents the challenging proposition that there are no longer any 'quick fixes' to complex systems. The provision of more powerful information technology tools, even though they are faster and more sophisticated, is increasingly unsuccessful in reducing or coping with the complexity.

Professor J. Boardman, in his paper *'A Theory for Decision Support in Technology Management'* (unpublished paper, Portsmouth Polytechnic) proposes a soft systems methodology for considering the problem of complexity. Boardman suggests that there are four quadrants (or approaches) currently available and being practised within the realm of systems analysis: messy, fixing, reflective and innovative.

Messy	Innovative
Fixing	Reflecting

FIGURE 4.3: *Boardman's matrix.*

Messy quadrant

In this world, things are accomplished, albeit usually inefficiently and ineffectively. This situation is ill-behaved and unresponsive. It requires the involvement of managers in the mess so that they can deal pragmatically with the issues as they are observed. However, involvement in the messy quadrant carries with it a loss of objectivity and the feeling of 'walking through treacle'.

Fixing quadrant

This world is populated by experts who continuously develop and offer a range of tools, techniques and products with which to provide a 'solution' to the problem. Although this approach sometimes solves a few problems, experts can be dangerously arrogant. They might 'know best', but more often they can add to the complexity of the overall problem and can lose sight of the merits of one solution over another.

Reflecting quadrant

The survivors of tough projects who have found time to dwell on their successes and failures and who are unconvinced of the 'latest breakthroughs' provide us with the population of this quadrant. These people are searching for frameworks and models upon which to base their reflective thinking.

Innovating quadrant

This quadrant exists purely to innovate and create products, tools or behaviours. These then provide a vehicle for the implementation of the findings of the reflectors, so that the inefficiency of the messy quadrant can be reduced, which enables the easier use of standard products and tools provided by the fixing quadrant.

In many companies, the attempt to improve the way activities and tasks are performed through the use of systems analysis are taking place within the 'messy' quadrant. Perhaps ultimately, they are being served by the fixing quadrant. In practice this usually means that the majority of development activities and projects are initiated, carried out, and finished relatively ineffectively and without the most complete and compatible tools, techniques, and processes being used.

Occasionally, you may encounter a unique response to a situation where innovative ideas are put to work on problems and processes which were previously in the patient but unproductive hands of the reflector.

One final point to bear in mind when evaluating the effectiveness of systems is the perceived value of the systems to the users. This, though, may not reflect the actual value of the system but may be more concerned with the personal defence mechanisms and individual preferences of the user. For example, a 'hands-on' practical person may react against what he or she sees as unnecessary paperwork. If genuine problems are being experienced, the engagement of an expert in systems analysis would be worthwhile.

The impact of new technology

These days the term 'technology' is increasingly used to refer to the equipment available for management, particularly computer equipment. As technologies are developing at a rapid rate and prices of equipment have fallen drastically, there is a major temptation to use it more often than is appropriate. However, the search for solutions to accounting, production and other management problems has revealed the power of new technologies to be highly cost-effective, not only in large multinational organisations but also in small or medium-sized enterprises.

If we take computer technology as an example, we can see a number of benefits:

- The computer is interactive. Unlike books, tapes, films, radio and television, the user's response determines what happens next. People may see the computer as a friend, enemy, opposing player, counsellor or tutor and develop a very personal relationship in which both parties react.

- Computers are fun. We love to respond to challenges and to make things happen. At dazzling speeds the computer can produce responses not anticipated by the learner and this capability has a strong arousal effect.

- Computers have infinite patience and make no unpleasant judgements of the learner or the speed (or slowness) of the learning. This capability is of great importance with adults in fields where their self-confidence is very low, or with slow learners who need to take time to ensure understanding of concepts.

- Good computer programs can offer effective positive reinforcement. The mere incorporation of a person's name into the computer's screen responses produces a feeling of bonding and support.

- People can work with a computer in privacy and are not embarrassed by their mistakes. This produces a level of confidentiality which can be of vital importance to some people.

- A computer, with colourful and lively animation, can illustrate concepts more effectively than words or diagrams. Demonstrating the working of a 16-valve 4-stroke engine with electronic ignition becomes quite feasible with a good graphics package.

- Computer simulations are very powerful and compelling, offering users the chance to use their skills without being exposed to the dangers and risks of real life. As faster computers are now available, simulations are increasingly realistic and are being widely used for training purposes in process industries where much of the production takes place within very hot, highly pressurised or radio-active containers.

THE IMPACT OF
NEW TECHNOLOGY

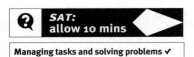

SAT:
allow 10 mins

Managing tasks and solving problems ✓

ACTIVITY 9

Identify a number of instances when a new technology is being used in your company or learning institution.

Commentary...

You might have suggested:

- management presentations
- video-conferencing
- technology-based training
- simulations
- interactive video
- computer management.

Let us take a closer look at each of these applications in turn.

MANAGEMENT PRESENTATIONS

When a manager is presenting information, audio-visual aids support the hearing and seeing aspects. Many improvements have been made and the miniaturisation of solid-state switches means that audio-visual equipment can be fitted with sensors and timers to control the presentation. In general, this gives more freedom to the presenter but greater care has to be taken to ensure the hardware is correctly set up.

The faithful flip-chart is unbeatable for a small group. It is less distracting than a bright overhead projector beam. Conversely, the handwriting and informality can look quite unprofessional in front of a large audience. This situation would call for the latest overhead projection technology and a machine which could withstand being turned off between visuals, together with plenty of bright colour.

To project the contents of a computer screen to a large screen you can use an LCD overlay (a liquid crystal display like the face of a digital watch) placed on the overhead projector. This is excellent for presenting to an audience a series of 'real-time' computing applications.

The spoken word is still a very powerful tool. Occasional use of a simple audio cassette tape, well recorded and easy to hear, can create a very high level of concentration. The material should be short and sharp, e.g. a five-minute case study, short story or other piece of fiction, a recording of a meeting, a discussion, a sales pitch or a description of hazardous behaviour on a site.

VIDEO-CONFERENCING

This system of bringing people together by video link is now available on a world-wide network. The primary purpose is to allow people to take part in a discussion while avoiding the cost of travelling to a meeting.

Attention to the subject matter can be closely focused, and visual clues to understanding may be made available. Intimidation may be lessened and multilingual problems of comprehension can be reduced. In addition, meetings can be more tightly structured, discipline improved and team building strengthened.

TECHNOLOGY-BASED TRAINING

The generic term now used to describe all training which incorporates the use of a microprocessor in its delivery is technology-based training. Under this banner you will find a number of applications:

- computer-assisted instruction (CAI)

- computer-assisted learning (CAL)

- computer-based training (CBT)

- computer-managed learning (CML).

There are so many terms because they reflect the numerous sources and different approaches of computer application that have been developed. Note that:

- ○ 'assisted' means the computer is used as an interactive learning medium

- ○ 'based' means the computer is used as the primary delivery vehicle for both learning and management

- ○ 'managed' means the computer evaluates the results of the learning and determines the learner's progress through the learning programs.

Of all these, the most commonly used is computer-based training which uses the capabilities of the computer to present learning sequences on the screen to the learner. As with the early programmed learning machines, you can present a combination of logical, verbal and graphical issues, together with colour and movement.

SIMULATIONS

Flight simulators are impressive machines that give trainee pilots a 100 per cent simulation of the 'feel' and control of an aircraft in any number of possible situations, varying from trouble-free take-off to life-threatening loss of power due to fire in the engines. Each simulator costs billions of dollars because it is physically built to replicate an aircraft cockpit and rests on a complex system of computer-controlled hydraulic rams.

While flight simulators give 'real' experiences, a microcomputer can simulate slightly less complex tasks and experiences which still exercise motor skills and knowledge. Using the computer as a tool to replicate, control or demonstrate a process is an effective approach to simulation. A person can view or take part in:

- ○ a production process, e.g. in plastic moulding where a machine operator has to understand the effects of variables like temperature, speed and pressure

- ○ a business application, e.g. in a car rental firm with many vehicles, clients and depots

- ○ problem analysis, e.g. where the learner's decisions affect the outcomes

- ○ machine operation, e.g. where the learner actually controls the machine in real time to improve motor skills.

Interactive video

An interactive video system enables a microcomputer to control a video disc player. The person 'views' a TV programme followed or overlaid by instructions or questions produced by the courseware. A branching computer-based training program enables the system to show different video sequences to the learner according to the replies given to the questions.

Video-disks are optical storage devices; the information is 'read' by a laser beam deflected by depressions in the surface. About 30—35 minutes of video can be held on one disc and it takes only a second or so to find any particular video sequence.

Computer management

At its simplest level, a computer management system compiles the results of the work undertaken by each worker and provides the manager with useful information about progress. This is just a record-keeping system. Only in very large organisations would such a system be cost-effective.

Further developments are taking place though. Eventually communication with computers will be in our natural language, not a programming language which attempts to bridge the gap between human languages and machine instructions.

In summary, then, there is a growing range of technical resources becoming available to support the manager. As long as the technology remains at the service of the manager, it can be put to good use. However, if the manager becomes a slave of the technology the whole future of the management function will be put in jeopardy.

summary

This session has looked at some techniques for reviewing and evaluating business activities. The core theme is to examine whether actual performance measures up to product or service specifications.

▶ Product and service specifications provide the basis for the achievement of quality standards. They should be clear and unambiguous.

▶ Product specifications are typically defined in terms of two key parameters: physical dimensions or specifications and performance criteria.

▶ In developing quality controls, companies need to pay attention to process issues as well as product issues. In other words, they need to consider 'how they will provide or produce a product or service' as well as detailing the particular product or service specification.

▶ As a general quality principle, prevention measures are to be preferred to detection systems.

▶ Competence-based vocational qualifications are being established throughout business and industry. These are based upon observable performance to agreed standards in workplace conditions.

▶ Value analysis is an organised approach to product and service design. Through evaluating alternative designs and methods, it aims to find ways of achieving the same (or better) performance at lower cost.

▶ Auditing provides objective evidence about business procedures. It provides the factual evidence on which to base improvements.

▶ Auditors need to be logical, precise and constructive. They need to have an understanding of the system under observation, an ability to report findings accurately and ideas for corrective action and improvement.

▶ Systems analysis describes the way organisations work under four main headings – messy (inefficient and ineffective), fixing (dominated by 'experts' but prone to overcomplexity), reflective (based on experience although sometimes too cautious and slow to respond) and innovative (creating new tools and techniques to overcome problems).

▶ New technology provides a way of speeding up work processes in a cost-effective way. It offers a way to present complicated information simply so it can be understood and manipulated easily. This means it can aid design, presentation and learning needs.